D1611732

Marxism and Christianity

Marxism and Christianity

DENYS TURNER

BARNES AND NOBLE BOOKS
Totowa, New Jersey

First published in the USA 1983 by
Barnes & Noble Books
81 Adams Drive
Totowa, New Jersey, 07512

Library of Congress Cataloging in Publication Data

Turner, Denys, 1942–
    Marxism and Christianity.
    1. Communism and Christianity.   I. Title
HX536.T84   1983   261.2'1   82-22713
ISBN 0-389-20351-3

Printed in Great Britain

Contents

Introduction

I have written this book with a view to defining a problem about the possibility of morality. It may seem excessively paradoxical to raise questions about the justification for a practice in which we so spontaneously and unproblematically engage, for whatever problems we may have about which moral judgements to make, it seems uncontentious that we can make some. But because of the reputation for credibility which morality as such enjoys, I have devoted a considerable part of this essay to the elucidation of the Marxist doctrine that morality itself is 'ideological'. On the Marxist theory, what you explain about a set of beliefs or about a practice when you say of them that they are ideological is both why they are radically problematic and why, in spite of this, they appear to be natural, spontaneous and self-justified. Morality, in my view, has that character. At any rate, bourgeois morality has it.

I also raise the question, but do not get very far with settling it, of the bearing which Christianity has on the problematic character of bourgeois morality. On the one side, I concede that there is much in the Marxist claim that Christianity is part of the same problem and is itself ideological. On the other side, Christianity resists – or can learn how to resist – this description, if it is prepared to learn how from Marxism. In short, on condition that Christianity can incorporate the Marxist criticism into its own doctrine and practice, then in turn a very necessary Christian critique of Marxism becomes possible, although I admit to a degree of tentativeness about this conclusion.

On the positive side, I argue that it is possible to define the conditions under which moral and religious language can be retrieved from their ideological forms and that Marxism is an indispensable tool in defining them. But as the author of a severely restricted argument, I am very conscious of the likelihood of its being read as intended to have a wider significance than it does or possibly could have. For instance I have no theological pretensions whatever. In no way have I presented an argument for any specific theological position, not, certainly, for a 'political' or 'liberation' theology. For the most part, I do not have any very clear notion as to the bearings of my argument on those of the liberation theologians and, where I think I am clear about this, my argument seems often to go in an opposite direction. In more general terms, I do not imagine myself to have done any theology at all in this book. In another book I hope I may be able to do some of the theological work which proper support for the rash theological statements of the last four chapters clearly requires. In this one I proposed merely to set theology a problem which, so far as I know, theology has grown accustomed not to set for itself.[1]

As for my account of the Marxist claim that morality and religion are ideological, it is in no way meant as a general theory of ideology in Marxist terms. Even as far as it goes, it is contentious not only in itself but also as a reading of Marxism. I have intended to present some hypotheses, but not the only possible ones, about the ideological character of moral and religious phenomena which are consistent with general Marxist criteria for the criticism of such phenomena. Even then I do not really try to prove the truth of these hypotheses so much as to elucidate them and explain what would appear to follow from maintaining them.

In these and in other ways, then, my argument is severely restricted in scope. It is indeed an austere, formal and conceptual argument. It is austere in the provision of the empirical support which would be required to demonstrate fully its main claims, and generally such empirical support as I do give them is meant to be illustrative rather than demonstrative. The argument is formal in that it is concerned with illustrating the shape of a Marxist theory of moral and religious ideologies and correspondingly of any possible Christian response to it, but it does not provide the substance of either. It is conceptual in that in the determination of the shape of the theory, the skeleton is decisive. And the skeleton of a theory is built out of the logical links between its controlling concepts — in this case, 'ideology', 'science', 'class', 'oppression', 'exploitation' and so on. I have tried to bring some clarity to the nature of these logical connections.

It may seem perverse of me to introduce my argument with so many disclaimers in view of the nature of the substantive theses which I propose, which must seem to be in equal measures pretentious and implausible to Marxists, Christians and those who are neither. The substantive theses are two. The first I call the 'identity' thesis, the identity in question being that between morality and Marxism. Bluntly, I maintain that the practice which morality entails for us in our engagement with our social world is none other than that which Marxism entails for us in that world. The second substantive thesis I call the 'strong-compatibility' thesis, according to which Marxism and Christianity are in asymmetrical relations of dependence on one another. I do not anticipate, or even welcome, instant agreement with these propositions, for they are of a kind that can be accepted only on the basis of an argument which succeeds. One such argument for them is what I offer here, and I offer it almost overwhelmed by a sense of its vulnerability to counter-argument and counter-evidence.

The only concession which I ask of the reader, in turn, is to share with me a sense of the very great difficulty of these matters. For any unnecessary complexities of exposition I apologise. I have no apologies, though, to those for whom the truth, in particular truths which have express bearings on practical matters, must be simple. There is absolutely no reason ever to suppose that the truth is simple and in the matter of the relations between Marxism and Christianity it is particularly hard to see how it could be, except in the view of those for whom all the truth is in one and none in the other, or else none in either.

The unavoidable complexity of my argument derives from my conviction that both Marxism and Christianity supply concepts and categories which, on the one hand, are indispensable if we are to make sense of the social world in which we live and, on the other hand, are concepts and categories belonging to incommensurable, if not exactly inconsistent, kinds of discourse. I have merely tried to think out the significance of these facts of equal indispensability and mutual dissonance at a theoretical level. This significance is hard to track down at all and I do not think it can be done within any single, overarching conceptual framework imposed upon both. There is no theoretical solution to the problems with which these facts confront us and most certainly there is no 'Christian/Marxist synthesis' lying to hand for theoreticians to discover. If the 'strong-compatibility' thesis means anything at all, it is that we may be able to recover some sense of the moral demands which our place in the modern world makes on us within the practice of living out the tensions and conflicts between the Marxist and the Christian perspectives. I have not supposed that the results of this practice can be anticipated by merely theoretical means.

I shall be happy, then, if it is accepted that this essay defines a problem concerning the possibility of morality. There are those who are profligate with moral language, and in such profligates I hope to provoke a sense of unease, at least with their moral profligacy. It is astounding how easy moral talk is commonly thought to be. Of course in the bourgeois world moral views come exceedingly cheap, and I have tried to show what it is about the bourgeois social world which has so reduced the price of morality. Moreover, it is worrying for a Christian that all too often it is Christians themselves who are in practice the meanest buyers in the moral market. They, who talk so readily and unproblematically about (of all things) 'love', seem quite to have forgotten that Christianity, embodied in the life of its founder, came not so much with news about love, but rather about its price. And if Christians have forgotten what that price is, they may reasonably doubt whether they have been trading in the genuine article, rather than in a counterfeit. Marxism may perhaps serve to remind them that the price of love is revolution and, ultimately, death.

In the meantime capitalism does not deny morality. It evacuates it as in the end it must evacuate itself, by the over-production of increasingly valueless choices. Moral talk has been made unserious and in the face of the moral vacuousness of capitalism it is necessary to impose what I call a *significant moral silence*, a silence relative to the vulgar garrulousness of bourgeois 'free moral choices', but a silence whose significance demands that it be sharply distinguished from the crassness of Stalinist amoralism. Anyone who, like me, feels crushed between the moral cynicism of a Brezhnev and the moral hypocrisy of a Reagan and who finds in both something rooted in the very structure of our moral world will have identified the controlling concerns of this book. Perhaps also they will be able to identify its governing symbol, that it is, as Terry Eagleton once put it, in the silence of Jesus before Pilate, in his refusal to talk morality with a frivolous moraliser, that the true significance of morality may be articulated.²

The task, then, is to discover and realise the conditions of the possibility of moral discourse. In this task I argue that Marxism is indispensable but insufficient. I learned first of the indispensability of Marxism from Terry Eagleton of Wadham College, Oxford. I have learned much of the nature of the insufficiency of Marxism from Herbert McCabe OP of Blackfriars, Oxford. It is inconceivable that this book could have been written except as a reflection, albeit insubstantial and distorted, of their influence. In addition, Herbert McCabe read and criticised a draft, as did Professor Kenneth Grayston, Professor John Kent and Dr Margaret Pamment of the Department of Theology and Religious Studies at Bristol University, and Dr Ian Hamnett and Dr Kieran Flanagan of the Sociology Department of the same University. Steven Lukes made available to me his very perceptive reader's report. Neil Stubbens helped compile the index. Margaret Horne sensitively edited the typescript. To all of these I owe a very great debt of thanks. They have all been to a great deal of trouble to get me to write a better book. The result certainly is better than it might have been, although still less good than they tried to get me to make it.

I owe debts to many others, particularly to my colleagues in my own department at Bristol University with whom I discussed several aspects of my argument with a persistence on my part which says much for their patience. But one special debt is now sad to record. Fr. Laurence Bright OP was the first to encourage me to write this book. In the course of so doing he was fortunately able to dissuade me from writing another far worse book which I was proposing to write. Whether he would have been pleased with this one I shall never know, for he died before I was ready to show him the manuscript. I am but one among very many who owe a great debt to the once tireless but now effortless work of this dedicated socialist and Christian.

It is, however, to my wife, Marie, that I owe most of all, too many debts to be calculable. If I have not attempted to calculate them, it is to my advantage and to her credit that neither has she. To her and to my long-suffering children I dedicate this book.

NOTES

1   Professor Nicholas Lash's work *A Matter of Hope*, London, 1981, appeared too late for me to take his conclusions into account in this book. Although I disagree with much of what he says, it is nevertheless one of the very few theological works written in this country in recent years which is in close enough contact with the real world to recognise that Marxism thrives every bit as much as Christianity does in most of it and creates radical problems for theology which must be indispensable items on any theological agenda.

2   T.F. Eagleton, 'Marxists and Christians: Answers for Brian Wicker', *New Blackfriars*, October 1975, p. 470.

1

The Problem

Marx has little to say specifically about morality and religion. Religious people often suppose that he must have said more about them than he did, partly because some Marxists have made so much of these topics and partly because organised Marxism has such a decidedly hostile attitude towards religion in particular. In fact, however, Marx wrote no book on either topic and what he did write is both small in extent and early.[1]

On the other hand, what is lacking in volume is made up for in vigour and comprehensiveness. Some of Marx's best-known *obitera* are about religion. It is 'the sigh of the oppressed creature', 'the illusory happiness of men'. It is 'the reflex of the real world' and, best of all, it is 'the opium of the people'.[2] In view of the largely unanalytical and rhetorical character of the typical Marxian polemic against religion, and in view of the scarcity of the sources and the early date of most of them, some have supposed that Marx either just lost interest in religion in his later works or else that he ameliorated his hostility. There is no evidence for either supposition. Dressed up a little, though, it is a little more plausible to say that Marx came to see the pointlessness of a polemic against religion as such, since he came to see that religion would just 'wither away' when the illusions which appeared to require it had been demolished by political criticism. He certainly held this view even before 1844, and never after that date do we find him saying what he said in that year, that 'the premise of all criticism is the criticism of religion'.[3] As late as in *Capital* I he insists that:

the religious reflex of the real world can, in any case, only then finally vanish, when the practical relations of everyday life offer to man none but perfectly intelligible and reasonable relations with regard to his fellowmen and to Nature.[4]

Engels, in turn, supports this reading when he complains that the Blanquists cannot see the futility of overt persecution of religion as such:

the only service which can be rendered to God today is to declare atheism a compulsory article of faith and to ... prohibit ... religion generally.[5]

In any case, as I explain more fully in chapter 10, there are two quite different sorts of hostility towards religion to be found in Marx's writings. The first sort is plain (and in Marx's case definitely vulgar) nineteenth-century materialist atheism of the sort which simply says: Demonstrably there is no God. Hence Christianity is false. The second kind of hostility says something vastly more complex and, since it is the purpose of this essay to elucidate it, I will report it here compendiously in the form of the mere slogan: Christianity and morality are 'ideological'. Marx did lose interest in the first line of attack. He never refined the vulgarity of the plainly absurd disproof of the existence of God in the third Paris manuscript.[6] The second line of attack, however, is the characteristically Marxist one. As I shall be arguing in chapter 10, when you see the point of saying that Christianity and morality are ideological, you see the crucial pointlessness of trying to prove that Christian beliefs or moral claims are in any straightforward way false — or, for that matter, of trying to oppose organised Christianity by force. Consequently, as the mature Marx came to see what the point of the second charge was, necessarily he lost interest in the first. In that case, though, why has he so little to say even about the ideological character of religion and morality?

The question betrays a misunderstanding. One of the results of reading Marx's corpus as a Holy Writ is that there is a tendency to read a significance of some sort into everything about it, as much into what is not there as into what is. If Marx wrote little about religion and morality at a time when he wrote much about many other subjects, does this show a relative decline in interest on his part? Perhaps. But even if it did, this would show nothing about what he would have said about them had he said more, and it would not indicate any lessening of hostilities. In any case what is in question is not a Holy Writ. I take the view that to Marxists Marx's writings *as such* should be unimportant. What should be important to Marxists is what they achieved, namely the articulation of the fundamental concepts and principles of the science called, after its founder, 'Marxism' — as Newtonian physics is called after its author. Strictly, however, a science is nameless because, strictly, science, unlike literature, is authorless. Science, to abuse a phrase of Popper's, is 'epistemology without a knowing subject'.[7] It is romantic nonsense to read significances for the science out of the gaps and omissions in the texts, as if those texts were some sort of diary of their author's intentions and as if it was those intentions which gave the concepts and principles their scientific character. When someone convincingly shows that Newton's *Principia* has the same relation to Newtonian physics that the Shakespearian autograph has to *Hamlet*, then it will be right to see anything more than biographical significance in the paucity of later Marxian writing about religion and morality.

It is true, of course, that Marx barely finished sketching the fundamental principles of his new science of society, and in some important areas he did not even do that. In any case he died before he could systematise the applications in all or even any of the areas to which he thought they could be extended: morality, art, law, politics, history, philosophy and religion. Subsequent attempts to carry on this scientific work are utterly misconstrued, if they are thought of as attempts to answer questions of the sort: 'What would Marx have said about liberation theology or the plays of Samuel Beckett?' To such questions, first, there is no possible answer. Second, were there any possible answer, it could only add biographical interest to what, if Marxism is scientific at all, we must already be capable of knowing on the basis of the science which he founded.

It is incidental to this point, although this is the occasion on which to say it, that these remarks may help to explain the rather odd combination of Marxist fundamentalism and revisionism which characterises the argument of this essay. I am fundamentalist enough to believe that Marx did found a new science of society — indeed, the only science of society — and that he founded it on an account of scientificity itself which radically departs from contemporary and subsequent models. The revisionism follows from this fundamentalism. A science, unlike a poem, has a life independent of the text in which it is first written. Although it is therefore an urgent matter to seek Marxist authenticity in respect of the fundamental principles of Marxist science, it can be of no concern to establish a point by point correspondence between my argument and the texts in the Marxian corpus — any more, as I have said, than it can be any physicist's concern to establish such correspondences with Newton's.

Returning, then, to the question of Marxism and religion, it is plain that Marx's early enthusiasm for the topic had slackened in his maturity. But what matters is how the scientific principles which increasingly occupied his attention are to be applied to religious and moral phenomena. Any answer to that question must begin with the statement that religion and morality are ideological. This, however, is to say no more than that a distinct subject-matter has been located within the critical theory of bourgeois society. In the first instance, to say that religion or morality is ideological is to isolate as a relatively autonomous area of bourgeois social space those regions which are occupied by religion and morality. Explanation begins with the process of setting these phenomena back into their places within that structure of social mechanisms which is capitalism, a structure which is characterised by two features mainly — by class oppression and by the failure to perceive it. When their roles within that overall mechanism have been adequately determined, then religion and morality are *known*: we have science.

Obviously, then, we need some account of what it is to say of any set of social phenomena that it is an 'ideology'. No doubt any reader today who is in the least acquainted with recent developments in Marxism will know how problematic and contentious a subject this is. With the exception of some necessary side-stepping around the views of the neo-Stalinist French Marxist, Louis Althusser, I shall eschew direct participation in the controversies about ideology which have so dominated Marxist theorising in the last decade or so. But no one who wishes to confront the topic with any form of honesty can avoid recognising its deeply problematic character simply as a concept within Marxism. There are problems enough about what social phenomena can be called 'ideologies', and we shall want to know in particular whether all forms of moral thought and all kinds of Christianity are ideological. A solution to this problem, however, is but simple compared with the general theoretical problem of what it is that you are saying about a social phenomenon when you call it 'ideological'. And in any case this latter is a problem on the solution to which depends all hope of solving the first — to the degree, one must suppose, that an identification of instances must depend upon a description of what sort of thing it is that we are seeking to identify.

We therefore first need an account not of what instances of ideology there are, but of what sort of phenomenon any such instances would be. In short we need an account of the structure of ideological thought or belief. More particularly, we will need an account of what we may call the *epistemological* structure of ideology, an account of the relations of ideological belief to 'reality'. That there is a problem here is not hard to see (at least in very general terms) if we now consider briefly just three of the fundamental properties an ideology may (provisionally) be supposed to have within Marxian theory.

In general, ideology is thought to be some form of 'false' or at least in some way 'deviant', consciousness of society.[8] Also, in general, an ideology is thought to be a society's false consciousness of itself. Finally, and also in general, ideology is thought to be a 'lived' form of social perception, to be, in a sense about which I shall later be clearer, a 'praxis'. The epistemological problem with ideology is that of reconciling all three properties within a single account; it is that of explaining how a society can be said to be *living* in a mode of *false consciousness* of *itself*. For one would have thought that, in so far as a society lives or practises the beliefs it has about itself, those beliefs will not be and could not be false. After all, it seems to go with the notion of 'lived' beliefs that they are internal to the life they are beliefs about and so, as it were, 'correspond' with that life. Contrariwise, in so far as a society has 'false' beliefs about itself, it would seem that those beliefs cannot be 'lived' beliefs and cannot figure among the determinants of its practices. Hence, it would seem, either social beliefs are 'true' forms of social perception or else, if they are 'false', they are not practices. Either way, ideology seems structurally impossible.

These are, of course, only intuitive remarks which do little more than register a sense of unease about the job which ideology is being asked to do: they hardly amount to a genuine objection, even if they do point the way to where the problem lies, not just with the notion of ideology but with the social phenomena, in explanation of which the notion of ideology is offered. Intuitively we should not want to deny either that some social beliefs are lived or that some of them which are lived are in some way less than 'true'. If, on the other hand, we are tempted to suppose that falsehoods cannot be lived, that the notion is inherently paradoxical, then perhaps we should attend to the fact that quite un-problematically we accept that, whatever about societies, individuals at least can and do live 'false lives'. And what we intend to mean when we say that (begging no questions about whether we can mean anything by it), is that in some way falsehood is internal to the life lived. At a point in this essay when it will have ceased to be misleading to do so, I will argue that there are certain partial analogies between the relation of an ideology to the society whose ideology it is and the relation of self-deception to the person self-deceived.[9] Here I wish only to say that much as the notion of a 'socially lived falsehood' may seem paradoxical, that notion still falls within our experience at an individual level. In view of this we may not wish to commit ourselves to an analysis of social belief which ruled out a priori the possibility of ideology so described. So long, therefore, as we do not wish to be so peremptory, we have an initial determination of our epistemo-logical problem: how are we to explain the possibility of social beliefs which are at once 'lived' and 'false'?

I propose to set about the solution of this problem in a long series of steps which will not be completed until chapter 10. I begin by pulling apart the elements in our preliminary characterisation of ideology (it is in no way a definition) and examine them separately. First, in the next chapter I will consider what relations in general there are between social beliefs and 'practice' by having a look at the notion of 'praxis' itself, but without special regard to the way in which we might expect it to figure in an account of ideology. In chapters 3 and 4 the epistemological problem of ideology is confronted directly: first, by considering how social 'praxes' can be internally contradictory, and second, by considering how praxes which are so might be socially functional. From that point on the argument develops in other ways and by other means, but because of the formalistic and abstract nature of the first three steps in this argument it might be worth mentioning that in one way this abstract starting-point might be misleading.

'Ideology' is a relatively recent word in the vocabulary of social theory. It predates Marx, though not by much. The topic is, of course, perennial, as I shall show; indeed it is certainly older than I shall show it to be, predating Plato in whose writings we find the first sophisticated account of something like ideology. Because I shall go to some lengths in chapter 8 to show the perennial, indeed universally necessary, character of ideology, the mistaken impression might very well be given that for Marx (or for me) there is some one phenomenon called 'ideology' which is recurrent in all societies and ages. This is not so. In all ages there is ideology. But there is no one thing which, in all ages, ideology always is. Since in the next three chapters I seek to describe some quite formal and general features of ideology, it may seem as if this is a description of some characteristics common to all instances of a perennial phenomenon. To remove this misleading impression at the outset, let me say that, although the ensuing discussion of ideology is general and abstract, what I describe is an aspect of the formal structure of that highly specific contemporary kind of ideology which we can call 'bourgeois'. Initially I make no attempt to account for bourgeois ideology in terms of historical origin, contemporary necessity or contingent effect. As the argument progresses in the following chapters, it will increasingly acquire the more empirical character which is due to it.

Forewarned, therefore, by these purely methodological remarks, we must begin by asking what a 'praxis' is.

NOTES

1   Most of what Marx and Engels have to say about religion is contained in the one-volume collection, *Marx and Engels on Religion*, Moscow, 1972.
2   Karl Marx, *Contribution to the Critique of Hegel's Philosophy of Right, Introduction*, edited and translated by T.B. Bottomore, in *Karl Marx: Early Writings*, London, 1963, pp. 43—4.
3   *Ibid.*, p. 43.
4   Karl Marx, *Capital*, I, part I, 1, i, iv, translated by S. Moore and E. Aveling, London, 1970, p. 79.
5   Engels, *Marx and Engels on Religion*, p. 127.
6   Cf. Marx, *Economic and Philosophical Manuscripts*, edited and translated by T.B. Bottomore, in *Karl Marx: Early Writings*, pp. 165—7, and my discussion of this argument on pp. 165—6 below.
7   Cf. K.R. Popper, *Objective Knowledge, an Evolutionary Approach*, Oxford, 1972, chapter 3.
8   We shall have reason to qualify this, however, in chapter 3 and later.
9   See chapter 8, pp. 119—22.

2

Praxis

I

I begin with the proposition that, if we are to understand what a praxis is, we must first recognise that, and then how, actions may be said to speak. We are familiar, of course, with the saying that 'actions speak louder than words', although it may be thought that this is but a metaphor. That it is not a mere metaphor is, however, made clear by the fact that if, in some literal sense, it is words which speak then it follows that, just as literally, actions speak. For words are but actions of making a medium vibrate or of making physical shapes on surfaces; and if these are actions, then actions speak *because* words do. Hence, if there is anything suspicious about the saying 'actions speak louder than words', it is in its suggestion that words are only in some metaphorical sense actions, not in any danger that the metaphor of actions speaking will be taken literally. It ought to be so taken.

Consider in amplification of this the differences between the words 'I love you' and a kiss between lovers. They are many. But they ought not to hog the philosopher's attention. For they reduce in the end to the difference between one way and another of saying the same thing with your lips. You say the same thing either way. You can show someone, say a child, what the words mean by kissing; or, alternatively, you can explain to a child that he has misunderstood what kissing means by saying 'kissing means "I love you": you don't do it if you are not really sorry'. You say the same thing, but in different ways. You can say by means of touching what the words say by means of sounds.

Now sounds (and shapes on a page) are perfectly ordinary

bits of matter, they come and go, wax and wane, are measurable, insurable and can be priced, just as kisses are and can. There is nothing less physical about verbal sounds and shapes than there is about any other sounds and shapes. Anything you can do physically with a non-verbal sound or shape you can do with a verbal sound or shape. Words, moreover, are just as much bodily functions as are kisses. Indeed, as I shall argue shortly, in the one really important sense of the word 'bodily', words are more bodily, not less so, than are kisses.

In the meantime let us note a persistent tendency to disembody the word relatively to the kiss, and, in the course of noting this tendency, note a terminological and conceptual confusion. We are inclined to think of the kiss as a more brutally material action than are the words which say the same. And we have this tendency because we are correspondingly inclined to suppose that the more bodily something is the more material it is. It seems obvious, after all, that the body is material; indeed it is nothing but a lump of highly organised and efficient matter. Now kisses, as it were, seem closer to the lips than are words, and so closer to the body. Words seem somehow less 'tangible', more suffused with meaning, to exist less as bits of matter than as bits of meaning. And, it is thought, meanings are not themselves bodily entities, although they have of course a close if mysterious connection with bodies.

To see how very nearly right this is — and at the same time disastrously wrong — consider the following analogy. If one is uncertain about how to spell a word, say 'parallel', it sometimes helps to try out the permutations of single and double r's and l's on a sheet of paper in the hope that eventually one of them will look right. Sometimes, however, the experiment misfires, the curious mental state being induced in which, so to speak, the meaning of the word and the physical shapes separate from one another, so that the shapes stop being a word, become *mere* shapes. It happens with children, too: they repeat a word out loud to themselves so often that the word becomes in the end a mere sound, that is, not a word. This is the condition which, one supposes, is normal for the dyslexic and in Sartre's view, is normal for the existentialist. In *La Nausée*, Roquentin is staring at a seat in a tramcar:

I murmur: it's a seat, as a sort of exorcism. But the word remains on my lips: it refuses to go and rest on the thing . . . Things are delivered from their names. They are *there*, grotesque, stubborn, huge, and it seems crazy to call them seats or to say anything whatever about them.[1]

Whatever the existentialist may think, the state is abnormal, but the structure of the abnormal experience is of some interest, shedding light on the character of the normal. Finding the meaning and the shapes to have split apart, you can be left wondering how the meaning can ever be got back into the shapes, or for that matter how it ever got there in the first place. Moreover, there are philosophical theories which, like Locke's, appear to regularise the predicament, for once you suppose that words are purely material entities and meanings are immaterial 'ideas', you are left with the quite general problem: how do meanings come to inhabit purely material shapes and sounds? However, the problem in this form is insoluble. Once words and their meanings are conceived in this manner as opposed kinds of entity, the one material and the other immaterial, the relation between them becomes, as Locke says, entirely arbitrary[2] and there is no way in which we can account for their synthesis in the meaningful utterance.

We can see why, if we return to our analogy. It is precisely in so far as the meaning does slough from the shapes that the writing appears as mere shapes. For when the meaning has evaporated, we are left not with *words* minus their meanings, but with *shapes* minus their meanings, that is, shapes which are no longer words. Likewise, a meaningful utterance is not spoken words plus a meaning. Rather, it is sounds plus a meaning, i.e. words. Therefore, in so far as the sound is 'merely material', it is not a word; in so far as the shapes are merely pencilled scribbles, they are not a word. It is only in so far as a sound is a meaningful sound that it is a word, and so with written shapes. And so we may say that it is not strictly *as material* that words are words, but as meaningful bits of matter. Hence, although they are of course material, words are precisely *words*, in so far as they materialise a significance, a meaning.

We ought not to conclude from this, however, that words

are bits of matter plus an *immaterial* significance, for if we do, we are still left with the philosopher's problem of how the immaterial meaning gets into the matter to form words. The difficulty with this conception is the same as with the more general proposition that minds use words as a means of communication, rather in the way that embodied people use pens or telephones as means of communication. As McCabe has rightly pointed out:

> It is important to see that the human body is not a means of communication in the sense that a telephone or pen may be a means we use to get in touch with others. The body itself cannot be such a means because we have to have a body in order to use such means . . . If the body itself were merely such a means, you would need another body to use it with.[3]

It is just the same with words. To be able to use material entities as means to communicate immaterial ideas, a mind would have to have a body in order to use those material entities with it. But to be able to use that body in order to communicate its ideas to the material entities, the mind would have to have another body with which to use the first body . . . and so on. Moreover, there is not just an analogy here between vocal sounds and bodies. The reason why we cannot think of minds *using* matter to form words is just the same as the reason why minds cannot be said to use bodies as a means of communication at all; namely that, as I said, words are just as much part of our bodies as are our lips. So, if we cannot be said to use our bodies as a means of communication, just for that reason we cannot be said to use words as a means of communication.

And now we can see why it is wrong to think that a kiss is somehow a more material and *therefore* more bodily way of saying what 'I love you' says. Admittedly it *is* easier than with words to think of kisses as purely material events, in themselves devoid of the significance of loving, this being given to them by means of a separate act of linguistic interpretation. This will certainly not do as an account of how physical gestures or contact find their significance in loving relationships, although there are evidently some for whom love approximates to this low condition of merely physical contact plus a lot of talk. On the contrary, thus far the case is just the same with kisses as with words and our analogy holds: in so far as the physical contact of the lips is merely that, a neutrally material event, it is not a kiss. In order to view a kiss as a material event — which it undeniably also is — you have to abstract from its being a kiss, which by no means goes to show that the material event and its significance are distinct sorts of entities, a material event plus an immaterial significance, which somehow get together in the kiss. Again, it is the same as with words. Just because, in abnormal conditions, the physical shapes or sounds can seem to be separate from the meanings, it does not follow that there is a general problem about how they fuse in the first place. And just because there are mock kisses which are not kisses, which are merely material events deprived of loving significance, it does not follow that the events and their significance are distinct entities which quite contingently merge in the gesture.

All this rests on a quite general point about the body and brings us back to the terminological confusion. We are apt to disembody meanings because of a combination of two tendencies of thought: the first mistaken, the second correct. The first and mistaken tendency is to identify 'body' with 'matter'. The second, which is correct, is to contrast 'meaning' with 'matter'. I have said enough about the second tendency to indicate why it is correct. But taken in conjunction with the first and mistaken tendency it yields the conclusion that, not being material, meaning is not of the body and being of neither is purely 'mental' or 'ideal' or some such. Now this inference is scotched, if we can show the identification of body with matter to be false, and I now propose to argue that it is. For although it is certainly true that anything which is a body is material, it is not precisely *as* material that it is a body.

We can see this if we return again to the lips. Clearly lips are material entities, bundles of muscle tissue, nerves, blood and skin. But it is not precisely *as* bundles of these materials that they are lips. Nor, as we have seen, are they lips in virtue of something immaterial — the soul — which *uses* the bundle of tissue as lips. It is rather that they are lips in so far as they are parts, or as we say 'organs', of the body; in so far, that is to say, as the bundle of tissue plays a part in the overall life of the organism. As with lips, so again with bodies: it is not exactly as material, nor yet as matter used by something immaterial, that a lump of matter is a body. Rather, it is as matter organised for a certain form of life that that material is a body. It is therefore precisely in so far as some material parts have a distinctive role in the life of the body that they are what we call organs of it, such as lips are: as lips they are not material, but body.

But it is as lips that they kiss. For lips play a number of distinct roles in the life of the body (which incidentally is why they are not strictly organs in their own right), one of which is their role in the life of loving, a role which they have only in virtue of the place they have in that bodily life. It is thus in its role within a specific aspect of the life of the body that the physical contact of the lips has the significance of 'I love you'. In short, it is because of the body that the material event has that meaning. Consequently, although it was right to say that it is not as material that the kiss can speak, it is quite wrong to conclude that it is as somehow disembodied that it can do so.

This should lead us to ask whether the same can be said for words. The answer to this is yes and no. There was, I said, something nearly right in thinking of speech as being more disembodied than kissing — and yet something disastrously wrong. What is nearly right about this is that words (written or spoken) are, in a sense, less 'material' than kisses are; what is disastrously wrong is to conclude from this that they are less embodied than are kisses. On the contrary, they are not less but more strictly bodily than kisses are.

One way of explaining the difference between words and kisses is to say that words are more 'abstract' than kisses are. This, I think, is correct, so long as we do not misunderstand the force of the word 'abstract'. There are two ways of using the word, only one of which is helpful — the other is thoroughly misleading — in our attempt to find the differences between the way words and actions speak. The misleading use of the word is such as to mean by it the isolation in thought of features of experience from all its rich complexity.

In this sense of the word we often speak of 'abstract ideas' meaning the isolation in thought of one feature from others, as when we isolate in thought the colour of a shape from its shape. An 'abstract idea' in this sense is simpler than that from which it abstracts, as, to take another example, the abstract idea of 'the state' is thought to be a formal, definitional affair, capturing, as it were, the highest common factor of all actual states, thus being far less rich and varied in its content than the manifold variations, overlappings and discontinuities between actual existent states.[4]

The helpful use of the word has almost entirely fallen out of both technical and everyday usage. It enjoyed a heyday in Aristotle, then again in Aquinas and much later in Hegel and Marx — and I propose retrieving it for the purposes of the argument. On this conception of abstraction everything is reversed. What you abstract *from* is not the rich variety and complexity of experience, but, on the contrary, from its limitedness — or, which is to say the same thing, from its gross materiality. Whereas on the highest-common-factor theory you have the abstract concept of colour when you have grasped just that which distinguishes any colour from any shape, on the older account you have it to the degree that you have experienced the richness and complexity of the spectrum, when you are sensitive to the possibilities of colour combinations and effects, when you have a grasp equally of the physics of colour and of the poetry of colour metaphors and when you have discovered some coherence, some order in all these differentiations. Likewise with the state: you have that abstract concept not when you have found the highest common factor of all states — if there is one — but when you understand the connections between power and the state, the relationships between class-interest and state-power, between the economy and the state, between revolutions and the state. The possession of the abstract concept of something or other is an affair of greater or lesser adequacy, adequacy both of differentiation and coherence. An excessively narrow concept of something is a concept whose coherence is bought at the price of insufficient differentiation. An excessively diffuse concept is one whose differentiation is incoherently constructed.

Concepts so understood may be called 'abstract' in that they abstract *from* the limitedness of particular instances. The concept of 'the state' is the account that can be given of the state in all its forms, or in as many as we know about; it is richer in information than any amount of data about a particular instance, for the concept of the state contains all such data implicitly in the account it gives of what potentialities for statehood there are and which of them and how far any particular state realises them. It is, therefore, quite unsurprising that for Hegel and Marx the concept or idea of the state includes an account of how the various actual states have *historically* realised what the state is; and there is, moreover, a very good Aristotelian precedent for this view, since, for Aristotle, the concept of something is the grasp you have of what it is. And what a thing is, its nature, is what you would have to say about it, were it a fully realised instance of the sort of thing it is, something which can be determined only in and through its temporal development.[5]

Concepts, therefore, may abstract from the *limitedness* of the particular instance, but not from the differentiations which particular instances exhibit. In fact the test that we have the concept of something or other is precisely our ability to apply it in particular instances, when we can place a particular instance within the pattern of differentiation. Concepts are exercised in judgements about particulars, when we can say of this or that particular: this is what it is and this is why it is said to be a thing of that sort.

Now the common medium of judgements is language. The skill we possess when we understand the concept of the state is, as I said, that of being able to make a vast number of highly differentiated and coherent judgements about states. Another way of putting this is to say that the skill is exhibited in our command over the 'language of politics', the precision and coherence of that language being the test of our command over the concept. To have the concept of something is to know how to talk about it and to know how that talk relates to talk about other things. And here the most striking paradigm is given by Plato, whose answer to the question 'what is justice?' is neither an enumeration of particular instances of just actions, nor a one-line statement of minimum conditions, but the elaborate description in several hundred pages of the conditions, political, economic, intellectual, religious, aesthetic, educational and sexual of the form of social life implicit in the concept; plus an account of the mechanisms governing the rise and decline of that form of social life. The *Republic* does not just include, it *is* the definition of justice.

Now I have argued that kisses can speak in the sense that they can convey the meaning which is conveyed by the words 'I love you'. They can do this because the physical contact becomes a kiss through its role within that dimension of the body's life which is the life of loving. But the expression 'the life of loving' is equivalent with the expression just introduced, 'the language of loving'. Granted that a great deal of the language of loving is non-verbal in character, consisting in gestures, looks, tones, embraces, even silences, none the less the capacity of this profoundly bodily language to speak as it does is rooted in the character of the human body as linguistic.

I have no axes to grind on the question of whether the equivalent gestures of animals can be said to speak. I am rather in favour of the view that they can, although only non-linguistically and without that density and differentiation which characterises the human gesture. For human gestures are, as it were, impregnated with the meanings over which only language can give us a command. We can rightly think of a kiss as being pure poetry, but only because we can read and write poems. We can rightly think of a kiss as ironic — as Judas' was — but only because language makes ironic discourse possible in the first place. Because our bodies are linguistic organisms their organic activities acquire all the density, differentiation and coherence of language itself, that is to say, they become more 'abstract'.

For language is not, indeed, *dis*embodied, but rather is an intensification of the bodily powers. Through language our bodies become cultures, so that language, through its role in which the kiss says 'I love you', is the human culture of sexual love itself. Every kiss, therefore, can condense everything which that culture says about love into a gesture. Every kiss can betray the ironies and ambiguities of that culture, can find its place within the differentiations and coherences and, equally, confusions and incoherences which that culture establishes. For our bodily powers get their capacity to signify not just from the individual organisms whose powers they are, but also from the results of their insertion into language and therefore into culture. That insertion is, as I have said, an intensification of the bodily functions, and because of it the human kiss is certainly more 'abstract' than the equivalent gesture in an animal, but for that reason is more, not less, bodily in character. In short, because they are linguistic human bodies are more bodily, less tied to the particularities of their matter, than are those of brute animals. For this reason we can after all say that our bodies as bodies are less material and more abstract; but not for either reason that they are less bodily.

Language, then, is an intensification of our bodily powers; but it is also their extension. Because they are linguistic, our bodies are social bodies. For our bodies are the mode of our presence to each other, the form of our body being the form of that presence. Therefore, because of their linguistic character we can be present to each other not simply in terms of our basic natural desires — as animals are present to each other as food or competitors for food, as sources of warmth or protection, as threats or as companions — but also in institutional and ritual terms, as 'father' to 'son', as 'wife' to 'husband', as 'buyer' to 'seller', as 'capitalist' to 'worker'. Through language the roles in terms of which our bodily powers 'speak' are institutions or praxes, enormously extending the significance of what they say, as, for example, the satisfaction of the desire to consume goods can become what it cannot ever be for an animal, namely a contribution to the rate of inflation. That desire can become that contribution because by its insertion into language it acquires a role within that form of the social body which we call the 'economy'. To call the economy a 'form of the social body' is not a mere metaphor. We can call it so not because the economy is *like* a body. The economy is not 'like' a body at all, it *is* the body extended by that language which we call the language of economics.

Furthermore, because our bodies are inserted into language they are inserted into ambiguity. Because of language we can lie, cheat and deceive ourselves. But just because we can do these things we can tell stories, write poetry, construct ironies, jokes, pretences, play games and laugh. If we could not do the one, we could not do the other. If we can laugh at all, we can laugh derisively; if we bargain, we can cheat; if we can tell the truth, we can lie. And if language can give us this capacity, it also necessitates its intensification and extension. Institutions and social practices can embody lies, fictions, distorted self-images, as some marriages are structured upon, intensify and extend the self-ignorance of the partners. Whole societies can do this too, at any rate they can do this if there is anything for the theory of ideology to explain.

And so we may conclude that actions may speak as kisses do, but they speak only with the accents of language itself. Our bodies are organisms inserted into language, acquiring from the abstractive power of language an intensification and extension both of coherence and ambiguity. Thus it is that a simple gesture of kissing can become a symbol, can become the bearer of a dense concentration of overlapping meanings and ambiguities. Now I should want to say, with Marx, that it is in the intercrossing of our actions towards and our relations with each other that our primary forms of social consciousness are to be found. In other words, it is precisely within that capacity which our social action has to speak that we primarily communicate our awareness of our social world, for, as Marx puts it, 'Life is not determined by consciousness, but consciousness by life.'[6] And this, it seems to me, has the force of an elementary truth, not that of an exotic theory. The first form of our thought is that which is integral to the forms of our social life, to the praxes of our social relations.

II

I promised that if we could understand how actions speak we could come to understand what a praxis is. Merleau-Ponty, following Marx, described a praxis as:

the meaning which works itself out spontaneously in the intercrossing of the activities by which man organises his relations with nature and other men.[7]

This will do as a promising start, although it will need some qualifications before we can let it stand as a definition, as we will see.

The first thing to note is that Merleau-Ponty describes a praxis as a 'meaning'. It is a meaning in some way generated by socially organised activities, but a praxis is not those activities taken by themselves, it is those activities in so far as they generate 'meaning'. In ways whose falsity has been made apparent in the last section, it is too common to adopt an over-theoretical account of meaning and, correspondingly, an over-'practical' account of practice. Just as it is wrong to split the word up into heterogeneous elements, a sound or shape plus a meaning, so it is wrong to split the praxis up into heterogeneous components, bare unmeaningful 'actions' and the interpretations or 'meanings' which human agents give of them. To use a metaphor, a praxis is an *incarnation* of a meaning or a set of meanings.

Second, Merleau-Ponty says, with less than complete clarity, that this meaning 'works itself out *spontaneously* . . .' The force of the word 'spontaneously' here is to suggest that the meaning is not something imposed upon the activities, but works itself out *in* the activities: if it is generated by the activities, it is none the less internal to them. The expression 'works itself out' would be quite misleading if it were taken to imply that in addition to an activity producing that which it is the activity of producing, e.g. a higher standard of living, it also produces a second result, namely the 'meaning' of doing that producing. For the 'meaning' which 'works itself out' in the intercrossing of the activities is nothing more than how we are to describe the activities themselves: they are, that is to say, the activities of producing a higher standard of living, that is their meaning. Hence all activities produce meaning, in so far as they are activities, 'spontaneously'. Or, in other words, as actions 'speak' so do praxes.

Third, what distinguishes praxes from actions generally is that praxes are organised sets of activities, not just single activities. For this reason we should not want to say that a kiss is a praxis. Rather we should say that a kiss is an activity whose meaning is worked out in the intercrossing of that set of activities — gestures, words, forms of physical contact and so forth — which earlier I called the 'language of sexual love'

and can now call the 'praxis' of sexual love. That language
has an organisation, a structure; it is what we might call a
'routine'. For it 'routinises', makes a number of ways of
doing things into so many ways of saying things *as a matter
of course*. And it makes them available as a given structure,
one which is 'to hand', a conscious form of life and a lived
form of consciousness.

This suggests a fourth point: the word 'routine', although
important in the characterisation of a praxis, is also easily
misunderstood. A praxis is indeed a public and stable structure
of behaviour which displays its regularities in the form of
intelligible rules. Just as a language is rule-governed, so is a
praxis, in fact the rules governing the regularities of the
behaviour are just the same rules as those governing the
capacity of the behaviour to speak. A person who knows how
and when to kiss is a person who understands the differences
between a formal kiss of greeting and the kiss of sexual
passion; and anyone who understands that difference understands the different connection there is between one kind of
physical gesture and what it says and another kind of physical
gesture and what that says.

Now such connections are rule-governed in the sense that
they can be grasped and understood publicly as being given
to those who engage in the behaviour. For of course it is only
in so far as the connection is publicly available that the
behaviour can communicate what it says at all. As I argued in
the last section, not to understand what a kiss says is not to
understand what a kiss is: you cannot kiss without understanding what it means to do so. For this reason we can say
that the praxis of sexual love routinises and internalises the
meanings of the behaviour which it structures.

On the other hand, to call a praxis a 'routine' is to lay oneself open to misinterpretation. For to many a 'routine' of
behaviour is but the bare unintelligent repetition of the
behaviour, behaviour performed out of the force of mere
habit. In fact a praxis is just the opposite of mechanical
repetition. As Merleau-Ponty says, a praxis is a meaning. Far
from it being the case that to engage in a praxis is a performance by rote, repetition without understanding; it is only
an understanding of the 'meaning' which a praxis incarnates

which makes any repetition possible. As I have said, it is only in so far as we can understand the connection between kissing and the display of affection that we can understand what it is to kiss at all. And it is only in so far as we can understand what a kiss is, that is, understand its role within the praxis of loving, that we can kiss at all, never mind do the same again. In summary, we learn how to perform the activities organised in a praxis by learning to understand what they say.

A fifth point is that a praxis is a social organisation of activities. To understand a praxis is to understand how those who engage in it form a community of some sort, as those who kiss form a sexual community and those who buy and sell form a community in their understanding of the cash nexus. Thus the meaning of a praxis makes a community of those who understand it. Learning to understand the meaning is what we otherwise call the process of 'socialisation' into a community in that meaning.

We are now in a position to say something more about how ideas can be socially lived. The forms in which men socially live ideas are their praxes. For any human interaction incarnates ideas, or, to put the same thing in a different way, whenever human beings interact with one another, they 'live' an idea or set of ideas. They do so in so far as their actions 'speak', and all human interactions speak in so far as their actions are the gestures of their bodies inserted into language. A praxis is but a social routinisation of significant human interaction, and the praxes of a society are but the forms of its significant life, they are its lived social language.

By now, too, we ought to be able to see more clearly what the epistemological problem about ideology is which was introduced at the end of the first chapter. It is hard, we said, to see how ideas could be *both* 'socially lived' and 'false'. And yet the classical conception of ideology involves saying both of these things about it. The difficulty is that, given what has now been said about how ideas are 'socially lived', there seems to be nothing for a socially lived idea to be a false idea *of*, for there seems to be no room left for any account of a social reality other than that which is already lived in the medium of ideas about it. Since, therefore, there seems to be no epistemic space between what is socially lived and the social ideas of it, there seems to be no room for a *false* relationship between the two. In short, it seems to follow from the proposition that praxes are socially lived ideas that such ideas are tautologically true.

Furthermore, as we will see in the next chapter, this is no merely artificial paradox contrived with its solution known in advance. The stress I have given to the internality of the relation between ideas and social praxes does genuinely put in question the possibility of that relation's being in any straightforward way a 'false' one. Certainly the theory of ideology does propose that this relation is in some way empistemologically 'deviant', but anything we have to say about the form of this deviance must, in my view, be qualified in advance by its internality to the social life of which ideology is the deviant perception. In short, if anything has to give under the pressure of paradox, it is not the internality of ideology to social life, but the proposition that the epistemological character of its relation to social 'reality' is that of falsehood. At any rate that proposition will have to be severely qualified.

NOTES

1   Quoted in Iris Murdoch, *Sartre*, London, 1967, p. 13.

2   J. Locke, *Essay Concerning Human Understanding*, III, 2, §8.

3   H. McCabe, 'Transubstantiation', *Ampleforth Journal*, LXXIV (I), Spring 1969, pp. 8–9.

4   See P.T. Geach, *Mental Acts*, London, 1957, for a sustained attack on what he calls 'abstractionism' and for the defence of an alternative account of concept-formation related to the one outlined in the next paragraph.

5   Aristotle, *Politics*, 1253 b 8.

6   Karl Marx and Friedrich Engels, *The German Ideology*, edited and translated by C.J. Arthur, London, 1970, part I, p. 47.

7   M. Merleau-Ponty, *In Praise of Philosophy*, Chicago, 1963, p. 50.

3

Ideology and Contradiction

If any way is to be found out of the impasse described in chapter 1, and if the internality of ideology is to be maintained, then the proposition that ideology is a form of *false* consciousness will have to be re-examined. The re-examination begins in this chapter, but only informally and by way of illustration or analogy. I propose, in fact, a pedagogical metaphor for ideology, an illustration which may serve its purely illustrative purpose even if, as many might wish to say, it is hardly an actual instance of it. For what is at stake for the time being is a strictly limited matter of whether it is *possible* to describe a state of affairs combining the two features, namely, first, that of being a social reality to which ideas are internal and, second, one in which those ideas are in an epistemologically deviant relation with that social reality. If we can manage bare plausibility, it will be enough to allow us the next step, which is to establish the form of that epistemological deviance. Such, then, is the purpose of this chapter.

I

We may suppose, first, and in line with the argument of the last chapter, that teaching is a 'praxis'; certainly it is an unambiguous case of speech-governed action and action-generating speech in internal relations with one another. More specifically, teaching is a form or routine of utterances which do something — although quite what the words of a teacher are supposed to do for the taught is, of course, a matter on which the theorists are hopelessly divided. But teaching is also a way of doing things which says something. Obviously some kind of problem arises if, in the actions of teaching, what the teacher's utterances do for the students conflicts with what his actions say to them — if the internal relations of the praxis of teaching are a disunity of word and action. Notoriously this is too often the case, and I shall have something to say shortly about what we may expect when this happens.

These are rather condensed formulae, but in the light of the argument in the last chapter it should not be too hard to grant that what teachers do says something. This, of course, is not the fact referred to by moralisers who, perhaps rightly, but not very relevantly in this connection, are concerned with what they call the teacher's 'good example'. Constituting the fact that what teachers do says something is the evidence that the materiality of the teaching praxis itself teaches many things — and often enough far more effectively than anything the teacher himself teaches. Rather more to the point is the very special case of this effect: the fact that the teacher teaches very largely *by saying things* itself teaches things other than, and more effectively than, *what* he says.

The action of saying can say things which the speaker's words do not themselves say. University teachers, the most word-centred teachers of all, are among the least aware of this fact. Obsessed as they usually are with the quality of their verbal output, they are at a loss to explain why the overt liberalism which they regularly preach so rarely rubs off on the average undergraduate. It hardly ever occurs to them to look beyond the quality of the verbal message at what their actions *of saying* say to the students. A university lecturer preaches his anti-authoritarian idealisms day in and day out, preaches the emancipation of minds through learning, through free inquiry, through the ruthless questioning of every dogma, and so forth. His saying these things will do little enough for the students if nearly everything he does by saying them says the very opposite, if the very lectures in which he announces these elevating principles of freedom are themselves authoritarian actions. Let us imagine him saying in his lectures 'speak your own minds'; then he says by his lecturing, 'but by no means interrupt'. If he says in his seminars, 'ask you own questions', may he not be saying in his examinations, 'you will fail, if you answer any but mine'? Is it necessary to insist that this is but an illustration? Those who doubt its plausibility even in that role might prefer to consult Malcolm Bradbury's *The History Man* a novel which is constructed upon the ironies of such cases. It is ironic, but at least plausible, to say that occasionally universities fall foul of the charge that the ideas they hold themselves responsible for teaching are subverted by the conflict they are in with what their praxes of teaching them teach. And where such conflicts have become routinised, then the consequence is that the conflicts themselves teach yet another idea of very fundamental significance. This is what could be called the 'second-order' idea, that ideas and practices are in purely external relations with each other, that the materiality of the mode of communication has no bearing on the quality of the ideas being communicated. After all, if it really is possible to teach freedom of thought in the medium of authoritarian teaching conditions, how can the quality of the idea itself be in any internal relations with the social conditions of its communication? But if a practice of communication itself communicates, then it will matter to the character of the ideas being communicated what that practice says. In the case, then, where the two sorts of things said fall apart, we have a paradox: the complex contradiction itself is a praxis which teaches that only ideas can teach, not practices.

Let us push the analogy one step further along the road to parody. Imagine the really progressive university lecturer making a meal of just these points in a lecture. It happens. Here is the 'verbal professor of freedom'[1] in the course of what is called a 'lecture'. There are the emancipatory things which he is saying which are, so to speak, the mind-occupying events on which attention is focused. At this manifest level 'the lecture', in its materiality as an enacted set of social relations, disappears into the purely ideal order of the meanings which he is attempting to convey. The 'better' his words, the more this is so. For the better his words — the more mind-engaging they are — the greater their capacity to draw attention from the effective pedagogy of the teaching relation itself, inattention to which has no tendency to reduce the effectiveness. On the contrary, precisely because it is not observed, the materiality of the teaching relationship — its authoritarian character, for the sake of argument — achieves an enhanced effectiveness, for its subliminal character puts it beyond the reach of explicit criticism.[2] The paradox is that what the professor's teaching materially says exhibits all that his words ideally criticise; he is teaching freedom in the material mode of a dominative relationship. Running within the explicit pedagogy of his words is a tacit, non-manifest but effective propaganda of the praxis of communication, a propaganda which contradicts the pedagogy.

I say that the one is pedagogy and the other propaganda on fairly conventional definitions of these terms. For pedagogy is a form of free explicit expression which freely engages the minds of the learners. Propaganda is a form of verbal causality which brings about an effect in the mind of the propagandised without freely engaging it. Where the pedagogy and the propaganda fall apart, where, as I put it, what is said by the words is contradicted by what their being uttered says, this contradictory conjunction of sayings and doings is a total result, a praxis, which is my first metaphor for ideology. That metaphor suggests about ideology that it is a routinised enactment of a contradiction between a meaning conveyed explicitly and a meaning conveyed by the act itself of conveying, where what is manifest is only the explicitly uttered meaning whose very translucence disguises its contradiction by the latent message of the meaning-conveying act.

II

Some comments are necessary on this metaphor. The first is that it is a (hypothetical) case of a form of enacted contradiction. But the contradiction is internal to the act itself, it is not that *between* men's actions and that they think about them, as if 'thought' and 'action' could be first described independently of one another, and then compared for 'fit'. Unfortunately many readers of Marx have been misled into the view that, for Marx, the relation of ideology to the 'reality' of which it is the distorted consciousness is in this way external. For example, many have taken Marx to be suggesting that the relationship is one-way and causal in character, that the social world causes those who participate in it to have distorted ideas of that world. Of course, Marx himself must be held partly responsible for this misunderstanding, for in a famous passage in *The German Ideology* he states that:

> . . . men, developing their material production and their material intercourse, alter along with their *real* existence, their thinking and the products of their thinking. Life is not determined by consciousness, but consciousness by life.[3]

Moreover, the origin of *ideological* consciousness is explained in even more grossly causalistic terms:

> If in all ideology men and their circumstances appear upside down as in a *camera obscura*, this phenomenon arises just as much from their historical life-process as the inversion of objects on the retina does from their physical life process.[4]

Taken simply as it stands, this conjunction of passages would amount to the abandonment of that feature which I said to be essential to the notion of ideology; namely, that ideologies are internal to the social relations of which they are the ideological representations. For the mechanistic language which Marx uses, on the contrary, suggests that the social reality can be described independently of the ideas which social agents have of them, so that the discrepancy between the ideology and the social reality can be detected simply by looking at the reality as it truly is. And Marx says what certainly seems to be as much when he states that he and Engels:

> . . . set out from real active men, and on the basis of their real life-process we demonstrate the development of the ideological reflexes and echoes of this life-process. The phantoms formed in the human brain are also, necessarily, sublimates of their material life-process, which is empirically verifiable and bound to material premises . . .[5]

Now to attend exclusively to these and other similar

passages in *The German Ideology* is absurd if we want an account even of Marx's early (and, incidentally, intentionally unpublished) views on ideology. They must be taken in conjunction with the argument of the whole work and at the very least in conjunction with as many other passages in it which suggest a very different reading. A little earlier in *The German Ideology* he insists that 'as individuals express their life, so they are'[6] and that:

language is as old as consciousness, language *is* practical consciousness that exists also for other men, and for that reason alone it *really exists* for me personally as well; language, like consciousness, only arises from the need, the necessity of intercourse with other men.[7]

In other words, Marx is very clear about the internality of men's consciousness to the social relations into which they enter; there is no easy contrast to be made between their *real* existence and their consciousness of it, for:

consciousness can never be anything else than conscious existence, and the existence of men is their actual life-process.[8]

And that is why, if ideology does represent social reality ('men and their circumstances') 'upside down as in a *camera obscura*', this misrepresentation is internal to the structure of the 'historical life process', not something externally imposed upon it.

Now I hold no brief to demonstrate the consistency of these sets of texts, prima facie conflicting as they are. In any case *The German Ideology* is an early work which Marx and Engels later wished to see 'consigned to the flames', and there is little to be gained from pursuing the matter exegetically. The point is that, although in this work Marx and Engels do not yet seem to have the epistemological tools for the task, none the less the task they have appointed for ideology is stated clearly enough: it is that of pulling together the features both of its internality to social relationships and of its misrepresentation of those social relationships to which it is internal. And this is what my metaphor illustrates. The contradiction is not that between a set of meaning-conveying locutions (the teacher's words) and a dumb, non-meaning-conveying 'reality' (the social relations of teaching), as if the ideological contradiction could be detected by empirical inspection of the pre-significant 'facts' and comparing them with the language used to describe them. The contradiction is between two sorts of thing said, the one said explicitly by the teacher, the other said implicitly by his acts of saying them, both being intrinsic factors of the total social 'reality'. Consequently, if anything is said to be that social 'reality', it is not the social relationships *rather than* the consciousness of them, but the contradiction between the two itself: the 'reality' consists in the facts of that contradiction.

Let me, therefore, conclude this comment on the pedagogical metaphor with another metaphor, this time religious, which will serve the additional purpose of typifying formally the general features of Marxist criticism of Christianity itself.

Let us this time suppose a priest delivering his sermon, as it were from the height of his authoritarian pulpit, on the equality of the people of God. No more in this case than in the last should we analyse this complex praxis into two separate factors, the egalitarian communication and the fact that, as it happens, it is delivered from an authoritarian pulpit. For the point about authoritarian pulpits is that they are already sermons. If you have one, you do not need to preach authoritarian sermons, for the authoritarianism of the pulpit will preach well enough within the words of the egalitarian sermon. The pulpit itself is part of the materiality of the priest's act of saying — it both internalises and exhibits the character of his relationship with the congregation — but for all that this materiality lies outside the realm of the conscious, intended communications of the priest, it is not for that reason external to the gross total of meaning achieved and communicated. For that materiality not only has its own significance — it *says* something — that significance practises its own hermeneutic upon the explicit meanings of the preacher. Hence his words become the bearer of a condensation of conflicting meanings which, precisely in so far as it lies outside the intentions of the preacher, is uncontrolled by those intentions, and subverts them. The total result is a social reality constructed upon the contradiction.

But it is in these facts of contradiction that the members

of the worshipping community are socialised. They perceive their relationship to the act of worship via the condensation of conflicting meanings, for at one level they attend, perhaps with approval, to what the preacher says *and in so doing* reciprocate the authoritarianism of his act of saying it. Consequently the preacher and the congregation engage in a mutual relationship with one another via the contradiction in which they are jointly socialised. Hence they socially live an enacted contradiction, a contradiction which is internal to their form of life.

III

It will appear from what I have said so far that ideological contradictions are some species of the general class of performative contradictions, as they might be called. Such is a case where a person is saying something, *p*, does something to do which is to say something which contradicts *p*. Arguing at tedious length for maximum participation in the discussion, reading the Riot Act and thereby provoking the behaviour it prohibits, creating racial harmony by means of lurid warnings against its dangers, disarming criticism of one's action by anticipating it — these are all ways in which people refute what they say by the act of saying it. Ideology, I wish to say, is a special case of this wider class, differentiated from other cases, including all the examples given, by the fact that whereas these are primarily actions explicable in terms of agents' intentions, ideologies are practices explicable in terms of their routinised structures and independent of any particular agent's intentions. An ideology is a praxis which internalises a systematic performative contradiction. None the less performatively contradictory actions do often share significant features with ideologies, and before attending to the crucial differences it is worthwhile mentioning one of the shared features which has a special bearing on my argument in later chapters.

In the Prologue to the Pardoner's Tale in the *Canterbury Tales*, Chaucer has the thoroughly cynical and hypocritical Pardoner describe in graphically meretricious terms the deceitful art of his trade in false relics. He addresses his fellow pilgrims roughly as follows:

My trade, as you know, is in false relics. I work on the fears and super-
stitions of my audience who believe that my relics are genuine. I
persuade them to part with money they can ill afford by preaching
them sermons, the main theme of which is that the love of money is the
root of all evil. Of course the joke is that their very gullibility enables
me to practise what I preach against. Well, naturally, this makes me a
thorough hypocrite, and I don't mind admitting it, I am. So what? My
customers think they are getting what they believe in and I for certain
get what I believe in: they my 'relics' and I their money.

The value of this illustration lies in the extreme character
of the Pardoner's perversity. He knows that his fellow pilgrims
regard him as a hypocrite. Hence, instead of denying it and
making a fool of himself, he turns the tables on them by
admitting it: now it is they who will appear naive if they
venture to criticise. Of course, in much ameliorated form it is
common enough for people to disarm moral criticism by the
open admission of its truth. It somehow makes it irrelevant
for others to press the charge. In any case to admit guilt is at
the same time a condemnation of one's own action and a
declaration of one's independence of, indeed moral superiority
to, the action one has condemned. I thus disarm the criticism
of me which another's condemnation implies, while sharing
with my critics the common basis of moral judgement on
which my action is condemned. I am at one with my critics
in condemning my past behaviour.

But the Pardoner's ploy goes much further than this. He
proclaims his unrepentant hypocrisy. In doing so he blunts
the critical edge of the moral word 'hypocrite' in the very act
of using it, thereby illustrating a certain truth in Sartre's
belief that no man can properly self-ascribe vice.[9] For,
Sartre argues, there are only two possibilities. You may
genuinely condemn yourself as in some way vicious, say, as
lazy, but such an admission is, in a way, self-defeating, for in
so far as your self-condemnation is genuine you are already
something other than a lazy person, you have already 'trans-
cended' your laziness. On the other hand, if, in calling
yourself lazy, you are not condemning yourself, but are using
the language of condemnation in an externalised, 'objective'
and uncommitted way, it is not vice that you are ascribing
to yourself. Thus the person who is 'happy to admit' that he

is lazy (or unscrupulous or a hypocrite) is either thereby not any longer the hypocrite he says he is or else is using the language of condemnation as a ploy to neutralise in the moral language any critical, condemnatory force. In fact this is what is so disconcerting about the self-proclaimed hypocrite or cynic or amoralist: he sets himself apart, not by refusing to use the common language of morality, still less by the mere eccentricity of his moral views, but by dislocating moral language itself in its use.

One form of ideology is characterised by something like this form of cynicism. Let us reconsider the case of our emancipated university lecturer lecturing against authoritarian teaching methods. His action is a performative contradiction in a rather straightforward way, but it is conceivable that a defence of his activity will be made out on the grounds that it is ironical in character rather than cynical. He might, like the Pardoner, admit the contradiction and thematise it. He might, that is to say, make just that contradiction the theme of his lecture, encouraging his students to see that it matters not what is said in a lecture in favour of libertarian teaching methods so long as the students' reaction is to take notes on it. The lecturer will admit that he is exhibiting the contradiction he is describing *in* describing it, but, drawing the lesson from this heightened awareness, argue that the only non-compromising mode of discourse in the university is this ironic mode.

None the less, there is no need to be deceived by this manoeuvre. If the lecturer means what he says, he will place alongside the 'arm of criticism' the 'criticism of arms'[10] — he will do something about it. And this, too, is for a reason which is aptly illustrated by his compromised circumstances: his own arguments prove that you cannot fight ideology by ideological means alone, even of this 'second-order' ironic character. If the lecturer tries to make a profession of this stance he will fail, his individualistic and purely rhetorical irony being pitted in a quite hopeless struggle with that structural cynicism which, after all, he has correctly identified. He becomes the Pardoner of the professoriate, a mere exhibitor of what he condemns in the very act of condemning it. If he hides himself at all, it is, paradoxically, by means of exhibitionism. In his very exhibitionism he, like the Pardoner, debases the language of criticism in the act of employing it. And now, at last, we come to the crux of the matter. We have seen in what way the contradictions of ideology are internal to the form of life of which it is the ideology, but so far we have said nothing explicit about the way in which ideology internalises 'falsehood'. Now, however, we can say something about this matter, but what we can say is disappointing from the point of view of the original formulation. For the deviance of the epistemological relation between ideology and 'reality' is not really a form of falsehood at all, but something rather more subtle. If we look again at our illustrations, we can see why this is so. Although cynical at the personal level, the lecturer's words are not false any more than are the Pardoner's. The Pardoner, after all, is what he says he is — a hypocrite. His admitting it does not make it any the less 'true'. The lecturer, likewise, is quite right to say that it is out of permanent, structural features of the relationship of lecturer to students that his paradoxical situation arises. Consequently, if in either case we wish to ascribe a form of 'false consciousness', it is not in relation to obvious facts which they refuse to acknowledge that their consciousnesses are false, for they do acknowledge them. It is not as if either were hiding *from* obvious truths, or, if they are, it is not by the means of their suppression. If anything it is themselves that they are hiding within the obviousness of certain truths. If it is appropriate to use the term at all in this connection, and we have seen reason to doubt that it is, what is 'false' about this form of consciousness is something epistemologically far more complex than logical falsity and does not even involve it. The 'falsehood' is rather that in this mode of the assertion of truth the truth asserted is sundered from its critical and therefore from its practical import. In a word, the nexus between truth and praxis is ruptured. In this respect the Pardoner and the all too self-aware lecturer are rather the shameless than the guilt-ridden. The guilt-ridden hides as much as he can, because he will not do what his standards dictate. The shameless exposes everything in order that he need do nothing.

It remains to insist that the difference between the Pardoner and the lecturer is crucial. It is the *attitude* of the Pardoner which is cynical and his destruction of moral language is in its reference to him personally. He causes a temporary hiatus, a suspension of the applicability of a discourse whose practical, critical force survives otherwise than in its reference to him. He can, therefore, restore the practical force of his admission of hypocrisy merely by coming to mean what he says. He thereby ceases to be a hypocrite. The lecturer, however, can change his attitude as much as he likes without destroying the general cynical force exerted by the situation of his exhibiting it. It is the relatively more 'objective' material praxis of the university and of his role as lecturer within it which robs his words of their critical power, so that the language of criticism itself is subverted by the praxis which, paradoxically, also makes sense of his speaking it. There is, therefore, a structural contradiction, a cynicism endemic to the praxis itself, it is a socially lived, practical form of the Pardoner's cynicism. It is as such that his situation is a metaphor for ideology in general, that capacity of a form of social life to neutralise, without suppression, the moral force of critical language.

To sum up, then, on the abstract and general features of ideology which emerge from this lengthy and by now much forced analogy. First, ideology is a species of lived, or performative, contradiction. The contradiction in question, however, is not that misleadingly described by Marx and Engels in *The German Ideology* as that between 'ideas' and 'reality', but is rather a contradiction between levels of ideas within a reality which lives in the medium of ideas. The kind of ideology which I have been illustrating is that which is typical in a praxis of communication where ideas communicated are systematically contradicted by the idea of communication itself. The total result for the form of social life in which such contradictions are lived is an ideological praxis, the social effect of which is the cynical undermining of the language of communication itself.

Clearly, then, the model for ideology developed in this chapter is designed for the explanation primarily of those forms of ideology which either are, or share significant features with, praxes of communication. It remains to be seen whether this model will serve in the explanation of those forms of ideology which also differ in important respects from praxes of communication, above all, of that most fundamental form of ideology, the economic.[11] For the time being it is enough that the model serves my narrower purpose in the explanation of those two forms of ideology which are the topic of this book: the moral and the religious. For they are, whatever else, essentially communicative discourses. But before considering how the model bears on these, it is necessary to fill out the model by reference to some further general features of all ideology, consideration of which will, incidentally, bring us somewhat closer to the terminology of Marx's formulations. In the next chapter I consider the first of these, 'mystification'.

NOTES

1   '. . . everyone talks of freedome, but there are but few who act for freedome and the actors for freedome are oppressed by the talkers and verball professors of freedome'. Gerrard Winstanley, *A Watchword to the City of London and the Armie* (1649), in *The Works of Gerrard Winstanley*, edited and introduced by G.H. Sabine, New York, 1941, p. 317.

2   I once second-marked some university examination papers in the philosophy of education in which candidates had been asked whether examinations are an authoritarian method of assessment. Many candidates answered in the affirmative without a trace of self-consciousness or irony.

3   Karl Marx and Friedrich Engels, *The German Ideology*, edited and translated by C.J. Arthur, London, 1970, part I, p. 47.

4   Ibid.

5   Ibid.

6   Ibid., p. 42.

7   Ibid., p. 51.

8   Ibid., p. 47.

9   See Margaret Gilbert, 'Vices and Self-Knowledge', *Journal of Philosophy*, LXVIII, 1971, pp. 443–53.

10 Karl Marx, *Contribution to the Critique of Hegel's Philosophy of Right, Introduction*, edited and translated by T.B. Bottomore, in *Karl Marx: Early Writings*, London, 1963, p. 52.

11 See chapter 9. It should not be inferred from this remark that the

economy is not, in the sense defined in chapter 2, a praxis which internalises ideas. In the sense in which, in common with every other praxis, it does so, the economy is a form of communication between people. But whereas the economy communicates production, a praxis *of* communication differs from it in producing communication.

4

Ideology and Mystification

In George Eliot's novel, *Felix Holt, the Radical*, Felix's mother, a poor widow, appeals to Harold Transome, a rich landowner and a radical candidate in the 1832 general election, to use his influence to secure the release of her son from prison. He has been wrongfully charged with having led a riot at an election meeting of Transome's, although he had in fact tried to prevent it. Forgetting her due position in her appeal to Transome, Mrs Holt becomes overheated. At length she realises that she may have overdone it, 'feeling', as George Eliot puts it, 'that she was now in deep water', she ends her outburst in a properly remorseful spirit with the remark:

. . . and I know as you're told . . . not to rail at your betters if they be the devil himself.[1]

In the last chapter I went some way towards explaining how ideology involves a species of performative contradiction within the structure of social reality, a contradiction which is not hidden in some way below the surface of conscious social behaviour but is exhibited at the surface where it is emasculated by a process which I have so far only metaphorised as a kind of 'structural cynicism'. I further argued that an ideological praxis is a routinisation of this ideological contradictoriness. We may now add the point that a person successfully socialised into the routines of an ideological practice is a person who accepts its contradictory character as a matter of course — with spontaneity and naturalness. Mrs Holt's remark to Transome exhibits both this spontaneous routinisation of ideological contradiction and one further feature of ideology, the role of class oppression in ideology. Both require detailed examination.

I

I consider first naturalness and spontaneity. Mrs Holt's quoted remark records her return to a sense of reality, as she understands it. So urgently had she appealed to Transome that she had forgotten her place. Indeed it might be more accurate to say that the anxiety and heat with which she appeals are symptoms of an anxiety about having forgotten her place, they are symptoms of her awareness of the dis-equilibrium between the language of her appeal and a system of stable tokens of mutual identification and class relation-ship. He is one of her 'betters'. There are modes of speech which are proper between 'betters' and 'inferiors', and naturalness in speech is possible only where the rules governing these proprieties are observed. Once these rules are transgressed there is only verbal anarchy — anything might be said and nothing would mean anything. Hence, her final words record, as I say, her return to 'reality', to that normality within which natural and spontaneous modes of speech restore meaning, value and with them, stability of relation-ship, a sense of knowing how things stand.

The sentence does not, however, merely enact a return to reality. It is also an inchoate description of the reality restored. Harold is described by Mrs Holt as one of her 'betters'. That is how things are. Of course the word is a rough, unspecific token for a social class. Its looseness as a description is, as we will see, one of its key ideological features, but its looseness is relative only to more 'scientific' accounts, in economic, political and social terms, of the class to which Transome belongs. As a token of identification, however, Mrs Holt can use it with exactitude. She may know very little in theoretical terms about what makes Transome's class a class. But she has no such uncertainty about his belonging to it, nor, in general, would she have any difficulty deciding who does and who does not belong to the class of her 'betters'. This is unsurprising, since it is generally possible to identify a case falling under a rule without being able to formulate explicitly the rule under which the case falls. So too with social identifications. Most people are quite capable of spontaneously falling into the modes of speech appropriate to a very varied range of occasions without any explicit reference to the rules governing this appropriateness: they will greet their wives with a kiss, their mates at work with a grunt and a nod, and their boss with correctness. They neither need to, nor probably could, work out just what rules determine the difference. We pay sociologists to do this for us.

There is, moreover, a specific reason why Mrs Holt need know nothing about the determinants of Transome's class position in her use of the designation 'your betters'. It is that this expression is less a designation of Transome's social place than it is a designation of her own in terms of his. Two points indicate this. The first is that 'your betters' is a lower-class designation of people belonging to a superior class. There are equivalent terms of identification used by Transome's class to designate those below them as a subordinate class, for example, 'inferiors' or 'the lower orders'. But social 'betters' do not need those terms to describe their own social status. Although to Mrs Holt Transome is one of *her* 'betters' and although in so describing him she is identifying herself, the relationship is not symmetrical. Transome knows, of course, that he is one of Mrs Holt's 'betters' and that she is one of his 'inferiors', but far from his needing to identify himself by reference to her inferiority, the mark of the gentleman is that he is unselfconscious about class. Men who know their superior social position do not need to stand on their dignity. In fact, rather more positively, they need not have to do this. They do not need to, because within the system of social tokens and identifications, their superior position rests on the acknowledgement of it by their inferiors, it does not rest on their own assertion of it. And they need not have to stand on their dignity, because to have to assert their social superiority could only be necessary in the absence of the acknowledgement of inferiority on the part of their inferiors. It is, then, not so much the designation of Transome's position which is acknowledged in the expression 'your betters' as of Mrs Holt's. Mrs Holt identifies her place in terms of its relationship to Transome's.

Second, Mrs Holt can designate her social position in

ignorance of the class structure which determines it, because she sees this relationship as much in terms of the moral obligations which it entails as through any sociological perception of class structure. Even this is to misdescribe her thinking. It is not as if, in recognising her class inferiority, she recognises the moral obligation of deference to be entailed for her by it. Her acknowledgement that she is told 'not to rail at one's betters' *is* her way of acknowledging the class structure. Her social knowledge takes the form of moral knowledge — or at least social description and moral obligation become inextricably fused. It is enough that she knows what her obligations are. She does not need to know very much about the social bases of her class position; indeed, from the point of view of the stability of the class structure, it is better that her moral sense is not disturbed by too much sociology.

This fusion of the description of class into the sense of the moral obligations which it entails has the ideologically important consequence of closing the gap between 'is' and 'ought'. If Mrs Holt could have separated out the social and the moral elements into two distinct items of knowledge — if, in other words, she could have identified Transome's social class and her *de facto* relationship with it independently of the moral obligations supposedly entailed by that class relationship — then she could, theoretically at least, have questioned the validity of the entailment. She could have asked *why* Transome's occupying the social position he does is supposed to entail her deference, and she could have framed the answer that the entailment is not justified at all. But she cannot do this, given the language she uses about that relationship. For the relationship is already 'described' in terms of the moral obligations it lays upon her. In any case there is a psychological reason why she cannot abandon the language of 'your betters'. As we have seen, she needs this language as her natural and spontaneous mode of *self*-identification. It was a matter of personal anxiety to her that she had come near to disrupting the fragile stabilities of her own discourse. For she needs, as being her natural language of self-identification, a language which defines her into a position of social deference.

II

So much for naturalness and spontaneity. Mrs Holt's remark serves to illustrate Marx's comment that the ideology of a society is its 'natural and spontaneous mode of thought'.[2] But of course ideology is not just that. We have seen that it is the spontaneous living out of social contradictions. Furthermore, it is, for Marx, the dissolution of *class* contradictions into this naturalness. This, too, is illustrated by Mrs Holt. The first and most obvious form of contradiction which is so dissolved is apparently straighforwardly verbal. It is the most obvious because it is totally at the surface and amounts very nearly, but not quite, to a contradiction in terms: one's 'betters' are said to be one's 'betters' even if 'he be the devil himself'.

So close does this sentence come to outright contradiction that the naturalness with which Mrs Holt utters it requires a slightly more nuanced account than that which I have just given. The force of the expression 'one's betters' cannot be exclusively moral, if the sentence is to retain any semblance of plausibility. It cannot be the case that the designation of sociological class has entirely disappeared into the recognition of moral obligation, for if it has the sentence becomes just too plainly contradictory. No one, not even Mrs Holt, is going to denote a rational ordering of things with a remark whose explicit meaning is: one ought to defer to those who are morally better, even if they are morally worse. 'One's betters' cannot mean *only* 'one's moral betters'. Nor, on the other hand, can that expression denote in a morally neutral way simple class position of *de facto* greater weight, for then transparently there is no legitimate entailment of her deference. Finally, granted that the expression does in some way fuse sociological class description with moral obligation, this 'fusion' does not bring the descriptive and the evaluative elements together under some explicitly acknowledged moral rule, such as that one ought to pay deference to those who *de facto* wield social power, regardless of their right to do so. Mrs Holt shows no sign of knowing any such general principle. The ideological effect of Mrs Holt's remark requires the presence on the surface of her utterance both of the sociological description and of the moral obligation, but in systematically ambiguous relations with each other, relations which allow for the elision of the one side into the other in defiance of the logic of surface meaning. 'One's betters' leans in both the sociological and the moral directions, but ambiguously, as shot silk is neither one colour or the other, nor the other colour only, nor yet exactly both, but either colour, depending on the angle of refraction.

In the analysis of the sentence as a whole it might help to clarify the ideological exploitation of its ambiguities, if we divide it thus:

1 Moral prescription

'You're told not to rail at | your betters | if they be the devil himself'

2 Sociological description

3 Ideological perception of class

Each of the two sub-sentences, 1 and 2, constitute a potentially coherent unit of sense when taken on its own. 1. One's *moral* betters can be represented with sense as deserving the deference of not being railed at, so long as those who are one's moral betters can be identified on agreed criteria of moral goodness. 2. Likewise, there is no difficulty in supposing that a certain sociologically defined class of people who are socially superior, say in the power they exercise within the political system, may contain many members who are morally reprehensible people, even morally worse than those they rule. 3. But in the whole sentence 'one's betters' stands at the point of overlap between the sub-sentences 1 and 2 and has to be read in both ways, in one way from the point of view of 1 (one's moral betters are due deference) and in another way from the point of view of 2 (your social betters may be morally worse than you). If the whole sentence is read exclusively in terms of either meaning, then it is either patently contradictory (if read throughout as a moral utterance) or else it contains a patently implausible and unjustified inference from facts to values (if read throughout as a sociological utterance). But when read as a whole which encapsulates both readings, with the two interpretations allowed to oscillate within the phrase 'one's betters' (holding back sociologically in 1 and morally in 2), the sentence pulls off a certain kind of plausibility, not by hiding the contradiction, for it remains there on the surface, but by a sort of inoculation of its irrationality.

So constructed, the contradiction is now fit for utterance. Mrs Holt, too, can express herself by means of it. She can place herself within its fluctuation of meanings. She now knows where she stands and what to do. Her reality is now structured, ordered. No longer is she without bearings, as she was when in an explosion of anxiety she transgressed the known boundaries of her social world. The condensation of the contradictory utterance into a sort of fused, but still oscillating, tension of meanings rehabilitates her, restores to her her sense of the way things are. And yet, secure as she may feel in that social space in which her sentence locates her, analysis has shown just how precarious is the ideological basis of her security. If it is put under too much pressure from the direction of either moral criticism or of sociological analysis, her carefully balanced tension of meanings collapses either into plain contradictoriness or else into manifest implausibility. It is, then, the capacity of ideological language to sustain contradictory elements in this precarious tension with one another which represents its defeat of logic and its capacity, in spite of the internal contradictions which it sustains, to 'represent reality', to normalise the irrational.

It is this feature of much of our social language which Ernest Gellner has in mind when he remarks that an expression such as 'your betters':

. . . is a conceptual device by which the privileged class of the society in question acquires some of the prestige of certain virtues respected in that society, without the inconvenience of needing to practise them, thanks to the fact that the same word is applied either to practitioners of those virtues or to occupiers of favoured positions. It is at the same time a manner of reinforcing the appeal of those virtues, by associating them, through the use of the same appellation, with prestige and power. But . . . this . . . is to bring about the internal logical incoherence of the concept — an incoherence which, indeed, is socially functional.[3]

'Your betters' works its ideological magic by ambiguously denoting both a social class and a set of virtues, thereby prohibiting the description of anyone as a member of that class without the simultaneous ascription to him of those virtues and at the same time prohibiting the ascription of those virtues to any non-member of the class. And yet, by failing to resolve the ambiguity in either direction − that is, by collapsing the description into the ascription, or vice versa − by holding them apart just enough that the one can be traded off against the other, such sentences as Mrs Holt's survive the threat to their apparent sense posed by too explicit an exposure of their contradictoriness.

III

It is now time to have a look at the social effects of such ideological condensations. But first a word about their pervasiveness.

The detection of such key ideological expressions is the detection of ideological symptoms, but not, by itself, of ideologies. Ideologies are languages. Expressions such as 'your betters' are but phrases in ideological languages. They live out such lives as the languages of which they are part accord to them. The verbal cunning of 'your betters' cannot be accounted for except by reference to a whole system of interlocking attitudes, perceptions and prescriptions together with the discourse which is their appropriate expression. It is in the novel, typically, that the variety and density of such shared perceptions are best studied, because novels − or at least many English Victorian novels − are structured out of what one might call the *inter*perceptions of one character by another. More particularly, in a political novel such as *Felix Holt*, where the political and social dimensions of these interacting perceptions are made explicit, we have a vehicle, *par excellence*, for the exhibition of ideological modes of social perception. On the other hand, although *Felix Holt* exhibits the ideological as a language of inter-action, it is a far less satisfactory genre for its analysis and criticism: a point which should remind us that in the preceding analysis of 'your betters' we have been concerned primarily with ideology as a mode of *perception* of class. What the novel is less well equipped to deal with is the disclosure of the actual mechanisms of class — its social reality as a force exerting pressure on the language of interaction itself. The novel registers the perceived effects of that pressure. It cannot, as a novel, so easily analyse the mechanisms whereby that pressure is exerted.

The fact of the matter is that Mrs Holt's dictum about her 'betters' is at once a declaration of her perception of class difference and a formula which obscures the relation. She does acknowledge that 'your betters' denotes a class of people who are defined otherwise than by the quality of their moral behaviour, for that is how it is possible that some of them should behave reprehensibly while still remaining 'her betters'. She acknowledges, furthermore, that they enjoy a richer life-style — they 'live in great houses and can ride in a carriage where they will';[4] and finally that they have greater political and social power at their command — that is, after all, the point of her appeal to Transome and of her demand that he 'ought to go to the King and get him to let off my son Felix'.[5] She does know her 'betters' to be a class. All the same, the expression by means of which she denotes this class is one which obscures its true nature as a class.

I have already noted how Mrs Holt's language oscillates between an inchoate sociological description and an expression of moral evaluation, so as neither to collapse the former into the latter without trace nor as to exhibit any explicit logical connection between the factual and the moral. Hence it effectively bridges the gap between 'is' and 'ought' without having to acknowledge that there is any gap to be bridged. It is important, however, not to misunderstand this point. It is not, as some contemporary philosophers of morals would have us believe, that the gap between 'is' and 'ought' is logically unbridgeable, so that this oscillation of language between the factual and the evaluative is an unjustified crossing of a gap which it is illegitimate in principle to cross.[6] What is illegitimate about the bridging which Mrs Holt's language achieves is the manner in which it is done, for it is achieved in a manner which inhibits the perception of a suppressed logical relationship between the description and the prescription, thus inhibiting also the criticism of that nexus. Consequently, Mrs Holt's relationship to Transome is presented as evaluative from one point of view ('betters'$_1$) and as based on the way things are from the other ('betters'$_2$) so that, in conjunction, the two dimensions present the contingent, conventional relationship as *naturally* evaluative.

This, however, is not the end of the mystifications which Mrs Holt's language achieves. Just as the systematic oscillation from the evaluative to the descriptive and back again inhibits the analysis and criticism of the logical connections between them, so each element of the sentence inhibits the analysis of the other. From the moral point of view (that is, from the point of view of the deference owed to them) her 'betters' disappear as an empirically defined class of morally variable people only to reappear as that empirically defined class exhibiting every variety of moral worth, but now beyond the pale of moral criticism. Hence, just as from one point of view the entailment of an evaluation by the facts is illegitimately achieved (being one of her 'betters' entails her deference), so another possible entailment of an evaluation by the facts is illegitimately ruled out (the moral criticism of the class behaviour itself). In a word, Mrs Holt's vocabulary constrains her to use moral language to characterise the empirical class and descriptive language to inhibit the moral criticism of that class. Her language colludes to her disadvantage. Her 'betters' appear as a class only to entail her deference. In face of the potential moral criticism of the class *as a class*, the class disappears into the individuals who compose it: *of course* some are good, some are bad.[7]

It is correct, then, to describe Mrs Holt's language as part of a wider language of domination as viewed from the standpoint of the dominated. This is shown also by the fact, already referred to, that whereas she needs the language of her inferiority to designate her social position, Transome does not need it to designate his superiority. It would be incorrect, however, to take this point as meaning that it is language which is somehow forced upon an unwilling user, for, as I have argued, it is language which appears to Mrs Holt to represent normality in a quite spontaneous way. To introduce a formula on which a number of variations will be played in this essay, the language of domination is a language which *exhibits* a dominative situation in the course of *obscuring* the dominative character of the situation from which it arises. If, as on the Marxist view it does, ideology is characterised by two features mainly, mystification and domination, then we shall have to say that it achieves the latter not by coercive means themselves but by means of mystification — with the result that coercive means are made unnecessary. Ideology abets a dominative class structure by means of its routinisation and normalisation. And in the sort of case which we have been considering, the word normality retains its etymological connections with 'normativeness'. What is made to seem natural is made to seem also to be morally required.

This ideological expression, therefore, both exhibits and at the same time misrepresents the realities of the class power-structure. Admittedly Mrs Holt is explicitly aware of the *greater* power of her betters. She knows Transome has a form of social power which she does not have. But she does not see Transome's power as related to her lack of it in any way other than as the excess of his over hers in relation to a common object — securing the ear of the king. She shows no sign of recognising that Transome's class-power is a direct function of her relative lack of it. More simply, she does not see that the power relations of class are not just relations of inequality in amount of social power, but are also, and primarily, relations of domination. At the very least the reality of such relations is obscured by *what* she says. They are, on the other hand, exhibited by the language in which she says it. Her language says more than what she says by means of it, indeed her language refutes what she says by means of it. In so far as this contradiction can be seen to live in the spontaneity of the language itself, we can make sense of the proposition that ideology is *lived* contradiction.

Moreover, the cunning of this lived contradiction has all the appearance of a social artifice contrived to produce its effect — even though it is not in fact attributable to any artificer or contriver. In my view it is inevitable that, in the explanation of ideologies, we should be forced to use functional, even purposive language which is bound to suggest something closer to a conspiracy theory of ideology than it is right to suggest. Inevitably we describe the effect of ideology as being its 'point' or as being, in Gellner's words 'socially functional', and we speak of it as a 'device', perhaps, as I did just now, of exceptional 'cunning'. Such language is inevitable in the description of ideology and is also pardonable so long as it is understood to be what it is, namely metaphorical language, and so long as clear limits are set as to the use of such metaphors. Functional and purposive metaphors are not extendable to the implication that ideology in any sense has an author, whether individual or collective. In particular, 'bourgeois ideology' is not the ideology invented by the bourgeois class which that class then collectively foists upon bourgeois society as a whole. Bourgeois ideology is the ideology of bourgeois *society*. It is the principle of its stability as an ongoing concern. It is the expression which denotes the 'natural and spontaneous mode of thought' of *any* individual in bourgeois society, in so far as he is an adequately socialised member of that society, whether as worker, housewife, stock-broker, manager, civil servant or whatever. It is also the expression which denotes those social mechanisms whereby this naturalness is won for the processes of socialisation, even in the case of those whose interests conflict with that society's survival as an ongoing concern. We have already detected one feature of that mechanism in Mrs Holt's language: arising out of the class domination of bourgeois society, it is language which contrives to obscure the domination from which it arises. No one, not even the collective 'subject', the bourgeois class, *invented* this language; no one invented *any* language.

It is by the fact that ideology has no author that it is chiefly distinguished from its poor relation, 'propaganda'. Whatever else may be required in the definition of this term, it is certainly at least the conscious use by a social agent, the propagandist, of the available social language with the intention of distorting the perception of social reality, a distortion which will normally favour that agent's interests. Here functional and even purposive language is quite literal. For propaganda has to be composed, usually to cope with just that situation in which the propagandist cannot count on spontaneous forms of mystification working in his favour. It is the mark of the relative instability of power relations if a ruling class has to authorise it own lies. Ideology, on the other hand, not only has no author, it does not usually need to lie at all. For the most part it can rely on the altogether more complex but spontaneous mechanisms of mystification. Whereas ideology is spontaneous, propaganda is artificial. It is only in the absence of the inherently stabilising mystifications of ideology that the precarious lies of propaganda are necessary. This, perhaps, is the unflattering reason why bourgeois societies are so hostile to propaganda. It does them good to take moral umbrage at the lies of 'Marxist' societies, when ideology has so effectively removed the need for them in their own.

Let us sum up the results which, so far, this analysis of *Felix Holt* has gained for us. First, ideology is a purely natural and spontaneous mode of thought and speech. Second, it derives its spontaneity and naturalness from the fact that it is not merely a discourse of social description but is also a discourse of self-identification within the social system: ideology is, as Eagleton has put it, the individual's 'primary mode of insertion into the social system'.[8] Third, it follows from this that ideology is a language, not merely a particular vocabulary within a language, since it is a vocabulary systematised (or at least systematisable) into a complete description of social structure and individual role within it. Fourth, it is an internally contradictory, irrational language, which exhibits in its use social realities that its surface meanings obscure. Fifth, the social realities which it both exhibits and obscures are those of class domination. Finally, in its authorless character (and connected with this, its spontaneity) it differs from propaganda, which is the designed attempt to counter or modify the effects of an already given ideology.

NOTES

1   George Eliot, *Felix Holt, the Radical*, edited by Peter Coveney, Harmondsworth, 1972, p. 532.

2   Karl Marx, *Capital*, I, translated by S. Moore and E. Aveling, London, 1970, p. 542.

3   Ernest Gellner, 'Concepts and Society', in D. Emmett and A. MacIntyre (eds.), *Sociological Theory and Philosophical Analysis*, London, 1970, p. 140.

4   *Felix Holt*, p. 544.

5   Ibid., p. 532.

6   See my discussion of this doctrine in chapter 6.

7   One is reminded of that rhetorical question often put to Marxists by their opponents, 'But surely not *all* capitalists are bad?'

8   In private conversation.

5

Ideology and Power

In the last chapter I made something, although clearly not enough, of two points. First, that an ideology is a language of social description and personal identification. Second, that ideology is spontaneous and authorless. More has to be said about both these points.

I

In what sense is an ideology a language? There are two ways of getting the answer wrong. The first is an error of under-restriction and is to identify the ideology of a society with that society's language. The second is an error of over-restriction and is to think of ideology as consisting in a set of agreed social beliefs. Both misconstrue the way in which ideology is a language, the first because it is only in an exten-ded or analogical sense true to say that an ideology is a language, the second by mistaking what it is to be a language.

First, then, a society's ideology is not its language, in either of the two senses between which this assertion is ambiguous. It is neither the case that language *as such* is ideological, nor is it the case that the natural language, which the majority of the members of a society speak, is identical with that society's ideology. Neither can be true for the same simple reason. The criticism of ideology will always be possible in the same natural language in which the ideology is exhibited. Since no ideology can be genuinely criticised in terms which derive their meaning from the ideology that they criticise, any natural language must therefore equally allow for the statement of an ideology and for its criticism. If, moreover, this is true for any natural language, it is true for language. The point is trivial and probably quite uncontroversial: the ideology of the English is in some sense a language, but it is neither the *English* language, nor is it language *as such*.

Second, in saying that an ideology is a language, we are not talking about what, since Wittgenstein, has come loosely to be called a language-game — a subset of any natural language determined either by what it is language about (as, for example, religious and economic languages are clearly *about* different sorts of phenomena) or by a special way of talking about the same objects (as there is, for example, a philosophy and sociology of religion). It is not as any such languages are languages that ideology is a language, since these are, in turn, subclasses within the general class of ideology. Any one of these languages can be ideological and, if it is, it will be in different sorts of ways: a given economic theory and a given set of religious beliefs may both be bourgeois and ideological, but it will not be either in the same way or in relation to the same set of objects that they will be ideological.

Although ideology is not any one 'language-game', it may be conceded that it is some kind of feature of our language generally which is related to a central or 'paradigm' case of ideology in the 'language-game' of social description. Ideologies are features of our *social* life, specifically. They are discovered in our ways of describing ourselves in our relations to the social system. But even this needs to be qualified. On the one hand, it would be at least misleading to deny that there are literary, philosophical or religious ideologies, even where these languages are silent, at any explicit level, about the relationship of the individual to social structure, for example, in the theological argument about nature and grace, or in literary discussion of the nature of Wordsworth's genius. In neither case is any reference thought appropriate, normally, to the bearing that such discussions have on the question of our modes of social description and identification. And yet clearly they do have such a bearing, as in the case of the literary theory of genius.[1] As for the theological case, it is worth reminding ourselves of the distinction made in chapter 3 between what is said in ideology, which may of course make no reference to social structure, and what is being said by saying it, which may be of direct social relevance. Doing theology is performing a social action, and is an ideological action precisely in so far as in doing it the theologian denies, as so many of them do, that their doing theology has any political implications — for example, in the assertion that the question of 'nature' and 'grace' has no political relevance but is a question concerning only the individual's relation to God. In such cases it is the fact of the denial which is ideological because it is to adopt a politically relevant distinction between the political and the 'individual' spheres of life, even though, *ex hypothesi*, no actual political judgement is asserted.

Not all ideologies are forms of language about society. But 'non-political' doctrines are ideological, or not, depending on the bearing that their non-political character has to the social system. This brings us back to the formula introduced in the last chapter: ideologies are shown in language by the way language is used to obscure, in what is said, that which is exhibited by the social fact of its being said.

So far, then, ideology can be seen to be neither identical with language itself nor to be just one 'language-game' among others, but to be a potential feature of any sort of language-game, a feature which is defined by reference to a central case, namely socio-political-economic language. What every form of bourgeois ideology achieves, in one way or another, directly or indirectly, is the mystified perception of that central socio-political-economic feature of bourgeois society, which is class oppression. It is this which ideology both obscures and exhibits. The reason, then, why it is worth saying, by analogy, that ideology is a language, is that this process of mystification appears to be replicated throughout *all* forms of bourgeois discourse, not randomly, but systematically. It appears to be the natural orientation of bourgeois language. This, once again, does not entail that ideology *is* language itself, since this natural orientation cannot be accounted for in linguistic terms. Rather, it is that bourgeois language succumbs to extra-linguistic pressures which, so to speak, bend it into this orientation: the language bends to the needs of a class society and is, as Gellner puts it, 'socially functional' for those needs.

For this reason, although ideology is, like a language, authorless, it is not without social origins. To recognise an ideology is to recognise, via the sort of distortions in language which I analysed in the last chapter, the pressure language is under from features of the social system itself. Ideology, in the strict Marxist sense in which I am now using the term, is that social mechanism which produces distortions in the very language we have for describing social mechanisms.

In view of this complex, recursive character of the ideological mechanism, it is understandable that some contemporary Marxists have borrowed Freudian terms to describe it, since the Freudian theory of the genesis of the 'ego' (the conscious self) involves an analogous mechanism. As Eagleton has put it, for Freud:

> ... the human subject is constructed only on the basis of the determinants which went into its making. This is the shattering, devastating paradox of human animals: that we become what we become — 'sexed' individuals — only by a massive and painful repression of the determinants of our making.[2]

There is an analogy between the Freudian mechanism of ego-production and the Marxian account of ideology production, since, for Marx, ideology is that distortion in our language of social description which is both produced by the needs of class domination and, by virtue of these distortions, is rendered incapable of describing what causes it.

The *source* of ideology, therefore, lies in class domination. The *effect* of ideology is to obscure the nature of its source. But before explaining this mechanism in more detail I should add one further point in clarification of the sense in which an ideology is a language: this point is contained in the denial that an ideology is a set of agreed social beliefs. Any language involves a certain sort of 'agreement' between its users, but, in the first instance, this agreement is over meanings, not over truths. The distinction here is easy to grasp, if it is recognised that people cannot be said to disagree over the truth of statements, over the meaning of which they do not agree. For if they do not agree about what a given statement means, they cannot disagree over whether it is true or false, since what the one asserts will not, in that case, be what the other denies. Hence, there will be nothing over which they disagree.

On the other hand, any agreement over meanings involves prior agreement over *some* truths: indeed, any disagreement over given truths presupposes agreement over some other truths. No two people can be said to disagree about *everything*. To be capable of disagreeing at all, both parties to the disagreement must inhabit the same linguistic world, because, if they do not, they cannot disagree because they cannot talk to each other. To agree over meanings (and thereby to be capable of disagreeing over some truths), agreement over other truths is therefore required. Most philosophers of language would concur in the view that any language, by virtue of its very logical structure, commits its users to some beliefs about certain very general features of the universe. Thus, the subject/predicate distinction in language commits us to holding some form of *de re* distinction between particulars and attributes of particulars.[3] Since we would not know what to make of a natural language in which this distinction did not occur, we literally could not describe *a world* in which the distinction between particulars and their attributes did not occur. In this sense, therefore, our language commits us to some truths prior to and as a condition of committing us to any meanings. Since agreement on meanings is presupposed to disagreement about truth and falsity, it follows that such disagreements in turn presuppose agreement on other truths.

Let us say, therefore, that a language commits us to agreement on those meanings in terms of which its users can express disagreements over 'first-order' truth and falsity. 'First-order' truth and falsity will be that which presupposes this agreement in meanings, in the way mentioned. A language as such does not, however, commit its users to any agreement on 'first-order' truths, but only to what we may call 'second-order' truths, which are those presupposed by the agreement over meanings which makes first-order disagreement possible. An analogy with the academic seminar helps us to see how an ideology shares with language this structure of relationships between meaning and truth commitments. A seminar is a social arrangement for generating and containing disagreements over the truth and falsity of the statements which are its topic. But, as with all social practices, the disagreements which the seminar generates presuppose a shared perception of the rules of the game of disagreeing which are specific to a seminar — the participants have to agree on how to disagree in the seminar fashion. Thus, the participants agree on the 'meaning' of what they are doing and must do so as a condition of their disagreeing appropriately on what are, analogously, the first-order statements, or topic, of the seminar. However, they cannot agree on what it is to call their activity a 'seminar' unless they agree on certain truths, truths which are, relative to the statements they disagree about in the seminar, second-order truths — for example, that the participants are rational agents, that they are language-users, that it is possible to convey disagreements linguistically, and many others besides.

I have said that ideology is in this sense a general feature of our language, that it is a pressure on language itself which is revealed in a certain kind of distortion. This 'bending' of language produces its effects at all the levels just mentioned, but primarily at the level of meanings. What an ideology does, in the first instance, is to determine the language of disagreement. It does not settle the arguments over (equivalently) first-order statements, but it does determine what it appears to make sense to disagree about. This, of course, is the reason why an ideology is not a set of *agreed beliefs* and is perfectly consistent with the maximisation of disagreement over first-order beliefs. What an ideology does settle is the question of the terms on which such disagreements are to be conducted, with the result that certain second-order truths are presupposed. Before providing illustrative material in support of this view of ideology, we can summarise my substantive thesis about bourgeois ideology thus. Bourgeois ideology is an orientation in our language of social description and evaluation which derives from the class character of bourgeois society. The effect of this orientation is to determine the meanings of terms in our social language so that the phenomena of class domination will not normally be described as *class* phenomena while still allowing their description as conflict. Just as in the seminar, a plurality of first-order beliefs and disagreements is permitted, even encouraged, on the question of social conflict, but by means of this agreement on the meanings of terms, substantive second-order agreement is secured in the denial of the *class* character of social conflict.

II

It is now time to be a little more concrete by way of completing this slender account of the Marxian notion of ideology. I shall do this by developing a little further the contention that ideology is a form of structural 'weight' or pressure and by taking a cursory look at some of the contemporary theories of political power. For it is in the gaps which are provided by what those theories fail to explain about the nature of social power-relations that we can identify both the need for and the general shape of a theory of ideology.

First of all, then, let us consider some of the analyses of political power to be found in the literature of contemporary political scientists. Steven Lukes has admirably summarised the main arguments in his monograph on the subject[4] and, following his classification, I shall look at three main theories of power in liberal–democratic political systems.

There is, to begin with, the 'behaviourist' theory. According to Dahl[5] and that group of political scientists commonly called 'pluralists', power should be studied 'scientifically', which, being behaviourists, means 'behaviouristically'. To study power 'behaviouristically' means, in the first instance, studying actual *exercises* of power, since they are the form of behaviour in which power relations can be identified. Of course exercises of power are actions, and actions are enacted by agents. Consequently, the unit of inquiry in a study of power relations is the action of exercising power performed by an identifiable agent, whether this is an individual person or a power group (elite).

Two further features characterise the behaviour in question. To be the object of empirical study, hypotheses about power relations have to be testable. They will be testable if and only if the behaviour in question involves actual and overt exercises of power. Exercises of power which involve *not-* acting (a plausible category, as we will see) have to be discounted from any empirical science of power relations on the grounds that non-actions are not a form of observable behaviour.

Second, exercises of power consist in an agent's making overt decisions, or in having overt decisions made in that agent's interest. On this definition, power relations are defined in terms of the success such agents have in securing decisions in their own interest in situations of explicit or overt conflict of interest. The qualifications 'explicit' and 'overt' are needed here, again for the reason that if hypotheses about power relations are to be empirically testable, then the conflicts which exercises of power settle must be conflicts between observably distinct interests. In short, all the theoretical terms permitted within an empirical theory of power must be observationally testable: power agents, decisions, interests and the conflicts between them.

Power, then, is identified only in its successful exercise and involves 'a successful attempt by *A* to get *a* to do something he would not otherwise do'.[6] Who has power is discovered by determining, 'for each decision, which participants had initiated alternatives that were finally adopted, had vetoed alternatives initiated by others or had proposed alternatives that were turned down'.[7]

The underlying model of the power system for the behaviourists is, it seems, the committee room. There are actors who are identifiable in a situation of 'conflict of interest'. The conflicts of interest can be observed in the disagreements between these actors over the items on the agenda. Decisions have to be made, one way or the other, and power is identified in — indeed identified with — success-rate in getting decisions made. As Hobbes put it, 'the power of a man is his present means to achieve some future apparent good'[8] and, as MacPherson adds, power, on this conception, will consist in the observable *excess* of one man's 'means' over all others in a conflict situation.[9]

The analogy of the committee room leads naturally to the second theory of power which Lukes examines, that of Bachrach and Baratz.[10] For them, Dahl's theory of power does not cut deep enough and, through its emphasis on overt forms of power behaviour, misses a more basic form of power.

60   *Ideology*

If one 'face' of power is shown by the success-rate in getting decisions made on those items of conflict which are on the agenda, another is exhibited by those who can determine what gets on to the agenda in the first place. Any experienced committee-person knows the decisive nature of this 'agenda-control' as a form of power.

What Bachrach and Baratz in effect note is that those with power in the committee room are in a position to ensure that only such issues as they want to allow disagreement about get to the meeting in the first place. 'Agenda-control' is too narrow a term to describe the forms which this sort of power can take. There seem to be at least two forms of this power. One form consists in *one* of the agents in the conflict situation conspiratorially contriving to prevent discussion of an issue which other agents in that situation have an interest in airing. The other form is illustrated in the case where *all* the parties present at a meeting agree not to disagree about certain issues and thus collectively prevent the issue being raised. In either case what Bachrach and Baratz call 'non-decision-making' has taken place. But there is a difference between them, which is important: it is the difference between power *in* the meeting and the power *of* the meeting. If it is at the meeting that the decisions are made, one form of power will be demonstrated in the successful attempt by a participant to prevent the other participants discussing an issue; the other will be demonstrated by the *meeting's* decision not to raise the issue.

Politically, both forms of power are much exercised. Government parties at Westminster have considerable power of agenda-control in Parliament, much to the disadvantage of opposition parties, whose opportunities to initiate debates are severely limited. But Parliament itself — the meeting — can collectively exercise agenda-control and just as frequently does. Given that, in the wider society, there is a sum total of conflicts of interest, the political parties can collectively determine which of the issues become what are called 'political' issues, that is, topics at issue between them. In this spirit the major British parties have agreed not to make the Northern Irish issue a 'partisan' issue. Clearly, there are major disagreements in the United Kingdom (and more obviously in

Northern Ireland itself) about the solution to the problem the British have created in Northern Ireland. Moreover, in any plain sense of the term, these disagreements are political disagreements. Consequently, in agreeing, as they say, to 'de-politicise' the Northern Ireland question these major British parties have not only succeeded in keeping the issue off the agenda of their own disagreement, but are exhibiting a mutual complicity over the more fundamental issue of what counts as 'genuine' politics. It is in the collective interest of Parliament so to restrict the notion of politics to the settling of those issues about which Parliament can contain disagreement. All other issues come to be regarded as, at best, marginally political, and at worst, dangerously subversive.

Power over the agenda, therefore, can be exercised in both of these two ways. In either case 'to the extent that a person or group consciously or unconsciously creates or reinforces barriers to the public airing of policy conflicts, that person or group has power'.[11]

So far, then, Dahl's theory of power emphasises its most overt characteristics when exercised in the overt behaviour of settling overt issues concerning the empirically identifiable interests of empirically identifiable agents. In the terminology which I have adopted, Dahl is concerned with 'first-order' disagreements, if not exactly over truths, at any rate over interests. Bachrach and Baratz, on the other hand, are rightly critical of Dahl's behaviourism, since by focusing as it must on decisions *made*, behaviourism has no place within empirical theory for those forms of power which consist in the exclusion of issues from the agenda, resulting in decisions not being made.

In turn, Lukes rightly insists that 'non-decision-making' is an ambiguous phrase. In one sense 'non-decision-making' is still deciding. The political parties at Westminster have formally agreed to keep the Northern Ireland issue off the agenda of 'politics'. The processes whereby they came to negotiate this agreement are, presumably, accessible to behaviouristic analysis. Furthermore, although Bachrach and Baratz are right to lay emphasis on the political fact of the *absence* of discussion of conflicts of interest, this 'absence' is still an observable absence in yet another way. For, in their view, the empirical study of the suppression of issue-airing is possible only when those conflicts of interest which are excluded from the agenda are accessible to empirical observation outside the arena of formal politics. It is relevant, that is to say, to note the exclusion of the Northern Irish issue from formal political argument only because it is possible to make empirical observations of the conflicts of interest being fought out in Northern Ireland. Only overt, explicit and empirically observable conflicts of interest can therefore be known to have been excluded from the agenda of formal politics.

Lukes, however, is not satisfied with this. For him there is yet a third 'face' of power, more fundamental than and even less apparent than 'agenda-control'. Power in this sense is exhibited in the capacity of a person or group to prevent the *perception* of conflicts of interest in the first place. Behaviourism, of course, can make no headway with such a notion of power, since, if there is power in this sense and it is effectively exercised, *a fortiori* its effects are non-apparent. For power in Luke's sense will so contrive things that a 'real' conflict of interests is made unobservable even to those whose interests conflict.

This is not to say that it is impossible to describe situations which match Luke's conception. In January 1979 British trade union leaders concluded an agreement with the Labour Cabinet which they called, somewhat mysteriously, a 'concordat'. This agreement was made in a period of bitter and hard-fought strikes by lorry drivers and local authority manual workers (among other groups) over pay-claims well in excess of government norms. The 'concordat', however, called on 'responsible' trade unionists to recognise that the primary interest of the British worker was to moderate wage-claims to a less than inflationary level, because the British worker had the same interest as any other citizen in keeping inflation down. 'Responsible' trade unionists, of course, always will recognise this truth. They are not 'responsible' if they do not. But Len Murray and the then Chancellor, Denis Healey, had more than this in mind when they, in particular the latter, described their equation as 'common sense'. All those for whom, as a matter of course, arresting the decline of the British economy is a goal, must accept the logic of the argument. After all it is true, so far as it goes, that high wage-settlements are inflationary and that inflation erodes the wages settled upon. Hence it is plainly irrational to settle for wages above the level at which their inflationary effect cancels wage-increases out. At any rate, so all the national newspapers and most of the politicians tell us day in and day out.

Let us suppose, then, that there were some trade unionists, heretofore tempted to irresponsibility and irrationality, who were persuaded by the argument of the concordat. Reluctantly, perhaps, but no doubt with honesty, they were brought to face up to the reality of the iron laws of economic life. They were persuaded to identify their true interests as being at one with those of their employers whatever their more particular class interests may be: they were persuaded that they can afford to fight the class issue only within the assumptions of the economy which determines their class position as wage-labourers in the first place. In so far as they are so persuaded, the Healey/Murray power agency had successfully exercised a form of Lukesian power, so long, of course, as it is demonstrable on some theory that, as workers, it is not in fact in their true interest to maintain that form of economy in which the concordat logic is appropriate.

I say that the interest which these trade unionists are persuaded to misconstrue must be determinable 'on some theory'. This is because, on the supposition that the persuasion is successful, they will themselves no longer be perceiving this interest. It is an interest, therefore, which cannot be open to crude empirical observation. Of course, this is not to say that the theory on which the unperceived interest is determinable is not itself an empirical theory. After all, although it is an *inference* from the 'facts' appealed to by the concordat argument, it is still a pretty immediate inference, that the laws of an economy which regularly determine that workers will fail to accept cuts in real wages only at the price of losing their jobs cannot be the laws of an economy in which those workers have any real stake. The effect of the concordat rhetoric is to get workers not to see this, to persuade them to behave 'rationally', to accept 'common sense'.

It may be that some readers will prefer to consult the less contentious illustrations of Lukesian power which Lukes himself gives in his book.[12] In any case, exercises of Lukesian power do occur, bringing about the perception of mutual interest in a situation where fundamentally there is conflict. This may be done in one or other of three ways: first of all, it may be brought about that social groups *A* and *B*, whose interests conflict, fail to recognise that they have the interests in question; second, it may be brought about that, although each recognises its interests, both fail to recognise that these interests conflict; or, third, it may be brought about that, although each recognises its interests and that they conflict, both are persuaded, falsely, that deeper common interests require them not to pursue their interests to the point of conflict.

Although it is obvious that where such exercises of power are successful the *effects* of its exercise must be unobservable, none the less the *act* of its exercise must, on Lukes' view, be observable. Bachrach and Baratz went beyond Dahl's analysis of overt decision-making in overtly 'political' conflict-of-interest situations so as to include political non-decision-making, while leaving the door open for the empirical observation of cases where overt conflicts are prevented, by overt actions, from getting on the agenda of politics. Lukes goes further, focusing on the power exercised in preventing such conflicts of interest even being perceived. But his concept of power is still capable of direct observational support, since the processes whereby this is contrived and the agents who do the contriving may still be directly observable. It is for this reason that, closely related as the effects of this power are to the effects of ideology, Lukes has still not quite got all the way to a satisfactory theory of ideology.[13] In fact what Lukes describes is what I have called 'propagandising'. For propaganda is the attempt to get people to want what the propagandist wants, and is necessary only when those people's wants or interests conflict with the interests and wants, the perception of which the propagandist wants to promote. Effective propaganda, then, succeeds in getting people to misdescribe their interests in a way favourable to the propagandist's interests — as when, for a while, the Pentagon came near to persuading the media that the mass bombing of North Vietnam was *pacification*. *Everyone* is in favour of peace.

Lukes, then, is not describing ideology, but propaganda. This is because he wants to retain a minimum of direct observational support for his notion of power — in terms, that is, of the overt actions of overt power agents. But ideology, as we have seen, has no author; it is a spontaneous bias in the social system which no social agency could be capable of producing. If it therefore follows that ideology is not itself a form of power, it is none the less a social factor which cannot be omitted from any account of how political power is exercised in the social system.

For Bachrach and Baratz's 'second face' of power is not just another form of power in addition to Dahl's. It describes a form of power-exercise which is a necessary condition of successful exercises of power in Dahl's sense. The power to have issues settled in an agent's favour in Dahl's sense depends on the power to have the agenda of politics 'fixed' in the first place. Similarly, the power to have the agenda 'fixed' partially depends on and is certainly abetted by any success a power agent may have in preventing groups in conflict with that agent from recognising what their interests are. Now, however, it is necessary to add that, in turn, Luke's 'third face' of power depends for its success on the ideological bias of the social system as a whole. To account for the consistent success-rate which powerful social groups have in their exercises of all three forms of power, we need to appeal to social facts which cannot themselves be called 'exercises of power' and are not the results of any.

This can be seen if we return to my own example of Lukesian power. There is something manifestly implausible in the notion that any social agents, however powerful, could, by the force of any overt persuasion alone, contrive the wholesale misperception of real class conflict-of-interest in the course of an economic argument. In so far as Len Murray in any way succeeded in persuading British workers of their common interest in 'beating inflation', it was only in so far as they could, and did, already perceive that the Healey/Murray inflationary law defines how things work in an economy run on capitalist lines. The question-begging 'common sense' of the rhetoric derives, therefore, from an assumption which no persuasion could conceivably induce, namely that the capitalist economy is the given, unquestionable social definition of 'rationality', so that only within its assumptions can rational argument take place. If the assumptions of that economy can be regarded as settling the terms of the argument about rational wage-bargaining, the 'second-order' truth which agreement on those terms presupposes is that no other terms could be rational.

In short, in describing an ideology we are describing a situation, not brought about by anyone's decisions or 'non-decisions' nor by anyone's contriving it in any way, in which people consistently and naturally tend to misdescribe their interests in a manner which is relatively harmonious with the interests of those who do exercise formal power. To understand a society's power relations we need to understand more than how the formal power of all three types is exercised. We need to understand that society's ideology.

NOTES

1   Cf. Francis Barker, 'Science and Ideology', *New Blackfriars*, October 1977, pp. 479–80.
2   Terry Eagleton, 'Marx, Freud and Morality', *New Blackfriars*, January 1977, p. 25.
3   Cf. P.F. Strawson, *Individuals*, London, 1964.
4   Steven Lukes, *Power, a Radical Perspective*, London, 1974.
5   R. Dahl, *Who Governs? Democratic Power in an American City*, London and New Haven, 1961.
6   Quoted in Lukes, *Power, a Radical Perspective*, p. 12.
7   Dahl, *Who Governs?*, p. 336.
8   T. Hobbes, *Leviathan*, I, 10.
9   C.B. MacPherson, *The Political Theory of Possessive Individualism*, Oxford, 1962, pp. 35–6.
10   P. Bachrach and M.S. Baratz, 'The Two Faces of Power', *American Political Science Review*, 56, 1962, pp. 947–52.
11   Bachrach and Baratz, *Power and Poverty: Theory and Practice*, New York, 1970, p. 8.
12   Lukes, *Power, a Radical Perspective*, pp. 42–5.
13   The argument from here to the end of the chapter owes much to Professor John Maguire's review of Lukes's book in *The Cambridge Review*, 96 (2225), 28 February 1975, pp. 116–18.

6

Ideology, Morality and 'Order'

Having now given some account, albeit mostly negative, of ideological 'weighting' in the power relations of a society, it is now necessary to fill in in a more detailed way the description of the mechanisms whereby this pressure is exerted on our social language. I do this in this chapter by examining an important moral element in the political ideology of the bourgeois state, namely its commitment to toleration as one of its constitutive virtues.

I

It is commonly supposed that, when viewed as a political morality, a central commitment of bourgeois political ideology is to toleration. In turn, toleration is connected with pluralism, since it is with a view to the encouragement of diversity that toleration is required. There is something in this. It is incontrovertible that historically one of Western civilisation's greatest gains from having passed into a capitalist phase is that the language of toleration is irreversibly with us, even if the track-record in practice is very uneven.[1]

Nonetheless, political toleration has a changing history. What it has meant — and also the social and political effects of our commitment to it — has changed with large-scale developments in our social and political history. R. P. Wolff[2] is, I think, right to emphasise one such change. In nineteenth-century English political thinking, typically in the work of J. S. Mill, 'toleration' is a term deeply embedded in the individualistic vocabulary of political liberalism and *laissez-faire* politics. In his essay *On Liberty* Mill's chief concern is with the relationship between the *individual* and the state, and perhaps even more with the relationship of the individual to wider social pressures than those which the state proper can exert — the pressure of public opinion, of conventional religion and morality, of education and of social custom.[3] One has the impression that Mill's liberalism would have caused him to object rather more to the 'closed shop' of contemporary British industrial practice than to support trade unions themselves as the collective representatives of a mass interest. For the focus of Mill's defence of toleration is on the individual in relation to corporate groups. The doctrine of toleration is the chief moral support for the *individual's* right of dissent.

What distinguishes advanced capitalism from its earlier nineteenth-century predecessors is, for Wolff, the decline of the immediacy of the individual's relationship to the state. Today all sorts of non-state groups 'mediate' that relationship; trade unions, vast industrial corporations, professional and house organisations, consumer and other sorts of pressure groups representing specialised interests, not to mention political parties themselves — all of which have a role to play in that process of agenda-control which was described in the last chapter. 'The individual' today is a far more socialised individual, in that it is rare that a person is to be found in some immediate relationship purely as an individual with the state. Far less than in Mill's day is there an obvious circulation of individual interests exchanging in a free market of politics, as on Mill's implicit model there was. What is much more apparent today is a plurality of interest — *groups*, trading power relations with each other within the machinery of the state.[4] Toleration as a moral principle of the liberal–democratic state has, therefore, also been redirected in its focus, away from the relations of an individual to the state and upon the relations of interest-groups to each other and to the state.

Two consequences appear to have followed from this shift away from individual pluralism to interest-group pluralism. We are made aware of the first when we note that the shift is not just a shift of emphasis. Interest-group pluralism is often defensible only at the price of actually lowering the toleration levels of individual diversity. The closed shop is a case in point. It is in the name of pluralism that Labour government legislation required many industries to enforce the closed shop — so that those industries are forced to accept union power as an essential factor in industrial organisation. But, of course, in order to guarantee the plurality of power relations in these industries, it is necessary to enforce union member-ship on all employees, willy-nilly. Interest-group pluralism and its attendant redefinition of toleration is actually hostile to the political individualism with which it was at first associated.

Second, whereas individualistic pluralism was a critical theory — it stated a principle on which the oppressive tend-encies of government and large corporations could be opposed — interest-group pluralism is, at any rate in practice, largely conservative in its political and social consequences. There are, in turn, two reasons for this, only one of which is noticed by Wolff.[5] This is that a society which has worked out the equations between the toleration of divergent interest-groups and the overall stability of the social order will generally be reluctant to extend the principle of toleration to new interest-groups whose appearance on the political stage could seriously disturb those equations. We return to the questions raised in the last chapter. Not only is there a form of power to exclude issues from the agenda, there is also a form of power, whose principle is 'toleration', which is to exclude actors from the meeting. Typically the justification for such exclusions takes the form of the rhetorical question: 'Can we tolerate the intolerant?' The answer is no, of course, because the intolerant undermine the principle of the society in which they seek a place. But in most instances what is in question is not the *principle* of toleration itself, but the 'principle' of the stability of the power equations of the established order. Toleration of and between established power-groups then becomes the principle of the stability of the sum of just those groups. Consequently, it comes to seem as if only that sum could be a stable order and, in turn, that only that stable order could realise toleration as a principle.

The second reason why interest-group pluralism is a conservative principle runs deeper and is, in summary, that the operation of the principle is not only effective in creating social order, it also presupposes what may in fact be false, that the sum of interest-groups within a society's power relations is in fact an *order*. It may not be, at any rate in any normative sense, an 'order' at all. On the Marxist view, of course, capitalism is, in one sense, an order. This is the sense that it is clearly an ongoing, relatively stable arrangement of social, economic and political relations, about which explanatory laws can be constructed such that falsifiable predictions can be made about its behaviour. But there is no prescriptive sense of the word 'order' in which capitalism is an order. It is, strictly, a *disorder*, since it is a form of society, economy, polity and ideology which collectively amasses contradictions — as we have seen at the ideological level at least. The principle of toleration, tied up as it is with the assumption that bourgeois society (whose principle it is) is an order, is itself part of that ideology, since it functions as a bit of prescriptive language — requiring toleration as a moral imperative — in a society which is constructed in fact on that basic disorder of class oppression. If toleration is a requirement of the liberal—democratic conception of pluralist politics, what it requires us to believe (as a 'second-order' truth) is that fundamentally opposed class-interests are ultimately reconcilable in a sort of vector-sum of forces, otherwise known as the bourgeois state. It is a form of ideology, therefore, because it is part of the natural language of bourgeois politics which imposes a redescription of conflicting interests in terms such that they are seen, ultimately, not to conflict. If we are to see in what way the principle of toleration has become, as a result, functional for the bourgeois state, it is necessary to look beyond that principle to the social origins of our contemporary moral language itself, at any rate in some of its more typically bourgeois manifestations.

II

It is a much-noted feature of our contemporary moral vocabulary that in it the word 'moral' has two quite distinct senses. The distinction can be partially brought out by noting that the word 'moral' forms distinct contrasts with *two* other words, namely '*im*moral' and '*a*moral'. Traditionally these contrasts were said to differ in that whereas to act 'immorally' was to act contrary to some moral principle or duty or virtue, to act 'amorally' was to act without regard to the question of whether there was any moral principle, duty or virtue governing what one did. The immoral man acknowledges the language which condemns his behaviour. The amoral man, like the Pardoner of chapter 3, rejects the language itself.

More recently, however, many moral theorists have drawn this distinction in a quite new, non-traditional and much sharper way. R. M. Hare,[6] for example, draws a distinction between what characterises moral language *as such* or *qua* moral, and what a man, speaking moral language, might commit himself to in terms of 'substantive' moral beliefs. This distinction acknowledges and re-enforces moral pluralism. Whereas, on the traditional drawing of the lines, a 'moral language' would have been said to be *constituted* by some set of moral beliefs, for Hare one must distinguish between actual moral beliefs and the language in which moral beliefs are espoused, since the language of morals is equally available for the espousal of quite different and even opposed sets of moral beliefs. *A* believes that racism is morally reprehensible and *B* believes that racism is morally defensible. If, in the course of expounding their disagreement, *A* and *B* both use language and arguments which satisfy certain formal requirements, *A* and *B* are both expounding *moral* beliefs, even though their moral beliefs are irreconcilable. For Hare this distinction is truistical. For moral language is a *language*. And, as we have seen, a language is a structure of shared meanings which makes possible disagreements over 'first-order' beliefs — and cannot, therefore, be a structure *of* 'first-order' beliefs. In the same way, for Hare, the language of morals is a structure of shared meanings of moral terms which makes possible disagreements concerning what it is good or bad to do. It cannot have 'substantive' moral beliefs built into it *as a language*.

What, then, makes moral language 'moral'? Since the publication of G. E. Moore's *Principia Ethica* at the turn of this century,[7] a very wide variety of answers to this question have been proposed, but by far the best developed and most broadly discussed has again been Hare's. For him two logical features essentially characterise moral language: 'prescriptivity' and 'universalisability'. Moral language is 'prescriptive', in that if someone grants that there is something which he ought now to be doing and he is not now doing it, then he is failing to use the word 'ought' in a fully moral sense. For to say that moral language is 'prescriptive' is to say that it is in a very strong sense 'action-guiding' language — in so strong a sense that it is a condition of your *meaning* 'ought' in a moral sense that you act as you think you 'ought' to be acting — assuming, of course, that you are not prevented from so acting.[8]

Secondly, moral language is 'universalisable'. This is to say that no singular judgement containing terms like 'good', 'ought' and 'right' is a moral judgement unless he who makes it is prepared to commit himself to the universal form of that judgement. Suppose I make the singular judgement that in these circumstances I ought to treat this man Baldwin differently from the way I treat Kruger in the same circumstances. This is a rational judgement only if it is made on some grounds, that is, I give reasons for making it. Let us suppose that in my case it is a rational judgement and that I do have reasons for making it and they are that Baldwin is black and that Kruger and I are white. This judgement is, for Hare, a moral judgement only if I am prepared to commit myself to the universal judgement that it is right for any white man to treat any black man differently from the way he treats any white man in all circumstances of the sort in question. If, in addition, my committing myself to this universal satisfies the 'prescriptivity' condition, then my judgement is, *ceteris paribus*,[9] a *moral* judgement. Summarising the two criteria into a single test, the test that my singular judgement was a moral judgement is that in uttering it I accept that I am committing myself also to the judgement that if *I* were black and Baldwin white then Baldwin ought also to discriminate against me in the same way in the relevantly similar circumstances.

Hare believes that the two features of 'prescriptivity' and 'universalisability' are purely 'logical' characteristics of moral language. By this he means, negatively, that the user of moral language is not committed by virtue of its possessing these characteristics to any actual moral beliefs. To hold his view of the logic of moral language is not to be committed to any moral answers, a fact which is illustrated by my example. Both the racist and the antiracist will be using formally identical language — universal and prescriptive — in giving expression to their moral disagreement: in fact they could not be *dis*agreeing in point of substantive morality, unless they were agreeing on the meaning of the terms in which they state their disagreement.

Connected with this point is another. Hare concurs with the vast majority of contemporary British and American moral theorists in the view that it is impossible, to put it compendiously, to derive an 'ought' from an 'is'. To be slightly less elliptical, it is thought to be impossible to derive any moral judgement only from non-moral judgements, in particular from 'descriptive' or 'factual' judgements alone. It is among the features which moral language possesses *qua* moral, that the judgements which are expressed in this language cannot be entailed just by statements of fact. This logical feature of moral language is said to follow (and clearly it does follow) from the belief that moral language as such commits its user to no substantive moral beliefs. For, if *the facts* determined what moral judgements were rational, then clearly there would be a determinable set of moral beliefs which alone were rationally supportable — i.e. those determined by the facts. In that case what beliefs were *moral* beliefs would also be determined by the same facts. There would be no language in which to express moral disagreements.

If it were to the point to argue the case philosophically, it would, I believe, be possible to show that there is no such morally neutral and purely logical account of moral language; that, in short, all moral language involves, *qua* moral, commitments to some substantive beliefs. But this is not how I propose to argue with Hare. Rather, I argue that Hare's moral theory is an ideological account of morality; or, if it is indeed true, as Hare claims that it is, that his theory is but a formalised reconstruction of the way moral language is *actually* used, that Hare's is a theory of an ideological moral language, and that the theory is ideological parasitically upon the usage which it reconstructs.

In order to show this, let us return to some remarks made

in the last chapter. I argued that an ideology is, in an extended sense, 'a language' and that one of the analogies between ideologies and languages lies in the fact that both are sets of agreed conventions in terms of which 'first-order' disagreements are made possible. The agreed conventions, however, are — broadly — shared meanings which, although they emancipate first-order disagreements, presuppose second-order agreement. It is characteristic of an ideology, moreover, that the agreed meanings which underpin first-order disagreements should so structure the issues disagreed on that second-order assumptions are obscured from view, that questions about them are inhibited. Perhaps it would now be a little clearer to say that the 'meanings' which an ideology constructs are a kind of systematic and authorless 'agenda-control' combining with this the Lukesian power-*effect* of obscuring the perception of more fundamental issues. It is in this sense that I claim that Hare's moral theory is ideological. He defines moral language as a morally neutral set of terms for the expression of moral disagreements. But this account of moral meanings rests on a 'second-order' *substantive* morality which it none the less obscures from view.

How is this? Alasdair MacIntyre[10] gives an account of the social history of contemporary British moral concepts in terms of two broad factors in nineteenth-century British history: secularisation and industrialisation. The latter, leading in the early nineteenth century to vast movements of population from country to city and thus to the uprooting of traditional ties of location, family and village religion, undermined with these the moral bases of a national religious culture. His argument about secularisation need not detain us here, except to say that, for MacIntyre, secularisation in the form of the declining capacity of national religion to give expression to the solidarity of the nation exhibits an already fragmented moral culture rather than causing it to come about. Religion declines because the common moral bases of its universal appeal have already declined, not, as is often supposed, in the reverse order of historical causation.

What matters, then, is the fragmentation of a universal moral culture. It matters because within the class of common perceptions necessary for the expression of any group solidarity, a very important subclass is that group's moral perceptions. This is because the possession by a group of common moral criteria, by which to identify legitimate social authority, is very fundamental to that group's perception of solidarity. Without these criteria different social groups within the larger body, will, where they possess their own distinct sources for the identification of authority, naturally make different identifications from each other. There can be no social solidarity, at any rate no perceived social solidarity, in such circumstances.

According to MacIntyre the Industrial Revolution brought about a fragmentation of the national moral culture into class-specific moralities in just this way. In fact MacIntyre assumes a much more uniform moral consensus in pre-industrial Britain than there is good historical evidence for. Likewise, there is little evidence for his assumption about a consensus, regarding which agencies exercised legitimate moral or religious authority. But in one way the actual historical evidence does not matter much from the point of view of my argument, or from the point of view of McIntyre's. It does not matter whether or not there was a more uniform moral consensus in pre-industrial Britain. What matters is that in industrial Britain it came to be *believed* that they had lost it. If the belief in a lost moral consensus was a myth, it was none the less an operative myth, which governed moral perceptions of the present. Whether or not industrial Britain was more morally pluralistic than pre-industrial Britain had been, at least it was true that *new* forms of moral fragmentation were evident and older appeals to collective solidarity had little purchase on the interests of new social and economic classes which industrialisation thrust upon a morally unprepared society.

There is nothing much wrong with the typology which MacIntyre offers of three broadly distinguishable 'class moralities' which came to dominate industrial Britain in the nineteenth century except that they are stereotypes, that is, classifications. They are an 'upper-class' morality of the 'public-school prefect', the puritan ethic of the middle-class entrepreneur and a trade union ethic. Each of these sectional moralities had its list of typical virtues — at least they were virtues within the pure form or 'ideal-type' of these moralities. In the first, there is combined a paternalistic self-confidence in the inherent superiority of the class, strict rules of conformity to the norms of a privileged group, together with the feeling that 'there are really no limits to what you may do to outsiders'.[11] In the second, there is a stress on the entrepreneurial virtues of thrift, honesty, self-help and self-advancement; and in the third, a contrasting emphasis on class solidarity, expressed in the view that a man can only better himself by bettering his class and in a stress on mutual help in the face of the uncertainties of working-class life.

MacIntyre's description of these 'class moralities' is, as he admits himself, a caricature. They are not identifiable for long in their pure form. But before considering the developments which eroded and modified all of them, it is important to note that in their pure form they constitute quite different moral languages, for the very good reason that in addition to being moral languages they are also social languages, languages of class solidarity. Each arises out of the shared experiences which are specific to distinct social groups and are expressive of distinct interests shared by members of those groups. They are, that is to say, moral languages, but not in Hare's sense, for they are languages of moral obligation and duty with quite specifically distinct sets of obligations written into each of them. In each case, furthermore, the obligations arise (and are clearly seen to arise) out of the specific social facts of the position of each class in society. And each morality provides the class which espouses it with a legitimation of the inferences required *from* the social experiences which typify their class positions *to* the appropriate substantive morality. Each 'morality' legitimates a set of inferences from 'is' to 'ought'.

Historically, however, none of these class moralities survived for long unadapted. Among the reasons MacIntyre gives for this, the one most relevant to my argument is the fact that the overriding requirement of social stability in a society which is inherently destabilised by conflicting class interests and moralities creates a pressure for the development, once again, of a *common* moral language. This moral language could command the allegiance of *all* classes in society and provide the basis for the shared perception of sources of legitimate authority in society. The problem, of course, is that no single class morality can itself provide a basis for common social perceptions, since, *a fortiori*, each is as moral and social language of class-specific solidarity. Nor, on the other hand, can any of the classes in question give up their own characteristic moral perceptions without sundering their allegiance to their class experience. To speak somewhat metaphorically, what was needed was a moral language which would do the job for morality which the market does for use-values. For example, in the market, the mechanism through which incommensurable use-values can be exchanged in equal ratios must be a measure of value, but not, at the same time, a value itself. In the same way, there is a need for a language of morals, which is an agreed medium for the expression of and transaction between divergent and incommensurable moralities, but which does not itself prejudge any substantive moral questions.

It was a consequence, MacIntyre argues, of the need each social group encountered for a common language of morality, that there was an increasing stress in British moral culture on the 'secondary' virtues of 'co-operation, of compromise, of a pragmatic approach, of fairness'[12] — and, we may add, of toleration. The increasing emphasis on these secondary virtues at the expense of the class-specific positive virtues reflects the society's increasing need for a language of social order *as such*, in face of the increasingly divergent and conflicting character of class interests destructive of social order. For whereas the class moralities provide a source of social solidarity within each class, to just that extent they inhibit the perception of common solidarity between them. But since the basis for a common morality could only be some shared social experience — which is exactly what is lacking in a class society — there is no room for a common *substantive* morality, but only for a purely formal, substantively contentless morality of the secondary virtues. And since, furthermore, a substantive class morality is normative for the requirements of social *order* within the class — and this is exactly what is lacking between the social classes — any morality which purports to cut across class boundaries will have to be linked with a purely abstract notion of *order as such*.

Given these requirements, it is easy to see how the effect of such contentless, morally-uncommitted moral notions, which exist alongside substantive class moralities, will be not so much to erode the contents of these class moralities as to undermine the absoluteness of their claims on the respective rival groups. Each class morality ceases to be for its adherents what morality *means*. It becomes, in view of the requirements of toleration (and its attendant abstract 'order') not 'morality' as such, but merely '*a* morality' — one among others. It is not long before the theorists are there to claim that the only language with genuine pretensions to a moral character is that in which the relativity of moralities is recognised. Then they will soon be found to be saying that moral language is a discourse in which disagreements between rival substantive moralities cannot ever be decided, because 'values' cannot be derived from 'facts' alone. Hare's 'prescriptivism' is but the formal theory of this social transformation, minus its history.

But if this is right, something very curious has happened. The liberal redefinition of moral language *says* that the language of morals is a morally neutral vehicle in which to conduct disagreements between rival substantive moralities; that as a medium of moral 'exchange' it is itself morally neutral; and that the principle of this neutrality is the logical (and therefore morally neutral) thesis of the impossibility of deriving values from facts. And yet we have seen that historically this conception of morality emerges as a response to a concrete social interest, the interest of social stability in face of the socially disruptive effects of unreconstructed class moralities. The power of Hare's thesis about moral language resides in the fact that it is a requirement of stability in a class society that its moral language should be capable of relativising the claims of class moralities, and that it does this. It does this by retaining, in fact, the essential link between morality and social order, but at a purely abstract level: as the definition of morality is morally contentless, so the conception of order with which it is linked is purely formal, not one to which the *class* experience of order can give any content. This 'abstract' bourgeois order is, then, an abstraction *from* that class experience (or, more strictly, an abstraction from the experience of class conflict), which can thereby provide a focus for the perception of a purely abstract solidarity, a solidarity which consists in little more than the collective failure to perceive the class conflict which underpins it.

The essential contradiction of ideology is therefore exhibited by this conception of morality. On the one hand, it *says* that values cannot be derived from facts. And yet the rationale for saying so derives from the substantive morality of social order, the basis for which lies in the need that a bourgeois society has for a language expressive of order in the face of the facts of class conflict. In what it says, therefore, it denies the origins which give rise to what it says. The thesis is proposed as an account of the logic of moral language as it is. In fact, as the history of its emergence shows, it is a value-laden account of the form of moral discourse which is required by the social facts.

To characterise fully the ideological nature of this moral theory, we need to add that in a society structured on unequal power relations between unequal social classes — as capitalist society is — the overriding interest in social stability is itself an interest unequally distributed between the unequal social classes. In the abstract, it is perhaps truistical that everyone has an equal interest in stability, but, in that case, the stability and order in which everyone has an equal interest, can only be an 'abstract' stability, as we have seen. But capitalism is not an order 'in the abstract'. It is ordered essentially upon inequality of access to the instruments of social and economic power, an inequality which takes the form of class oppression. Within that concrete *dis*order which is capitalism, it is clear just who has an interest in a *concrete order* beyond what capitalism can offer: those who lack social power and who are dominated by those who have it. It is just as clear that those who, as a class, have access to the instruments of political and economic power, will also, as a class, have an interest in the fiction of an 'order' which at once abstracts from the concrete power relations of society and at the same time is normative for all classes, whether they have access to power or not. That fiction of an abstract but normative 'order' makes its own contribution to the ideological effect whereby unequal class relations are perceived in the form of a mere 'pluralism of interests'.[13]

We can now complete the formal outlines of the structure of ideology which have been emerging in the last three chapters by answering the remaining unanswered question. I have argued that ideology is a distortion in our spontaneous language of social description and evaluation, which has the effect of misrepresenting the very social facts which give rise to its spontaneity. It is a disordering of our social language, on the one hand; on the other, the effect of this disordering is such that the language it dislocates becomes incapable of acknowledging that which dislocates it. Class conflict becomes represented within that language as legitimate pluralism, so that 'class' may legitimately be acknowledged, as indeed may 'conflict of interests'; but the perception of the society as being constructed upon the conjunction 'class conflict' is dissolved into the perception of the abstract solidarity in liberal-democratic freedom to dissent. Thus, exactly as with language as such, the social language of ideology is a set of shared social conventions which emancipate a certain kind of first-order disagreement while at the same time begging the substantive second-order questions which it suppresses. In this way ideology is a kind of agenda-control built into our social language, but of the Lukesian sort which inhibits the perception of class inequality and domination as being, precisely, class *domination*. The unanswered question, however, was this: if ideology is a language which suppresses its own origins and if, as I also argued, ideology, unlike propaganda, has no author, from what does it arise? The answer which we can now give is that, just as ideology distorts the facts of class domination, so it arises out of those very same facts. What bourgeois ideology may admit to is inequality. It may even admit to class inequality, and sometimes does. What bourgeois ideology systematically denies is the systemic character, within capitalism, of class oppression.[14]

NOTES

1   See H.M. Bracken, 'Essence, Accident and Race', *Hermathena* CXVI, Winter 1973, pp. 86–96, for an account of the complicity

of British empiricist philosophy in the theoretical defences of racist doctrines of man.

2 R.P. Wolff, in R.P. Wolff, B. Moore and H. Marcuse (eds.), *The Critique of Pure Tolerance*, London, 1969.

3 J.S. Mill, *On Liberty*, chapter 1, introductory.

4 On at least some theories of the state, the state just *is* the equilibrium of power relations between interest groups: it is, so to speak, the 'vector-sum' of these forces.

5 Wolff, in *The Critique of Pure Tolerance*, pp. 45ff.

6 Cf. R.M. Hare, *Freedom and Reason*, Oxford, 1963.

7 G.E. Moore, *Principia Ethica*, Cambridge, 1903.

8 Hare, *Freedom and Reason*, chapter 5.

9 The *ceteris paribus* clause is needed because other necessary conditions are required to complete the list of conditions which are, according to Hare, jointly sufficient. But none of these others are supposed to include substantive moral beliefs.

10 A. MacIntyre, *Secularisation and Moral Change*, London, 1967, particularly lecture II.

11 Ibid., p. 38.

12 Ibid., p. 49.

13 Of course it would be quite wrong, as my colleague Professor John Kent has pointed out to me, to suggest that working-class radicalism in the nineteenth century was defeated solely by means of an ideology of toleration, or, indeed, by ideological means of any sort alone. In fact, of course, it was defeated by, among other means, a good deal of brute state force, exactly the opposite of toleration. The role of the moral ideology of toleration was, however, crucial in at least two ways. First, it enabled those for whom it mattered to do so — the more morally sensitive intelligentsia, for example, George Eliot and Mill — to represent class oppression as necessary to 'order' *as such*; see, by way of illustration the 'Address to Working Men' of Felix Holt, (in George Eliot, *Felix Holt, the Radical*, edited by Peter Coveney, Harmondsworth, 1972, Appendix A). Secondly, it provided the moral principle which would justify the taking of means to maintain the capitalist order as a going concern: to this end *overt* oppression is no better substitute for ideology than is propaganda — see chapter 4.

14 In chapter 9 I hope to rectify the impression which the argument of this chapter may incidentally have given, namely that the aetiology of toleration (or of anything else) is, just by itself, a criticism of it. I do not hold this and I must ask the reader to be patient.

7

Morality and the Science of Society: A Classical Model

Having established, however sketchily, some terms for the discussion of ideology, it is now possible to raise the question of the relationship of Marxism to morality and, in the course of doing this, to raise the question also of the relationship of Marxism as a *science* to ideology. Marxists have often construed these relationships as follows: morality is as such ideological. Marxism, by contrast with ideology of any form, is scientific. In this and the next chapters I shall argue that this is a misconstruction of these relationships and, more positively, I will be arguing for the thesis that *morality is Marxism*.

I

There is something very odd about the way Marxists have conventionally construed the relationships between Marxism and morality, although admittedly in this they have generally been following some false clues given by Marx himself.[1] The suspicion that Marx was confused about these relationships concerns more what he called by the name 'morality' than what he offered as a method and substance for the analysis of capitalist society. The misleading confusion on Marx's part is that Marx (and subsequent Marxists) more or less explicitly define their stance as scientists by way of contrast with the status that the moralist or moral theorist is, on their view, supposed to have. I shall not discuss in any detail the various ways in which this false contrast has been made. Rather, I shall mention some guiding lines of thought which lead to it.

The hypothesis which I will offer as an alternative to this contrast is simply that it would do better justice both to the interest of conceptual clarity and to the history of moral thought if we were to agree on the following proposition: Marxism, as the critical science of bourgeois society and ideology, is — if indeed it is truly 'scientific' — all that we could expect morality to be under bourgeois conditions. Morality, under capitalism, is Marxism. Hence, the judgements about how to act which are based on the results of that critical science, if true, are moral judgements. If, however, the results of that science are substantially false, it is nothing but vice to act, or to want to act, on the judgements about acting which are entailed by them. The question, therefore, of whether Marxism is or is not what morality is under capitalism is a question of what 'the facts' are -- those facts, namely, which show Marxism to provide either crucially true, or else false, statements about bourgeois society.

It is possible, however, that some Marxists will find themselves strangely at one with various species of opponent in finding this hypothesis somewhat paradoxical. It is exceedingly strange when the grounds on which they do so are just those which provide the chief *bourgeois* stumbling block to the acceptance of my identity thesis. These are, of course, the grounds that scientific statements, *qua* scientific, are value-free and that moral statements, *qua* moral, are non-scientific, incapable of being supported by inferences from fact, are 'prescriptive', 'non-cognitive', and so forth. It certainly looks as if some Marxists do argue from these grounds, that for them morality *cannot* be made out scientifically. What is odd is that they should not notice how thoroughly bourgeois these notions are.

We have seen that one of the central elements of this supposed contrast between the 'scientific' and the 'moral' is the distinction which is made between the purely formal definition of what counts as 'morality' and the making of substantive moral claims, a distinction made with the effect of relativising the latter in the name of the former. In the spirit of this distinction it is said that the question of what morality is is a formal or conceptual question even if — and many would doubt this also — the question of what moral judgements are true is a factual matter. But outside the necessities of thought which bourgeois interests impose, there is simply no reason for accepting that there is any such distinction as that between what makes anything *moral*, be it agent, judgement, motive, reason for acting or whatever, and what makes it good to be an agent of the kind, or to enact the judgement, or to act for the motive or reason in question. Marxists, however, are presumably thinking in terms of these bourgeois distinctions, if they insist that on their science you can identify the relevant agencies and the judgements, motives and reasons relevant to that agency's actions, as *distinct* from the moral ones. Indeed, on my view of the matter, they can genuinely eschew morality only by also eschewing the idea that they can determine the relevant sense of these notions; which is to say, in short, that they eschew morality on pain of eschewing science.

No doubt most Marxists would be inclined to reply, and with some fairness, that they have no axes to grind either on behalf of or against *the word* 'moral' and that they merely want to be understood as far as concerns their own methods. The word 'morality' is hard to detach from bourgeois definitions and forms of thought which are quite incompatible with Marxist scientific methods, and if clarity is to be served it is served best by respecting this dominant usage and by denying any connection between Marxism and morality as construed by that usage. Marxism is, indeed, a theory about what those conditions are which entail judgements about how to act, but morality as conceived of within bourgeois thought is based on the denial that any set of conditions can, logically, entail judgements of that sort.

Although I recognise that there is something in this view, there is not enough to justify the wholesale disregard Marxists appear to have for the history of moral theory and, what is more, for the role in its development which Marxism has played willy-nilly. What there is in this self-ascribed amoralism can be simply stated: in so far as it has become merely a matter of terminology what one calls 'morality', nothing hangs on the question of whether Marxism is to be identified with it. Matters of terminology are not matters of substance, and, furthermore, given the contra-scientific associations of the word, nothing justifies calling Marxism 'morality', short of some quite arbitrary *prescription* to do so. Thus if my hypothesis that morality is Marxism amounted to nothing but that prescription, it would certainly be better to get along without it, as, in more general terms, it would be better if we could drop the entire conceptual encumbrance of the 'moral ought' and its allies, and get down to the question which alone counts: 'how are we to act, given the facts?'

I would readily grant this point, therefore, if indeed it were only a matter of terminology what one called 'morality'. But of course it is not just a matter of words. It is an error of substance to call by the name 'morality' what has been done under that name by philosophers from Kant to Hare. For what we now call morality is in radical discontinuity with that classical conception — of which Marxism is the inheritor — which was of a scientific investigation of the social order that can generate norms for action. The discontinuity of the contemporary bourgeois with the classical conception is, therefore, important at the very least from the point of view of the study of ideologies. One of the main points which any such study will be constrained to make is that it is no accident that we cannot now call Marx's scientific critique of capitalism by the name 'morality'. It is not an accident but, as we have seen, a conceptual response governed by the social pressure of a class society that we have to bifurcate the 'moral' from the 'scientific'. It is very important, therefore, that Marxists recognise what has happened: that 'morality' in its bourgeois sense has abandoned the role which was once assigned to it on the classical conception and has been redefined so as to work against that role. Contemporary 'morality' has become the ideological instrument for suppressing the connection between the science of society and judgements about acting, a connection which was the corner-stone of the classical view.

This bifurcation of facts and values cannot, as we have seen be regarded as a purely neutral, meta-moral thesis. From the earliest times in its history this doctrine has revealed its capacity to disable critical moral thought, a point which can be seen if we attend to one of its origins in the philosophy of

John Locke. Locke was simultaneously one of the major
theorists of toleration, as everyone knows, and, as Professor
Bracken has convincingly shown,[2] a thoroughgoing racist,
which nearly everyone forgets. Locke pulls off this seemingly
contradictory conjunction of attitudes via an apparently
innocuous metaphysical doctrine that there are, as he puts it,
no 'nominal essences'. This is the view, roughly, that there
are no fixed species or kinds of things. No attribute, therefore, is any more essentially a constituent of reality than any
other. From this it follows that there is also no reason why
one should not regard any particular attribute one chooses
as being essential. Consequently, both the argument for and
the argument against racism equally have a basis in the same
set of assumptions: on the side of toleration, if no characteristic essentially defines a human person, then there is no
reason why skin-colour should be taken as doing so. Equally,
and this is the permission granted to the racist, if any characteristic might just as well be an essential characteristic of the
human person, there is no reason why skin-colour should not
be made to be so. Generally, if every difference in point of
fact is equally a matter of indifference in point of morals, it
is never possible to show why I should not take any difference
I choose as making in point of morals *all* the difference.

From this, it is a short step logically to Hare's prescriptivism.
Hare, as we saw, defines the special 'moral ought' in terms of
an agent's commitment to take some reason for acting as
being, for him, 'overriding' or 'prescriptive'. The test that my
reason for acting is a moral reason is that I accept it to be
universally overriding; the test that I have done this is that in
the relevant circumstances I act on it. It follows from this
that there cannot be any reasons for acting which are, just
because they are those reasons, overriding, given that the test
of overridingness is actual performance. For that would
amount to saying not only that judgements about facts determine what moral judgements one should make (which Hare
would deny anyway), but also that judgements of fact logically
constrain action. And no one accepts that it would be impossible to accept some judgement of fact and not actually act in
a certain way. Hare's alternative is to say, therefore, that
what makes reasons for acting moral reasons is my being

prepared to take them as being overriding; which is to say that no considerations of fact are in themselves any more morally relevant than any others, except by virtue of my decision so to regard them. As a result, all Hare can say to the racist who decides that for him skin-colour is a morally relevant consideration of fact is that, logically, it is not incumbent upon him to do so; he cannot say to the racist that it is incumbent upon him *not* to regard it so.

It ought to be obvious, then, why the Marxist is going to view the whole enterprise of morality so construed as ideological — with its apparatus of the purely 'moral' ought free-wheeling about an established social order, with the consequent bifurcation of facts and values and the 'privatisation' of moral criticism. It would be wrong, however, to suppose that the Marxist objection to it as ideological derives from the moral unacceptability of its consequences. Even supposing the Marxist to accept the account I have just given, on which bourgeois moral theory must allow for the 'moral' defence of racism, it would not be exactly for the reason that racism is made morally defensible that the Marxist would call the moral theory which allowed for it ideological. Rather, what makes the bourgeois moral theory ideological is the fact that on it *both* the racist and the anti-racist positions are *equally* defensible, as being, albeit opposed, none the less equally moral positions. For this means that even the anti-racist (such as Hare himself) is right on entirely the wrong suppositions about the relation between his anti-racism and the social facts. If, in other words, his opposition to racism is 'moral' on some sense of that term which also allows racism to be moral, then 'moral' opposition to racism cannot be of the slightest consequence as a response to the problem which racism poses.

One can go further than this. The fact that the racist and anti-racist views can equally be regarded as moral options means not only that there is no moral way of settling the question, but also that the question cannot even be *raised* in moral terms. All morality may do, on this account of it, is to raise the one question which it can settle: namely, what formal argument procedures I may adopt which would guarantee my deciding impartially — whether I was deciding to be a racist, an anti-racist, or even, just to ignore the whole business. (On Hare's account, there is a way of deciding 'morally' not to see any moral issue whatever, whenever one is prepared 'impartially' to accept being treated without regard to moral considerations by others.) But the question of racism is not a question about how I would decide to strike, or, for that matter, not to strike, attitudes towards it, but is a question of what racism and racist forms of society do to human beings, as a matter of fact. If all morality can require a person to do is decide, *whatever* he decides, in an impartial manner, then the question of racism, and *what it is*, cannot be raised as the moral question.

It is, therefore, in the sense earlier defined that this conception of morality is ideological. For it defines as 'moral' a language in which one can disagree, while at the same time it so determines the rules of disagreement that the fundamental questions cannot be raised at all, and are, meanwhile, all begged. It is not, therefore, because a certain morally objectionable position is statable within that language that it is ideological, but because that position is as legitimately statable within it as is its contrary; because, in brief, it is a language incapable of articulating what those issues are of which it purports to speak. It is ideological because it provides a vocabulary for *not* saying things in.

But, to put the matter simply, the bourgeois definition of morality does not exhaust all the possibilities, as we shall see. None the less, the upshot of this mistaken identification is the traditional Marxist view that morality always and necessarily has been chronically incapacitating within any scientific critique of society. This, as I argue in the next section, is an unhistorical view which has done a great deal of harm in respect of Marxists' assessments of their own claims to scientificity in their social criticism.

For the result has been that Marxists have felt compelled to deny that their scientific critique can, *qua* scientific, be touched by moral considerations of any sort. Consequently, in their accounts of their own methods, they have tended to play down and even sometimes to exclude, so far as they consistently can, some crucial features of the classical conception of morality which they have inherited, above all, the teleological features. But Marxists cannot afford these omissions without dangerously misconstruing their own methods. If, on the other hand, Marxists could be got to see that they are, in fact, nothing but the historical successors, under capitalism, of the great moralists of earlier ages, then it is possible that they might be more disposed to learn from those moralists truths which they nowadays seem disinclined to acknowledge that they need to learn. They would not, in particular, offer strongly positivist theories about their own methods, as some do, when, in consort with their bourgeois opponents, they pose the question of the possibility of social science in terms of the rejection of all forms of teleological, and therefore moral, considerations.

It is in illustration of this view that I wish now to propose a reading of the origins of that classical conception in the debates about morals in sixth- and fifth-century Athens.

II

In the *Protagoras* Plato has the sophist of that name report a version of the myth of Prometheus. Zeus, according to Protagoras, created mortal creatures out of varying mixtures of earth and fire and charged Epimetheus and Prometheus to equip them all with appropriate powers. Epimetheus persuaded Prometheus to let him do their job, which he does, as Protagoras tells, 'on a principle of compensation, being careful by this device that no species should be destroyed'.[3]

However, Epimetheus stupidly exhausts all Zeus' gifts, all the possibilities of inhibition and suitable aggression on the brute animals, leaving humans 'naked, unshod, unbedded and unarmed'. They have, when Epimetheus has finished the task, neither the inhibitions necessary to prevent them destroying one another, nor the aggression sufficient to protect themselves against their enemies. Prometheus plans to save the day by stealing fire from Hephaestus and Athena and together with it the gift of 'skill in the arts'. Through these gifts 'man had a share in the portion of the Gods', and thus 'men soon discovered articulate speech and names, and invented houses and clothes and shoes and bedding and got food from the earth'.[4]

But they had, for all that, no political skills or virtues so that, in one way, the Promethean fire did more harm than good, for it only reinforced man's tendencies to social dislocation.

They sought, therefore, to save themselves by coming together and founding fortified cities, but when they gathered in communities they injured one another for want of political skill, and so scattered again and continued to be devoured. Zeus, therefore, fearing the total destruction of our race sent Hermes to impart to men the qualities of respect for others and a sense of justice, so as to bring order into our cities and create a bond of friendship and union. Hermes asked Zeus in what manner he was to bestow these gifts on men. 'Shall I distribute them as the arts were distributed . . . or shall I distribute justice and respect for their fellows . . . to all alike?' 'To all', said Zeus. 'Let all have their share. There could never be cities if only a few shared in these virtues as in the arts.'[5]

It should be noted how very easily this version of the myth of Prometheus is made to play into the hands of the sophist. In particular, is it significant that we have in this version the germs of that classical sophist doctrine of the contrast between *physis* and *nomos*, between nature and culture, between the socially disruptive individual energy represented by the fire of Prometheus and the countervailing force of the common social order represented by the gifts of Hermes. It is significant, furthermore, that the Promethean gifts are guilty goods, because they were stolen. The theme of the 'unhappy consciousness' is a commonplace since Hegel, but in the Protagorean version it is given a marked individualistic emphasis. For the sophist the Promethean gifts are pre-social, they represent the divine element in man as a form of anti-social guilt. That self-consciousness, which is the unhappy consciousness, is both what raises man above the non-reflective order of the brute animals and what provokes him to inhuman anarchy. Self-consciousness is both art, raising man above the brutes, and guilt, which sinks him below them.

For 'nature', according to the sophist, is brute, pre-social, animal-like instinct, a biologically given fact. It is value-free and to that extent the Promethean consciousness of nature is a guilty force, in itself it is pre-moral because it is pre-social. The gifts of Hermes, by contrast, are an extra-natural, conventional remedy for this defect in nature, a defect which is the combined result of Epimetheus' stupidity and Prometheus' rapacity.

Now Protagoras stresses the universality and equal availability of Hermes' gifts. By contrast, men may be by nature similar, but their common nature does not imply for them any common form of social life, for the instincts which, as natural, they share in common are, in the unrestrained pre-social form, forces of competition and mutual destruction. The propensity to sociality which they received from Hermes is not given in human nature but is, on the contrary, a counter-force to nature; it is the capacity to contain a guilty nature by virtue of a collective contract. The *polis*, for Protagoras, is not a redemption, but a contrived backlash. In being an afterthought to nature, the *polis* is contrasted with the natural as conventional. The capacity for political virtue which Hermes distributes he makes equally available to all; this being so, Protagoras points out, men become a possible object for instruction. They are not beyond the capacity of anyone. Indeed it is just that conventional, potentially common knowledge which the sophist professionally claimed to teach. For the sophist claimed to teach men the knowledge which they would need to be good members of any *polis*, of any social order.

But if political virtue is distributed equally to all, why does it need to be taught? If political virtue is convention, is it not learnt simply in the processes of socialisation? The answer to this question shows just how far the sophists shared with Plato and Aristotle, indeed with all Greek intellectuals of the time, a perception of the rapidly changing role of social — and therefore moral — knowledge consequent upon a variety of factors, including the very rapid development of inter-city commerce and the ravages of the Peloponnesian War. Let me illustrate this by reconstructing as a model that myth of a perfect social order which tended to operate as a preconception for political argument of the time. The chief methodological directive for this reconstruction is that on this model there is no distinction available between social knowledge and social reality — for the society is such that everything in it is exactly as it is understood to be. By contrast, of course, we are unceasingly and embarrassingly reminded of the fact that, in our society, that is not so. The fact is that the way in which we spontaneously and even quasi-naturally perceive our social relationships can be quite inconsistent with the sorts of causal forces which govern their actual operation. Indeed much social science is actually premised on the assumption of this gap, for it sees itself as having the role of filling it. Whatever the causes of it may be, we cannot take it for granted that what we understand our relationships to be is the chief factor in determining what they are, for we recognise the ideological misperception of our social relationships as a possibility built into the structure of those social relationships themselves: we are socialised in and by these ideologies. Consequently we need to be informed by specialised techniques about the nature of our social relationships; we need, in other words, to create a dimension of theory-making activity, which will generate systematically guaranteed knowledge adequate to the reality of our society in a way in which the spontaneous social symbols are not or may not be.

But imagine, I suggest, a society in which this possibility of discontinuity between social perception and social reality does not exist and so does not raise those critical questions which generate the need for social theory. In such a society the true nature of all social relationships is immediately available to every member in and through his primary socialisation. Each one understands what he is, what his society is and what his role is in that society via shared perceptions which are exactly continuous with that individual and social reality. In that case all social relationships would be an immediate embodiment of the social interpretations of them, and the social interpretations of them an immediate expression of those social relationships.

In such a society, furthermore, each man would have immediate, unproblematic criteria of action available, for they would be implicit in his transparent understanding of his society. The given social world and the moral world would be identical, not because they would have been identified, as by a conventionalist, but because they would not be distinguishable. A man would be good if he performed well his role in the social order. No distinction would be apparent between being a good member of one's *polis* and being a good *man*, because in the role-governed language of evaluation there would not be any distinction between the role a man might have *qua* man and the role he has as a member of his community.

Imagine, then, the perfect simplicity of this society beginning to break down, for whatever reasons. Social changes begin to alter social roles and relationships, while at the same time the spontaneous symbolic representations of them do not change in the same way or at the same pace. The result is that the beginnings of a discontinuity between social perception and social reality for the first time emerge. If the simple model which I described could be taken to explain what the later Greeks understood by a social *order*, then the social world which confronted the sophist in the fifth and fourth centuries was a social order of this kind in the final throes of collapse. The situation presented the Greeks with a challenge, and it is in meeting this challenge that they offered their most characteristic political doctrines.

The challenge was offered by the inconsistency which had appeared in Greek social life between the level at which their moral *concepts* worked, where they retained their connection with the fulfilment of social role, and the level of social *reality*, where the old roles and relationships had for the most part disappeared. To put the matter at its simplest, if the moral question was answered by the definition: a good man is a man who is a good member of his *polis*, it was no longer just obvious what was to count as one's *polis*. Put in yet a different, that is contemporary, way, moral language retained its prescriptive, action-guiding force, but it was no longer clear what descriptive force would give it content. Thucydides has a very vivid description of how the relationship between the prescriptive and descriptive forces of moral language had become quite arbitrary by the second half of the fifth century. He comments:

The meaning of words no longer had the same relation to things, but was changed by each man as he saw fit. Reckless doing was held to be loyal courage; prudent delay was the excuse of the coward; moderation was the disguise of unmanly weakness; to know everything was to do nothing.[6]

The challenge, then, which faced all Greek intellectuals alike can be reconstructed in the form of a dilemma. Either some non-arbitrary way of fixing a descriptive meaning for moral language had to be found, or, in the absence of this, moral and political virtue would have to be taught as a way of living well in a pluralist moral world, where the nexus between fact and value had been ruptured so that mere prescription was the basis of morality — which, in Plato's view, would be to reduce morality to the status of mere 'rhetoric'. But in either case the fact remained that virtue would have to be taught.

Those who, like Plato and Aristotle, opted for the first alternative were faced with the problem generated by their adherence to the old assumption, that the descriptive meaning of moral language was determinable only by reference to some social order, some *polis*, to be a good member of which was to be a good man. But the very fact that it was now problematic which *polis*, or indeed, whether any actual *polis*, was adequate to the definition of the good life meant that the search for moral knowledge had to be seen as the proper object of a specialised form of inquiry, the inquiry, that is, into the question of what those forms of social life are to understand which is to understand how the good man acts.

Moreover, and this is where the distinctively Platonic ontology comes into the picture, whatever doubts Plato thought we should have about whether any actual *polis* can adequately determine the nature of the good life are doubts also about whether any such *polis* can make possible any form of contact with 'reality'. A *polis* which is less than fully good entails a form of life for its citizens which is less than fully 'real'. Consequently, the search for the form of the *polis* life in which is the good life, is also and simultaneously the search for that form of life which alone is in touch with reality. The 'virtue' which the sophists taught was, in Plato's view, but a socialisation into what we have learned to call a kind of 'lived unreality'.

Thus it is that, if political virtue can be taught, it also needs to be taught. It can be taught because everyone knows what the universal virtues of the political life are and that they are virtues, for, as Thucydides had emphasised, even bad men justified their vices in the language of those virtues. But it needs to be taught because, in the situation in which the spontaneous perceptions in terms of which citizens live out their relations to their *polis* are suspected of being inadequate to 'reality', political virtue will correspondingly be but the requirement to live out an inadequate relationship with 'reality' — to be, in short, a form of socially lived 'falsehood', or, as Plato called it, *doxa*, opinion. Justice, for *doxa*, will be whatever meets the requirements for an 'unreal' order. By contrast, to know under what conditions 'justice' will denote a form of life adequate to reality is to know the real definition of justice. At best what the sophist offered as an account of 'justice' was a nominal definition, an account of how the word is conventionally used in this or that empirical society. Hence, for Plato, to know what justice is, its real definition, is to know that form of *polis*, a life in which is a life lived in relation to 'reality'. And, in turn, to come to a knowledge of the form of that *polis* one needs to penetrate beyond the conventions of *doxa*, one needs a critical theory which can move dialectically from how things present themselves in empirical appearance to what they really are. In a word, to establish a real content for political virtue, we need to know in what form of *polis* those virtues would establish contact with 'reality'. In that recognition was born, of moral parents, the need for a form of social knowledge which is 'scientific'. Plato called such knowledge *episteme*.

At any rate this was Plato's response to the dilemma about moral language. Admittedly he stated the matter in terms with which Marxists are traditionally unhappy, as the search for a timeless and absolute definition of knowledge such that it can be put in clear contrast with *doxa* or opinion. But Marxists have less reason for dissatisfaction than they know, for Plato's epistemology of this distinction is implicitly subject to historical conditions in a way in which many of our modern epistemologies in principle are not. The assumption of much contemporary meta-science is that purely formal and extra-historical methodological characteristics of science determine what will be its proper objects. Whereas for Plato exactly the reverse is true: what we need knowledge *for*, the tasks which the world sets for it, determine what will be its proper objects, and they, in turn, determine for us an appropriate method. For Plato, the teleology of knowledge, in the form of the governing, or, as Habermas puts it, the 'constitutive' interests[7] of knowledge, are determinative of the methodology. And even if Plato did not think so himself, it is at least consistent with his position to suppose that those teleological interests may set for knowledge the different tasks which different historical ages generate.

In the first place, on Plato's view, the pursuit of the definition of *episteme* required the determination of those *objects* of thought to grasp which was to know. The basic distinction between *episteme* and *doxa* was made not on formal grounds, as if the utterances which are the expressions of each were subject to different logical laws; nor on psychological grounds, as if they were grasped in distinct forms of mental act; nor yet simply on the grounds that they are more or less rationally supported. Still less, as we will see, does this distinction coincide with that between logical truth and falsity. That basic distinction is forced upon us by the problematic nature of reality itself, by the failure of the world, in particular of the social world, to correspond to spontaneous perception. And in the *Republic* that distinction is made out in response to the failure of conventional morality to examine self-critically its relationship with reality, and to the fact that all contemporary societies were, for Plato, but the praxes of that failure, living out that uncertain relationship with the 'real'. Thus is the distinction generated between the 'objects' respectively of *episteme* and *doxa*, 'the good' and 'the apparently good', a distinction which, as we have seen, meant the difference between the perception of the world determined respectively by the good and the apparently good *societies*. Scientific knowledge, then, is knowledge of the 'good society'. But it is also the cause of the good society which it knows. For not only is *episteme* knowledge of the real definition of justice, it is also the knowledge of those social conditions, the *polis*, in which that knowledge is the social praxis, the form of social perceptions. *Episteme* is the ideas which are lived in the praxes of the good society.

Of course, knowledge of the good society is possible prior to its achievement as the form of life of that society. But this knowledge, acquired dialectically in the criticism of the *doxa* of less than fully just societies, must be an imperfectly realised, theoretical criticism and we will want to know — in particular the Marxist will want to know — what is the nature of this 'critical' relationship between *episteme* and *doxa*, and on what basis Plato is going to distinguish between 'the real' and 'the unreal', whether in respect of 'the good' in general or of 'the good society' in particular. Marxists commonly suppose that Plato in fact makes this distinction only in ways which are to them unacceptably absolutist and un-historical. And, subject to some important qualifications to be made in the next chapter, I accept that this is true of Plato's account of the dialectic between 'the real' and 'the unreal'.

For Plato absolutises his just society. Its contact with 'the real' is vicariously achieved for the society as a whole by a priesthood of contemplative philosopher—rulers with speculative access to the eternal 'form' or 'idea' of 'the good'. That 'idea' stands in a one-way relationship to the goods pursued in and by actual empirical societies, for the latter goods merely 'imitate' or 'participate', to a greater or lesser degree, in the abstract model which is their paradigm. The dialectic of Platonic criticism would, however, be a true moral dialectic only if the just society were some dialectical *function of* imperfect societies, instead of being, as for Plato, but an ideal 'lying beyond' the appearances given to us in everyday experience. Thus because the objects of *episteme*, the 'ideas', are ontologically distinct entities which are only logically related to the copies of which they are the models, the criticism of *doxa* is the criticism of external comparison: the two, *doxa* and *episteme*, and correspondingly their objects, 'appearance' and 'reality', are in no *historical* relation with one another.

We can put all this in slightly more familiar, ethical terms. If the knowledge of what is 'really good' for man is at least partly a matter of determining what man's 'real' wants are, or of what would truly be in man's interest, then it is essential to recognise what Plato missed, namely the *historicity* of such knowledge. What a man can be said 'really' to want must be some function of what he actually wants; what can be said to be in a man's 'true' interest can be established only on some interpretation of what it is that he *believes* to be in his interests (his *'doxa'*), even if there are reasons for denying that what he believes is indeed what is in his interest — at any rate in the form in which he believes it.

This, in a way, is what Aristotle saw. He argued that Plato's merely external critique of conventional morality was incapable of generating alternative norms for action. Reasons for acting, to be such, must in some way touch on a man's actual desires. In moral argument it is worthless to tell a man that, although given his current desires, he cannot want a just society, none the less, if he were in a just society, he would then be socialised into having the appropriate desires. Besides, we recognise all too easily in that argument that kind of fideistic, Stalinist revolutionarism which merely tells a man how all will be well when things are otherwise, but is utterly incapable of informing us why we should now want to be the sort of people we will become when things are otherwise. An argument why a person *should* want something — if it is to offer a genuine reason — must offer him a reason why, on some interpretation of his present desires, he *does* want it.[8]

None the less, although Aristotle certainly recognised the force of this point, his own account of the method of this interpretation is itself thoroughly non-dialectical. His hermeneutics of the diversity of men's actual desires is straightforwardly inductive. Roughly speaking, if, at the level of what people will say about the desires which the good man should have, there is great diversity, the philosopher's contribution to the hermeneutics of this diversity is simply to make the best compromise with it:

Our proper course with this subject as with others is to present the various views about it, and then, after first reviewing the difficulties they involve, finally to establish if possible all or, if not all, the greater part and the most important of the opinions generally held . . . since if the discrepancies can be resolved, and a residuum of current opinion left standing, the true view will have been sufficiently established.[9]

In contrast with Plato, therefore, the major premisses of Aristotle's moral arguments are not provided by knowledge of the 'best society'. Aristotle's own descriptions of the 'ideal states in principle' in the *Politics* are mere exercises in model construction, not, as with Plato, the objects of rational thought as such. For Aristotle, it is indeed 'reason' which tells us what men should seek, but by means of an inductively established compromise between what, in the given society, they actually do seek. If, for Plato, knowledge of the good was knowledge of the best form of society, for Aristotle it was knowledge of the best one could make of actual society. If Plato's science is non-dialectical because it bypasses ordinary experience, Aristotle's is non-dialectical for the opposite reason, that it merely offers an inductive resolution of inconsistencies at the level of that ordinary experience.

If these were the responses of Plato and Aristotle to the challenge which faced them, the response of the sophists was utterly different from either. The sophist took the other way out of the dilemma created by the loosening of the nexus between description and evaluation, which is simply to accept it and therefore to accept the bifurcation of social science and morality. For the sophist, social knowledge was irrelevant to moral knowledge, for what the sophist claimed to teach was the knowledge which any man would need if he was to be a good member not of his *polis*, nor of the best *polis*, but of any *polis*. And thus it was that the purely formal, non-moral art of rhetoric is the skill which the sophist thinks the good man needs.

For clearly, given the sophist conception of the good man, the skill needed was one which would serve a man well anywhere, the value of which skill is not derived from the acceptance, in any absolute way, of the laws and conventions of any particular *polis*. If a man was good, *qua* man, only if he could do well in any social conditions, then his *techne* would have to be one which is neutral as between the aims, the value-judgements, norms or virtues which are demanded in terms of any particular set of social conditions. In thus detaching the wisdom which he taught from every kind of end that wisdom might be held to serve, the sophist argued for a kind of wisdom which could be exercised in the pursuit

of any end a man might choose to serve. There is nothing
unhistorical in regarding this stress on the formal, and so fact-
free, universality of moral judgement as an early version of
that theory of which Hare's version is but one of the latest.

The sophist conception of political virtue represents, then,
a radical departure from the mainstream of the Greek tradition
from which Plato and Aristotle never really strayed at all. The
sophists explicitly rejected the doctrine that there is some
polis, or, more broadly, any determinate way of conceiving
social relationships, an understanding of which specified the
nature of the good person's virtues. Their answer to the
question I proposed as crucial — 'What is one's *polis*?' — is to
say, 'It might be any, depending on local custom and convention.' In practice, for members, like them, of the educated
elite or of the merchant classes who might be expected to
travel, this meant that they saw the problem of how to be a
good man as the problem of how to be moral in a world
where there are only moralities. Exactly as with Hare, this
came to mean the search for a form of judgement one can
make *in propria persona*, which will be both a moral judgement and not in any necessary connection with any particular
sets of facts, social or otherwise. Negatively, then, the sophist
response to the situation in which everyday knowledge of
one's *polis* can no longer be regarded as the source of social
value is not, as with Plato and Aristotle, to argue for a form
of social knowledge which could give access to universal
values. Instead it is to argue for that form of universality of
value which is neutral as between any value whatever and so
for the detachment in general of value from social knowledge.
It therefore amounts to something very like the argument
which today we know so well for unscientific, indeed 'non-
cognitive', a-social morality and, as its mirror-image, a-moral
social science.

Now it is the argument of the next chapter that Plato's
rejection of sophism meets at some significant points with
the response which Marxism theoretically could and certainly
ought to be making to its contemporary analogue, bourgeois
moral pluralism. The point which Marxists ought to be able
to take from this analogy, although they are generally not
taking it, is that the grounds on which they can properly

frame their central criticisms of bourgeois morality are such as to make that criticism a genuinely moral one. They could learn this lesson from a more adequate account of the history of moral thought than they commonly possess; they could even learn this lesson from Plato. But until they do, there is little chance that they will shake themselves from the grip of that moral positivism which is but a bad habit they have picked up from their opponents.

NOTES

1   Compare, for example, Karl Marx and Friedrich Engels, *The German Ideology*, edited and translated by C. J. Arthur, London, 1970., part I, p. 47: 'Morality, religion, metaphysics all the rest of ideology and their corresponding forms of consciousness, thus no longer retain the semblance of independence. They have no history, no development . . .'
2   Cf. H.M. Bracken, 'Essence, Accident and Race', *Hermathena*, CXVI, Winter 1973, pp. 81—96.
3   Plato, *Protagoras*, 321 A, translated by W.K.C. Guthrie, Harmondsworth, 1956, p. 52.
4   Ibid., 322 A, p. 53.
5   Ibid., 322 B—D, pp. 53—4.
6   Thucydides, *Peloponnesian War*, III, 82, translated by B. Jowett, Oxford, 1881, p. 222.
7   J. Habermas, 'Knowledge and Interest', In D. Emmett and A. MacIntyre (eds), *Sociological Theory and Philosophical Analysis*, London, 1970, pp. 36—54.
8   But see the next chapter, pp. 120—1 for an important qualification on this.
9   Aristotle, *Nicomachean Ethics*, VII, 1, translated by H. Rackham, London, 1926, p. 377.

8

Morality is Marxism

In this chapter, therefore, I argue that there is an analogy to be drawn broadly between the Platonic polemic against sophism and Marx's against bourgeois society. Analogies, however, are notoriously dangerous in the absence of rules specifying what inferences may legitimately be drawn by means of them. In this chapter my aim is to elucidate the very general proposition that whatever can claim to be the science of a particular form of society can claim also, and on the same grounds, to be moral knowledge for that form of society. I do this by showing in very general terms how the analogy can be extended from Plato to Marx, and I do this in the not very confident hope that some Marxists may be convinced by it. If, however, any of them are convinced, it is my still less confident hope that the first conviction will pass over into a second, namely that what the analogy shows is that there is a historical role for whatever can claim, for a particular form of society, to be the 'science' of it and that that role is the moral one.

The analogy, however, is meant to have precise extension only so far as to suggest that Plato gets three important truths about social knowledge and morality in general terms right; and that Marxism satisfies criteria analogous to Plato's for the determination of what will count as science, and therefore as morality, under capitalist conditions. First of all, Plato is right in his view that the 'objects' of knowledge — what is to be known — have priority over methodological criteria in determining what is to count as science. Second, he is right in his view that it is the *telos* of knowledge which determines what are to count as the objects of science, for it is what makes it necessary to know at all which determines what it is that knowledge will be knowledge of. Third, Plato is right that the *telos* of knowledge is such that that understanding of society which is governed by it *eo ipso* meets essential conditions of scientificity and morality simultaneously. Hence, by analogy, in demonstrating its scientific character, Marxism also demonstrates that it is morality.

The analogy, however, may be legitimately extended no further than to establish these general epistemological connections. Marxist science is functionally equivalent to Platonic *episteme*, since it serves the same end of knowledge for bourgeois society that, in principle, Plato's *episteme* was intended to serve for his. It is quite consistent with maintaining this equivalence to hold also that Plato's actual account of the 'just society' met his conditions in his age far less satisfactorily than Marx's criticism of capitalist society does in ours. I hold no brief for the provisions of Plato's republic. Even at the general epistemological level, I do not maintain that Plato and Marx give the same account of the relationship between 'reality' and our perceptual and conceptual distortions of it, or that Plato's distinction between *episteme* and *doxa* is the *same* distinction as Marx's between 'science' and 'ideology'. The argument is only that the social need which Plato seeks to meet in his distinction is analogous to that which Marx meets, in my view more satisfactorily, with his. It is in this sense, therefore, that they are 'functionally equivalent'. They are *not* synonymous.

I

Let us first consider the question of the priority of the 'objects' of knowledge over methodological criteria in establishing scientificity. Marxism denies, with Plato, the contemporary assumption that science is defined as science by the methods which it uses. Rather, 'science' in the sense in which Marxism claims to be scientific is nothing more than knowledge, and knowledge is, truistically, a grasp of reality as it is in itself, which is also a reflexive grasp of that reality. We have knowledge when we know not only what is the case, but also that our knowledge has met the conditions required for knowledge of what is the case. To possess knowledge we must know what we know: we must be in possession of an account of the conditions for the possibility of knowing and know that they have been satisfied.

These are dark and condensed formulae and are in need of elucidation. First, let us note the general fact of 'descriptive pluralism'. For any given event or state of affairs there is, in the abstract, an indefinite number of descriptions which are true of it, each of them constituting a potential 'fact' holding of that event or state of affairs. Most of these facts are wholly uninteresting, although which turn out to be interesting and which do not depends, both etymologically and in substance, on what the 'interest' of the inquiry into that event or state of affairs is. There are, that is to say, no 'brute' facts, descriptions which describe facts but independently of any interest in terms of which they are relevant. It is only in so far as inquiry is governed by an explanatory interest that there are any *facts* for that inquiry; and there are no facts which are not *facts for* some inquiry.

The specification, therefore, of the controlling interest of any inquiry is crucial to the determination of what will be the facts relevant to its investigations and to the general description of the sort of facts which constitute its 'object', i.e. that of which it proposes to generate knowledge. It is therefore essential to note that the objects of knowledge are not objects, events or states of affairs which are given to knowledge already constituted as knowable. The objects of knowledge are objects only in relation to some knowledge-generating inquiry. For 'objects', being 'facts *for*' some inquiry, are classes of events or states of affairs *under some description*, the descriptions in question being, as I have said, determined by the controlling interest of that inquiry. Thus there are not and cannot be any objects of knowledge which exist *as objects* prior to and independently of some knowledge-generating inquiry.

Thus, purely in the abstract — abstracting, that is, from the controlling interest of Marxist theory — there is any number of *possible* descriptions of that form of social organisation which Marx regarded as being crucially capitalist. For any society which is capitalist is also, necessarily, an 'industrial' society, and any modern industrial society which is capitalist is modelled, at any rate fundamentally, on market relations and so can be called a 'market' society. Most market societies are politically 'liberal-democratic'. Furthermore, each of these descriptions is linked, conceptually and causally, with appropriate systems of evaluation, or to be a little more precise, each allows for a determinate range of moral options, the range being specified by an appropriate moral language. There is a set of moral questions and a range of possible moral answers which arise from the recognition that our society is an industrial society — for example, there is the moral problematic of the appropriate 'work ethic'. Similarly, there is a separate set of such questions and range of answers which arises from the recognition that ours is a market society — in this case the moral problematic represented by the notions of 'freedom' and 'equality', derived from the market notions of the free exchange of equivalents. Finally, as we saw in chapter 6, there is the political morality of toleration, which is linked causally and conceptually with the description of bourgeois society as 'liberal-democratic'. The meta-moral theory that the range of alternative moralities is a range of free options is itself a consequence of the meta-scientific theory, according to which the range of possible descriptions of bourgeois society is a range of free options. In much the same way as 'morality' has come to be thought of as neutral between moralities, so the range of possible social descriptions is held to be a range of free options the choice between which is not determined by our notions of scientificity. For 'scientificity' is said to be defined by reference to method, which is neutral as between these possible descriptions. Contemporary notions of scientificity, in social as in natural science, are characterised by strictness as far as concerns method, laxity as regards what is known, so that, at the worst, it is now possible to make a case for the 'scientific' study of the relations between race and intelligence so long as the inquiry is conducted along properly empirical lines.[1] Marxism inverts this order of priorities. The question of method becomes a secondary, derived question, the answer to it being determined as a function of what is required, methodologically, if science is to grasp what it exists to give knowledge of.

So far the analogy between Plato and Marx is relatively unambiguous. One of the ways in which Plato most frequently drew the contrast between *episteme* and *doxa* is on the grounds that the former is knowledge of the *necessary* connections between things, whereas the latter fails as knowledge precisely because it can apprehend phenomena only under descriptions which are in contingent connections with each other. To 'know' is to be able to see how things *must* be so. *Doxa* can see only what *happens* to be the case. Clearly, then, on the general principle underlying Plato's views on morality — that what is said to count as goodness depends on what the social 'facts' are said to be — there will be for *doxa* as many equally plausible moralities as there are social descriptions which happen to be true.

Plato very clearly illustrates the connectedness of descriptive with moral pluralism in a passage towards the end of the *Republic*,[2] in which he considers the various forms of political constitution which lapse in progressive degrees from the ideal republic. In descending order, these are the oligarchical, the timarchic and the democratic. We need not be detained by his account of these forms of political constitution. What signifies is that each constitutional description is paired off systematically with a corresponding description of the political psychology of the typical member of the society in question. The force of the word 'typical' here is that of 'good' member, where 'good citizenship' is taken relatively to the demands made on its citizens by that form of society. For example, then, the typically 'good' member of the oligarchical society is a man who has strongly acquisitive and competitive desires. This is because an oligarchical society is one which is politically organised around the compensation of desires of just that sort.

It is not irrelevant to note that there is no suggestion of social determinism in Plato's account of the connection between the political and the psychological descriptions. He by no means holds that a given form of society determines what desires its citizens will *have*. Rather, a given form of political organisation determines which desires (and more generally qualities of character) will be functional and which will be dysfunctional for it, and thus it determines the kind of psychological make-up which will typify the successful and 'good' citizen. In short, a political constitution of a given sort will routinise and reward modes of social behaviour which are the typical behaviour of citizens with a given, appropriate character and in this way will determine what will count as moral goodness for that political constitution.

Moral pluralism, then, is a consequence of the fact of descriptive pluralism itself, plus the doctrine that the range of possible true descriptions of a social order is a range of equally contingent truths. As such moral pluralism is, for Plato, the natural morality of *doxa*. In one way *doxa* concedes the fundamental doctrine of Platonism, that the determinant of morality is what counts as the facts. But in another way it departs altogether from Platonism since, for *doxa* there is no set of facts, nor any scientific account of them, which is such as uniquely to determine what morality is. Plato, no doubt, is right as to why the two positions diverge at just this point. It is because for the merchants of *doxa*, the sophists, the 'facts' — the *real* — are simply identified with the way things *happen to be*, that is, with the contingently true. But for Plato, that alone can count as knowledge which knows not merely what contingent social truths there are but also why things must be as they are, that is, what the truths are which explain why it is that the contingently true descriptions are true at all. When we know not merely the contingent truths about society but also the grounds upon which such contingent truths rest, then we know what are the facts which determine how we should act.

Whereas for bourgeois social theory the pluralism of social descriptions of contemporary society is left unhampered by restrictions in the name of scientificity, for Marx we do not begin to know or explain a social formation until we have begun to impose an order of systematic and necessary connections between these different descriptions. Knowledge begins when we have located the social mechanisms which determine the fact that our society *can be* described as 'industrial', as a 'market', as 'liberal-democratic' and as 'capitalist' and has discovered the laws governing the relations between these descriptions. In brief, 'scientificity' is defined within Marxism in terms of greater fundamentality, when we know not only how our society *can* be described, but also what those conditions are which *determine* that it can be so described and what laws govern the relations between the different possible descriptions. Science explains *why* those different descriptions explain at all.

Of course, for Marx, the ultimately determining description out of the given range of possible descriptions is that contemporary British society is 'capitalist'. It is that description which explains why the other descriptions explain, since the controlling mechanism of that form of society and of the descriptions which we can give of it is the class conflict which is based on the economic conflict of capital and labour. This is his discovery, not an a priori assumption. But why, for Marx, is it necessary, in point of scientificity, to describe that society as, fundamentally, 'capitalist'? Just why, to take up Marx's own question in the *Grundrisse*,[3] does it matter whether we regard modern economies as being systems of commodity *production*, structured on the relation of wage-labour and capital rather than, as did his bourgeois contemporaries, as being systems of distribution, that is, as *markets*? We know, of course, in what way the two points of view differ as regards their results. The notion of a 'rate of exploitation' is a relevant concept at all only within a conception of these economies according to which they are fundamentally systems of capitalist production. Within a conception according to which they are, essentially, systems of market relations, there can be no 'exploitation' (and therefore no *rate* of exploitation) in wage-labour, since on the market, all exchanges, including that of labour for wages, are necessarily free exchanges of *equivalents*.

But even if Marx believed that capitalism was most fundamentally a system of production based on a relationship of exploitation, he never denied that it is also a system of market relationships. And if that is the case, we are confronted by the truth of two descriptions of capitalist society which, prima facie, are mutually exclusive; descriptions which, it would seem, cannot both be true. For apparently one and the same social process cannot be constituted simultaneously both by relations of freedom and equality and by wage-slavery and exploitation. And yet, as Marx read it, classical economic theory did appear to want to say both, particularly in the form which Ricardo gave to that theory. Classical economics proposed the market mechanism as the account of how wealth exchanges hands, and something which at least foreshadowed his own theory of surplus value (and the consequent theory of exploitation) by way of explanation of wealth production. But what Marx believed classical economic theory could never do was to reconcile, within a unitary account, the inconsistencies which there appear to be between these explanatory models. This Marx thought he could do, and on this claim rest the credentials of his theory to greater fundamentality — to be 'science'.

No doubt Marx's solution to this problem is extraordinarily complex, and I summarise his arguments for it in the next chapter. But the broad lines of it are in accordance with the description of capitalist society as 'ideological', on that account of ideology which is sketched in the earlier argument of this book. Capitalism, as an economic structure, is a socially lived contradiction. In the briefest possible formula for this contradiction, we could say that, for Marx, capitalism is the inequality and exploitation of the wage-relationship socially lived in the form of the equality and freedom of the market. The contradiction itself, Marx believes, is the economic mechanism whereby capitalism 'lives'.

To understand this formula, let us first consider the character of these competing descriptions as 'lived'. On the one hand, the descriptions of the market mechanism and of exploitation are 'explanatory models', they are scientific constructs on real-life economic relations between people. But they are not just categories of theoretical explanation, justified, as they would be on a purely Popperian account of explanation, by their explanatory power and falsifiability. They are in the first instance lived categories, categories in terms of which real people actually relate to one another in their economic transactions. The market is a real social process: it is, as we have come to call such things, a 'praxis', embodying the ideas and perceptions in terms of which people relate to one another. People really do live their relations with the economic system via the perception of themselves as markets agents — as buyers and sellers of commodities, including their own labour[4] and that of others — and in so perceiving their relations with the economic system they are not deceived. They really do so relate.

Likewise, the abstract concept of 'productive labour', which is crucial, as Marx saw, to the structure of classical economics as an explanatory theory, is found within that theory only at the point when, in real history, it had become a widespread fact of economic life that labour is 'abstract', a uniform relation of all labour to capital and independent of qualitative differences in kind. It is a *real* phenomenon of capitalism that it treats all labour as uniform, that is, as having the single form of the commodity. The abstraction 'labour', therefore, is a lived reality before ever there is the concept of it available to theoretical economics as an explanatory category.

Thus Marx says that in capitalist economies:

not only the category labour, but labour in reality has here become the means of creating wealth in general, and has ceased to be organically linked with particular individuals in any specific form . . . Here, then, for the first time, the point of departure of modern economics, namely the abstraction of the category 'labour', 'labour as such', labour pure and simple, becomes true in practice. The simplest abstraction, then, which modern economics places at the head of its discussions . . . achieves practical truth as an abstraction only as a category of the most modern society.[5]

Hence, both categories — 'the market' and 'labour' — are first praxes and only secondarily categories of explanation. Furthermore, the contradiction between the models of explanation is also, and in the first instance, to be found in the social reality which they explain. For 'labour' is not only a commodity, freely bought and freely sold in relations of equality with its price (wages), but it is also the opposite of this, the source of a value which is in excess of what is paid for it in the form of wages, a surplus from which capitalist profit is constituted. Again, quite how this can be so is a matter which must await consideration in the next chapter. Here what concerns us is, first, the fact that, for Marx, the reality of capitalism, its structure as a social process, is constituted by this contradiction; and second, that 'science' or 'knowledge' is defined by its capacity to identify the mechanisms whereby this contradictory reality is generated and sustained, those mechanisms whereby, as I have put it, the relations of exploitation and dependence are lived in the form of equality and freedom.

Now in so far as Marxism offers itself as the 'science' or 'knowledge' which has this explanatory power, it does so on grounds which in their general character would have been familiar to Plato. In the last chapter we saw that Plato's distinction between *episteme* and *doxa* was constituted not on a priori grounds of logic or methodology, nor on psychological grounds, still less on the footing of the distinction between truth and falsity. That distinction, I said, was but the distinction which he believed to be forced upon him by 'the problematic nature of reality itself, by the failure of the . . . social world to correspond to spontaneous perception'. Analogously, these are the grounds on which Marxism must distinguish between 'science' and 'ideology'. No more is Marx's an a priori distinction, defined, for example, by some purely philosophical preference for a dialectical over a non-dialectical (say phenomenological) method. What social knowledge under capitalism is will be defined by what the contradictory reality of capitalism requires it to be. For capitalism is, ideologically, a structure of spontaneous social perceptions to which its reality fails to correspond, even if we have to say that that reality is lived in and through the perceptions which misrepresent it. Marxism, then, is 'scientific' if and only if it is adequate to the very same reality to which ideology is inadequate; if, that is to say, it can determine what the social processes are by means of which capitalism generates and sustains its own ideological character. In so far as it succeeds in dissecting those processes, it not only generates 'knowledge': it also knows itself to be that which is required of knowledge by the character of its own object.

It is in so far as it possesses this capacity for *self*-knowledge — the knowledge of the conditions governing its own constitution — that Marxism will differ as 'science' from ideology. For among the formulae which have been generated to characterise ideology in the course of the previous argument is the formula that ideology *cannot* know that which gives rise to it. In what it says ideology misdescribes that which causes it, as Mrs Holt's language about her relations with the class system misdescribes the very class relations which generate that language. On this account there is no sense to that conventional platitude that Marxism is just one more 'ideology' among others. For Marxism claims to 'know' ideology. If this claim is justified it is more than ideology, for it is the necessary tool of the criticism of ideology. Whereas if that claim is unjustified, it is less than ideology, it is but a pretentious falsehood.

<h2 style="text-align:center">II</h2>

In this way it seems to me that there is a legitimate analogy between Plato and Marx on the first score mentioned at the outset of this chapter, namely that it is the character of what is to be known, the 'objects' of knowledge, which determines what is to count as knowledge and not vice versa. But now we must turn to the second point of analogy, the Platonic doctrine that it is the *telos* of knowledge, its 'constitutive interest', which determines what those objects of knowledge are. If anything is to count as knowledge, we need to know to what end that knowledge is required, why it is that we need knowledge of just those objects.

For an answer to this question we must turn to none other than those conditions which were relevant to the last discussion. Just as Plato was confronted by a social world in which the given, conventional categories of social perception had become clearly inadequate to the realities of the contemporary social world, so Marxism arises out of the awareness of similar structural discontinuities between social perception and social reality in his world. Likewise, the reason why the critical theory of Marxism becomes the necessary form of knowledge — knowledge, that is to say, which is necessary for social agents in that world — is a need which is at once utterly primitive and general: to fail to 'know' in the relevant sense is to fail to be free. If our conceptions of the social world which we inhabit misrepresent that social world, and if, in particular, we inhabit just that sort of (ideological) social world in which, short of the appropriate critical theory, we are spontaneously caused to live in a false relation with it, then there is no possibility of our being able to control that social world. And the price of not being able to control that social world is the slavery of being controlled by it. But the first condition of controlling one's society is being able to understand it. To be able to understand it requires that one has the theoretical instruments adequate to that task. In short, the need for a critical theory of ideology is nothing but the human need for emancipation; emancipation, that is, from the determinism of the social processes which, in ideology, cannot be known. Here again we return to Plato's conception. Not to understand the nature of the human interest which such a critical theory serves is to fail to understand why we must regard it as knowledge and why we regard knowledge as worth pursuing at all. We want to know, because we want to be free: and from time to time we learn to call by the name of 'knowledge' those forms of inquiry which we need if we are at all to free ourselves from those time-encrusted conceptions which, in the course of history, have degenerated into the anachronism of ideology.

Thus it is that the different forms of theoretical inquiry which have, in the course of history, passed in and out of the canon of 'science' have done so as the result of social changes which have caused us to redefine and reorientate the perspective of that search for emancipation. For just where and just why, for any given society, the rupture occurs between the given symbols and perceptions which govern our social relations and the forces which determine how we perceive and represent them is a historical matter. It is, therefore, a *historical* matter what is to count as 'knowledge' and what 'opinion' — *pace* Plato. But, in every case, that alone is to be counted as 'knowledge' which not only knows what those forces are, but also knows itself to be that which is required by what it knows (required from the point of view of our emancipation from the determinism to which ignorance of those conditions would subject us).

As we have seen, there is something like a continuum of ideological possibilities, defined at one extreme by that simple model of society in which human relationships are nothing other than what they are socially perceived to be. In such a society theory is dispensable, a critical theory is irrelevant, art is a mere embellishment of everyday life, never a protest in terms of alternative symbols against it, morality *is* everyday life, and religion is not distinguishable from either. Emancipation in such a world from everyday symbolic understanding would be an unintelligible, idiotic fantasy.

Strung along the continuum is all actual history in which now, as in the time of the sophists, it is possible to see the lived perceptions of everyday life as being in so contradictory a relationship with its reality that the only way of describing that relationship is as mystification. In such circumstances the unmasking of those false relationships which govern social reality becomes the single most important task for knowledge — and as we will see, for morality — for it is the task demanded of knowledge by the stake all people have in their own autonomy, their emancipation.

That task would become finally redundant only under a condition which falls at the other extreme of the continuum, namely the emergence of a single, indisputably true body of social knowledge which was the normal and everyday form of social perception. For if such a body of knowledge were available and if its truth were 'realised in practice', then it would once again be the case that the symbols of everyday life would be perfectly continuous with the social processes which generated them. What people interpreted their social relations to be would be perfectly continuous with what they were, not in the primitive sense, that thought could not 'transcend' social conditions and would be a 'mere reflex' of them, but because knowledge would be the perfectly adequate instrument for the control of them. Such a society is what Marx meant by 'communist society', whose form would be in a *historical* relation with capitalist society, not, as with Plato's republic, in a purely 'ideal' relation with a deficient copy. None the less, as with Plato, even if it were not the case that such a society were ever to be achieved — and there is nothing in Marx to suggest that it could not fail to be achieved — the general conditions which it instantiates determine the criteria for scientificity, as its *telos*. Equally, as I argue next, those are the conditions of the possibility of morality.

III

We have, then, to consider the third element in our analogy; that the *telos* of knowledge is such that whatever meets it and so qualifies as 'scientific' thereby qualifies as morality. And it may be thought, and, if so, with some justice, that if the argument of the last section showed anything at all, it must also have shown this. If what determines knowledge to be scientific is its relation to the governing interest of 'emancipation', then that same relation to that interest must determine knowledge to be also moral knowledge. For what interest could have the character of morality more than emancipation? What in Marxism has a more explicitly moral dimension than the goal it seeks of 'communist society'? Of course this double character of the argument should not surprise us. All along it has been the central claim of the 'morality is Marxism' thesis that whatever, if anything, showed Marxism to be 'scientific' *eo ipso* would show it to be morality.

And yet it is here that we meet for the first time — although by no means for the last — a style of objection to this thesis, forthcoming chiefly from Marxists, who will protest that far from showing Marxism to be the necessary form of science, this thesis reduces Marxism to the status of an idealistic moralism. The objections can take many forms, and in this final section of the present chapter I consider some of them in the course of seeking to clarify what exactly the identity thesis does and does not maintain.

The main complaint is against the apparent 'absolutism' of the moral *telos* of emancipation, the tendency which may seem to be present in my argument to represent 'communist society', the concrete form of that emancipation, as being a non-historical moral principle or Platonic 'idea', at once detached from history and, as it were, its standard of comparison. Would not the 'morality is Marxism' thesis, construed on this basis, entail morally pretentious claims for Marxism? Would it not entail that Marxism is in a position to claim some privileged knowledge of an ethically absolute principle of 'emancipation'; or, worse, that Marxism claims to be able to predict the necessary emergence of a fully emancipated ('communist') society? If this were my interpretation of

Marxism, then there would be strenuous objections to it from all quarters of Marxism, and rightly too.[6] If the 'morality is Marxism' thesis postulates the abstraction 'emancipation' as the common criterion of scientificity and of morality, then it is certainly un-Marxist: Marxism must decisively reject the notion that the scientificity of its methods (as also its identity with morality) can be deduced from some wider, non-historical notion either of what counts as science in general or of what counts as 'emancipation' in general. In fact, however, my argument commits me to no such 'absolutism' either in science or in morality.

Connected with this potential source of misunderstanding is another. It may seem that my argument equally absolutises the Platonic social ontology of the contrast between the 'true' social needs which science knows and the 'false' social needs which men ideologically perceive. This, too, is an un-Marxian notion. Equally, my argument does not, in fact, involve it.

What, then, is the 'morality is Marxism' thesis? It is that, under the social and economic conditions which determine that Marxism is the science of society, morality is Marxism. For to fulfil the conditions for scientific knowledge of society is to fulfil the conditions for morality.

But even if this identity holds under these specific conditions it does not follow that the identity holds timelessly, as if Marxism were the timeless *definition* of morality. For, on that version of the identity thesis, it would follow that at no time prior to Marxism was there any such knowledge as moral knowledge. This is clearly absurd. It would in any case have the further, even more absurd, consequence for any consistent Marxist that at no time prior to the emergence of scientific socialism was morality even conceivable. For a consistent Marxist recognises, as I argued in the last chapter, that Marxism itself was not a possibility under any other conditions than those historically contingent conditions which we call 'capitalism'. Morality may be Marxism under those conditions. But in no way is it an intelligible view that Marxism *invented* morality unconditionally.

The argument, then, is that morality *is* Marxism under those conditions which determine its scientificity, but I am denying that it *defines* morality. Does it follow from this, as some have supposed that it must, that I am proposing the thoroughly un-Marxist notion that there is some timeless definition of morality which, in the capitalist epoch, it *so happens* that Marxism satisfies? Were it any part of my argument to suggest that the emancipatory interest of scientific and moral knowledge is some ideal, timeless standard or a utopian state of affairs to be achieved, then the identity thesis would collapse. In that case, far from morality being Marxism, Marxist science would be reduced merely to the status of knowledge of the means relevant, under capitalism, to the achievement of a morally defined utopian goal. I neither hold this, nor does it follow from what I do hold.

What, then, is the nature of the identity being claimed between morality and Marxism? It could be called a 'substitution-identity'. Morality is that form of knowledge which, in relation to a given form of society, can be called the science of it. There are no a priori standards which such knowledge has to fulfil in order to qualify as scientific. The point of my discussion of Plato's doctrines was to reject two such views on which there are a priori standards of scientificity. First, I argued, on mainly Platonic grounds, that there are no abstract *methodological* features which are timelessly distinctive of scientific knowledge. Second, I argued against Plato that there is no a priori distinction between 'reality' and 'appearance' which could timelessly dictate the distinction between science and non-science.

Nevertheless, although there is no one set of methodological criteria, nor any one ontology which for all time defines science, any given form of science will have to be in some way methodologically distinctive and will be underpinned by some form of contrast between 'reality' and 'appearance'. As Marx himself says, 'all science would be superfluous if the outward appearance and the essence of things directly co-incided';[7] and again, 'That in their appearance things often represent themselves in inverted form is pretty well known in every science except Political Economy.'[8] Of course, it is not enough to recognise this general fact in its general form, for the important question about science is the following: just what determines, for a given epoch, the distinctive methodology and the distinctive ontology?

The answer to this question, in part already given earlier in this chapter, is that a given form of social organisation is characterised by the human needs which that social formation typically generates — whether or not it is capable of satisfying them. The teleology of knowledge comes in at this point, because in the satisfaction of human needs there is, as elsewhere, a division of labour. If human beings have any sort of socially generated needs at all, then they have at least one socially necessary meta-need: the need, that is, to know what those needs are. The need to know what our needs are is simply a corollary, for human beings at least, of our having any needs at all. The point which is borrowed from Plato is that scientific knowledge of society is whatever form of knowledge it is that is capable of distinguishing between true and false need. For that is the kind of knowledge which we need to have, given that we have any needs at all.

This, however, entails no commitment to a Platonic timeless ontology of human needs. There is no one set of needs which is, for all men and all time, the set of 'true' human needs. There is, in consequence, no one form of the contrast between true and false needs which is, for all men and all time, the adequate definition of the contrast. As needs are socially generated, so too are the forms of contrast between their true and their false versions. The contrast, then, between what is a true and what is a false need is itself historically contingent; an 'ideological' form of society is, therefore, some form of social structure built upon a mechanism whereby needs are generated in false forms, a mechanism which is specific to it.

There is, therefore, no Platonic 'reality' underlying the 'appearances' of ideology, as I have already shown in chapter 3. If I am committed to any form of social ontology — that is, to an account, in general terms, of 'social reality' — it is one on which that reality consists neither in some supposed ideological 'surface' of mystified perceptions of need; nor, by contrast, in some 'deeper' reality of 'true' human needs hidden from us by the surface; nor even in some absolute contrast between 'surface appearance' and 'reality'. Rather, the social reality consists in *the mechanism itself*, whereby a social formation generates human needs in misperceived or ideo-

logical forms. Specifically, capitalist society *is* (its 'reality' is)
the processes whereby it reproduces a cycle of needs and their
satisfactions, *both* socially existing only in misperceived forms.
And 'scientific knowledge' of society is not, as Plato imagined
it, some kind of access to an absolute and normative truth
about what is good for man, ideology giving us access only to
counterfeit copies. To 'know' capitalism is to know the laws
governing that cycle of misperceived need and misperceived
satisfaction which it generates. There is no timeless knowledge,
since there is no timeless form of this cycle.

If there is no normative 'truth' to be discovered underlying,
as it were, the falsifications of ideology, in what way is
Marxist science 'emancipatory'? It seems to me that as self-
knowledge is to self-deception, so is Marxism to the capitalist
structures of ideology. A man who is deceiving himself is a
man who, for self-interested reasons of which he is unaware,
believes in a false self-image. In one sense, therefore, he is not
what he believes he is, since there is a gap of misrepresentation
between what he is 'really' like and what he thinks he is like.
On other other hand, it would be quite wrong to infer from
this that one could separately identify, say, a man's 'true'
desires, as if they were occurrent, actual desires, then identify
the desires which he thinks (but deceives himself) he has and,
so to speak, hold up two distinct sets of occurrent desires for
comparison. Self-deception is not a veil of obscurity spread
over an actually existent reality, any more than unmasking
one's self-deception is a matter of stripping away such a veil
so as to leave revealed something which was already there.

Yet this is only half the story. It seems to be necessary to
say two sorts of thing about self-deception, each apparently
incompatible with the other. We need to say that when a man
deceives himself he is bound by a false picture of his desires
and beliefs and feelings and that he is not 'really' like what he
has brought it about that he thinks he is like. On the other
hand, we also want to deny that the expression 'what he is
really like' refers to actual desires and beliefs and feelings
which 'exist' independently of, but concurrently with, that
false self-image. Why do we need to deny this? For two
reasons mainly. The first is that the self-deceived person is,
really, self-deceived. That is what he is really like. He acts,

feels, desires in accordance with his state of self-deception. What he does, feels and thinks is determined both by what he believes about himself and by the fact that in his beliefs about himself he is deceiving himself: his actions and reactions are caused by his state of self-deception, by the mechanism whereby he interestedly goes on believing in his false self-image. The self-deceived man lives, acts, feels and thinks out of his false consciousness.

The second reason is that there appears to be no sense to be made of a desire or belief's being occurrent when the desirer and believer is not aware of it. When it is said that a person does not know what he wants, we ought not to suppose that there is something which he wants but that he does not know it. What is meant is that there is something that the man would want, were he not captivated by a false picture of himself as being a person who does not want it. Similarly with self-deception, when we think of a man as 'really' wanting X when he prefers to believe in an image of himself as wanting not-X (or as not wanting X), it is wrong to suppose that below the surface of his perceived desire for not-X (or non-desire for X) there is some actual, but unperceived, desire for X. We mean only that, if he could be rid of the false image in terms of which he misdescribes his desires, he would come to see that he does want X and would have wanted it all the time, if he had not been deceiving himself. We cannot, however, in any other sense say that all the time he *did* want X. 'False' desires, then, are desires misdescribed — and interestedly misdescribed in the case of self-deception. They exist, or are occurrent, *only* in their false form. And they are 'false' only in relation to what a man would want and know that he wanted, if he were to come to see that he had been deceiving himself.

Consequently, we are in a position to say *both* that the only occurrent 'reality' in self-deception is the mechanism of self-deception as such *and* that the self-deceived image causes the self-deceiver to perceive false desires, where this 'falsity' is a relationship between how a person describes his desires to himself within the self-deceived image and how he would describe them if he were not self-deceived. On what grounds, then, it may be asked, is it shown that the first self-image is 'false' and the second self-image 'true'? Why should one not merely say that the two self-images are just different and optional patterns of self-description, one neither more true than the other?

It has to be admitted that no one can ever be sure that he is not deceiving himself in some way at any time. It is therefore always possible that the replacing self-image is in its own way as much a product of self-deception as is the image which it replaces. None the less, although we can never be sure that we are not now deceiving ourselves, it does seem possible sometimes to be virtually certain that we were once deceiving ourselves in some respect in which we now are not: that all along what I 'really' wanted was the power which professorial status brings, not the service which I could do for scholarship. In the end such awareness is based simply on the greater explanatory power of the succeeding over the preceding self-image. In terms of what I now see about myself, I can explain not only what my previous picture of myself explained, but also what it could not explain — what, in connection with that previous self-image, I had to explain *away*.[9] And further even to that, it is convincing to claim that I have successfully undeceived myself, if, in terms of the greater self-awareness which I have achieved, I can incorporate an explanation of why I needed to and how I was capable of deceiving myself in just that way — when I can say 'I can now see that I am just the sort of person who will deceive himself thus'. Admittedly, I cannot be sure that in some other way I am not deceiving myself now. But I can be reasonably sure that I was deceiving myself then.

It thus seems plausible to say that in cases of self-deception I can recognise, *post factum*, that there was a 'truth' masked by the self-deceived image without being committed to any view that some 'true self' was lying there, occurrent, but unperceived. To have deceived oneself is to have had an interest in not knowing oneself as one might have been. It is like having missed an opportunity. An opportunity is only *there*, if it is *seen* to be there. And so too with ideology. It is not a consequence of my account of the relationships between science and ideology that somehow, underlying the 'false appearances' of ideology, there exists a level of perceptible-in-principle occurrent 'reality'. This is exactly the account, given in *The German Ideology*, which I rejected in chapter 3. It is therefore a misconstrual of this contrast to suggest, as one Marxist critic has,[10] that on my view there is, within ideology, a 'normative truth which ideology falsifies *as if that truth were somehow in the ideology* needing only to be released — like Ariel from the tree — in order to work wonders'. On my account, in ideology, the reality consists in the 'falsification', itself although as I have argued, this word is hardly the most appropriate. To contrast man's 'true' needs with his 'ideological' needs is merely to point to what could be perceived as man's true needs in conditions of liberation from the distorting effects of ideological misdescription. We do not know now how we would describe our needs under such conditions, precisely because the emancipation from ideology would leave us in a relatively freer position to describe our needs for ourselves.

How, then, does 'emancipation' function as an interest determinative of scientificity? It functions 'heuristically' and the knowledge of it which is both scientific and moral is heuristic knowledge. Marxism 'knows' its own constitutive interest of emancipation in the way in which a writer, struggling to find the words in which to formulate his thoughts, 'knows' the words he is looking for. In a sense he does not know what the words are — in that sense in which he will know them when he finds them — for they are still 'on the tip of his tongue'. But for all that he does not know what the words are, he is perfectly capable of saying what they are not. 'No', he mutters to himself, 'this, that or the other word won't quite do, none of them say exactly what I want to say.' In this sense he does know what the words are, for he knows that the rejected candidates will not do the job he has in mind.

It would be a mistake, all the same, to infer from the naturalness of the expressions which I have just used — that the writer is looking for the words to 'formulate his thoughts' and that the right words will 'do the job that he has in mind' — that somehow the writer has a thought there 'in his mind' and that he is merely lacking the words for it. The notion that a man can know what he wants to say but cannot find the words to say it is as misleading as the notion that a man who does not know what he wants wants something but does not know it. Just as in the latter case the man will know that he wants X *when* he wants X, so in the former he will know what he thinks when he finds the words. From the fact that he knows what words do not express his thought, it does not at all follow that there is some occurrent, already formed thought there waiting for its verbal expression.

When, therefore, I say that he knows the right words 'heuristically', I mean only that he knows, prior to his finding the right words, which words will not do and that he will know both what the right words are and what the thought is which they express *when he finds them.*

It is only in a way analogous to this that Marxism can be said to 'know' its constitutive interest of emancipation. This knowledge is not knowledge of some non-historical absolute or utopia, a standard by which, for example, capitalism fails and Marxism succeeds. This 'emancipation' functions, in relation to Marxist scientificity, as that which the critique of capitalism is a process of discovering. It is not that Marxism knows what emancipation is and proposes to itself the moral task of 'smashing capitalism' to achieve it. Rather, it is that, in his response to the exigencies of the class struggle, the Marxist is seeking to dissect the mechanisms of capitalism which sustain it and in that dissecting he is seeking to discover what the possibilities of emancipation are and what emancipation could come to mean. On the one hand, then, the scientific critique of capitalism is morality, because it is governed by the constitutive interest of emancipation and, on the other hand, morality is this critique because it is only in and through the engagement in this critique that we can piece together the fragments of that new story which tells of emancipation, tells of what it might come to mean and of the conditions under which it might become history.

It is the same with the Marxist understanding of 'revolution'. Any revolution is the struggle with oppression in the name of a liberty which the revolutionaries know that they will be unable to describe until the oppression has been overthrown. For a revolution is not merely the extending to all of liberties which are already the privilege of an elite. Indeed, it is not that at all. It is a matter of revising what we mean by liberty itself. The ruling class know only too well that to concede their liberties to all would be 'the end of society as we know it' and the end of liberty itself as they know it. On the other hand, those who, for the Marxist, have the power to wage a successful revolutionary struggle, at least *ceteris paribus* — concretely, the working class — are often reluctant to shoulder responsibility for the revolutionary implications even of their reformist demands. In any case, they do not have and cannot have demanded of them an alternative programme of freedom. Yet just as the writer's struggle to write is both motivated and governed by the text he is as yet unable to construct, so the revolutionary struggle is motivated and governed by the demand for a freedom whose concrete form he cannot yet envisage. The normativeness of the freedom his revolution will achieve is not that of an already written text which already interprets his action. It is the normativeness of the as yet unwritten text of liberty which *has to be written*. It governs his refusal to compromise, his self-critical cancelling of the unsatisfactory phrase, sentence or paragraph — even chapter — of the revolutionary draft, and at the same time it governs his quasi-intuitive acceptance of the isolated fragment — sometimes as little as a word — which he knows points, as yet ambiguously, to the text in which it will later find its unambiguous place.

Marxism has a claim to be morality, not as being a moral programme or as being a given set of moral goals — goals, that is to say, given to it in advance of the revolutionary struggle. There is only one *given* morality and that is bourgeois. Marxism is its criticism. Marxism cannot know the morality which it is the struggle to articulate. Morality, in so far as we can know it, is the struggle that there should be morality, in so far as that struggle is governed by the emancipation which the present conditions both demand and suppress. Marxism is morality, not as being but a rival set of answers to bourgeois moral questions, but as *the condition of the possibility of morality*.

My response, then, to the charge of ethical absolutism and to the criticism that the identity thesis proposes 'emancipation' as an absolute moral standard is that the word 'standard' is ambiguous and that in one sense the answer is yes and in another no. In the sense of 'standards' in which they are abstract, non-historical, metaphysical, methodological or moral imperatives, it is true that there are none which Marxism can be required to satisfy — and certainly there are none which it is incumbent upon both Plato and Marx to satisfy. But my argument does not entail this conclusion. The teleological constraint which any social theory has to meet if it is to be scientific is the sort of constraint which, as a result of their both satisfying it, makes Platonic and Marxist 'science' necessarily *differ* from one another, in method, in social ontology and in the moral imperatives which are derivable. Just because, to be scientific, both Platonism and Marxism had to satisfy the same teleological requirement, they had to differ in their ontological and methodological standards of scientificity.

In the second sense of the word 'standard', therefore, the word denotes a respect in which forms of science in different historical conditions differ, not a respect in which they are always the same, regardless of historical conditions. The teleology of knowledge, therefore, far from being a covert 'absolute' definition either of science or of morality, is what systematically and in relation to differing historical conditions generates the differences between conceptions of science and morality out of the exigencies of those differing historical conditions. The teleology of knowledge is, in short, nothing more nor less than a special case, in its application to the notions of scientificity and morality, of the materialist theory of history itself.

NOTES

1   Cf. H.A. Eysenck, *Race, Intelligence and Education*, London, 1972.
2   Plato, *Republic*, 543—92.
3   Karl Marx, *Grundisse*, translated by M. Nicolaus, Harmondsworth, 1973, pp. 95—8.
4   Strictly speaking, as we will see in the next chapter, this is inaccurate. What the worker sells is his 'labour-power', not his 'labour'. But see chapter 9, pp. 132—7 for the significance of this distinction.

5   Marx, *Grundrisse*, p. 99.
6   Cf. Francis Barker, 'The Morality of Knowledge and the Disappearance of God', *New Blackfriars*, September 1976, pp. 403–14. This is an Althusserian critique of my article, 'Morality is Marxism', *New Blackfriars*, February 1973, pp. 57–66, and March 1973, pp. 117–25.
7   Karl Marx, *Capital*, III, translated by S. Moore and E. Aveling, London, 1970, p. 797.
8   Ibid., I, p. 537.
9   See my article, 'Self-Knowledge and Self-Deception', *New Blackfriars*, July 1975, pp. 294–305.
10 Barker, 'The Morality of Knowledge and the Disappearance of God', p. 407.

9

The 'Rescued Truth'

The argument so far can be summarised in the following points.

1   An ideology is a praxis characterised by a form of contradictoriness, in which the modes of social perception and relationship which it routinises misrepresent the social processes which generate them.

2   At the political level, the social determinants of ideology consist essentially in the phenomena of class conflict. These phenomena, however, can be represented within bourgeois ideology only as facts about class or else as facts about conflict, but in either case they are perceived to be the spontaneous phenomena of an abstract 'pluralist' order. They cannot, within ideology, be represented in the form they have as *class conflict*.

3   At the moral level, those same ideological necessities (to live out relations of class conflict in the form of 'pluralist' order) generate as imperatives correspondingly abstract virtues of relationship with that order, the 'abstraction' of the virtues consisting in their socially functional abstraction *from* the realities of class conflict.

4   At the economic level, this ideological structure takes the form of the contradiction whereby economic relations of exploitation and inequality are socially lived in the form of the market relations of freedom and equality.

5   The 'science' of capitalist society is, in general contrast with all ideology, that which is capable of dissecting the social mechanisms of ideology, of laying bare the constituents of the contradictory reality of that social world.

6   Hence, that alone is to be called by the name of 'knowledge' or 'science' which can demonstrate its own necessity, the necessity whereby it is that which is demanded by the problematical, contradictory nature of its own ideological object.

7   The necessity to which such knowledge responds is a form of teleological necessity, for that is knowledge which is the contact with reality we need to have in view of the historically contingent goal of social emancipation.

8   Consequently, that which is shown contingently to be the appropriate form of social knowledge is also shown to be, contingently, moral knowledge.

9   Under capitalism, Marxism uniquely satisfies these conditions.

It follows from this that morality, under capitalism, is Marxism. No doubt, however, this will be thought a very paradoxical conclusion, and indeed it is, at least for the reason that Marxism appears to be, if anything, *amoralistic*. I shall make no attempt to bring out the full force of this paradox until the third part of this book, since much difficult argument lies between this stage of it and the point at which it can be adequately done. In the meantime, let us state the paradox in its most obvious form: morality, on my argument, is Marxism. And yet Marxism, strictly as such, has no moral vocabulary of its own nor any alternative moral insights to offer in place of the bourgeois moral doctrines and values which it shows to be ideological. We begin to move towards a resolution of this paradox as we clarify what this critical relation of Marxism to bourgeois morality consists in and what we may expect of it by way of results. My argument is that Marxism stands to bourgeois ideology as its 'rescued truth'. I consider, in order, the criticism of economic and of moral ideology.

I

The first and wholly negative point about the critical relationship of Marxism to ideologies is that this relationship does not consist in any straightforward contrast between Marxism as 'true' belief and ideology as 'false' belief. For ideologies are not mere bundles of false beliefs, still less of meaningless propositions. We have already encountered most of the arguments to this effect. In fact, somewhat more positively, Marx's views about what logical and epistemic properties could be assigned to individual ideological beliefs and propositions are surprisingly elastic. This can be seen, for example, in his attitude to classical economic doctrines. Although he regarded them as, in the long run, 'ideological', Marx was quite happy to allow that many of the claims of Adam Smith and Ricardo made good empirical sense; at least some of them, he held, were actually true empirical assertions. Others he claimed to be false, indeed he claimed to have refuted them on empirical grounds. Yet others he clearly regarded as being pseudo-empirical assertions which were but covert tautologies, as he did with J.S. Mill's economic assumptions in the Introduction to the *Grundrisse.*[1] In other words, it is clear that for Marx at least some propositions within some ideological discourses could genuinely be assigned the unambiguously ordinary truth values which they purport to have, and that the truth or falsity, as the case may be, could be established by conventionally inductive methods of verification and probability, or else by conventionally deductive methods of falsification. To the extent that this is so, then, there is nothing very special about the relationship of Marxist science to ideology: it is superior just to the degree that it is capable of greater explanatory adequacy.

That not all ideological utterances could be assigned unambiguous truth values in this straightforward way is shown by the centrality of the role within any ideology to which Marx ascribes, among other non-logical properties, that of 'fetishism'. This property, and several others such as 'reification', 'de-historicisation' and 'naturalisation' are, as is well known within Marxism, very puzzling properties from the point of view of the epistemology which they entail. I cannot hope to do justice to them, but at least this much can be said with relative clarity: a concept which is the 'fetishised' form of another concept, or a social process which is a 'fetish' for other social processes is not a concept or process which stands in the epistemological relationship either of truth or of falsehood to that which it fetishises. On the contrary, the relationship between a fetish and what it fetishises is one which is precisely *ambiguous between* true representation and misrepresentation.

What, then, is the process of 'fetishisation'? Marx's brief formula in *Capital* is that it is the process whereby 'a relation between persons [is] expressed as a relationship between things'.[2] It is relatively easy to provide partial illustrations of this process from the economic sphere: money is one. A coin is an object, a bit of metal with physical properties. Although in any currency there is a fixed number of determinate forms which the bits of metal and paper of its coinage must have to be valid currency, clearly *as money* — as say '2p' — the coin is a *value*, not an alloy of metals in a particular shape. The physical properties of units of currency are conventionally necessary, but in no way sufficient conditions of their values. Just as a spoken word is both a physical event — a specific sound — and a meaning — a sign; and just as the physical event acquires its significance or value as a symbol from a set of linguistic conventions, so a piece of metal of determinate physical shape acquires the value '2p' — becomes a symbol — only within a set of economic conventions and relationships, namely those of exchange. Of what, then, is the value '2p' a symbol? It is the symbol of the abstract power to command certain values in exchange — it is the symbol of the economic power of its owner over those commodities of equivalent value which are available in exchange for it. It does not symbolise any commodities in particular, but rather a power over any commodities at all which are of equivalent value. For just as it symbolises in abstraction from any particular owner his power in exchange, so it symbolises his power over commodities in the abstract. Consequently the 2p coin symbolises a certain degree of abstract social power within a particular set of economic relationships, viz. exchange relationships. It is, therefore, a particular form of social relationship between persons, i.e. one of economic power, expressed as a relationship between things, i.e. between the physical coin and the commodities for which it can be exchanged.

To this degree money is, on the Marxist formulae, a 'fetish', although, as we will see, it only partially realises the full definition of fetishism in the sense of that word in which it is, within Marxism, paradigmatic for ideologies. But even in this case it is important not to be misled by the words 'expressed as' in the Marxian formula. It is not as if there existed, as some more basic economic fact, the bare power over commodity values, a relationship between persons (buyer and seller) which in a money economy becomes 'expressed' in the fetishistic form of relations between things. In a money economy 'power over commodity values' exists in and *only* in the form of relationships between things. The ownership of values in exchange *is* ownership of money. There is no secret form of economic relationship which is somehow translated into fetishistic form by the magic of money. Just as, in the last chapter, we saw that the man who deceives himself about what he wants is not to be described as having some wants about which he deceives himself, so here, the fact that the relationships between persons are said to be 'expressed as' relationships between things does not imply that underlying the money form of purchasing power there is some 'purchasing power *simpliciter*' which is fetishised in the money form.

Having made this precautionary observation, let us look at a much more complex case of economic fetishism, the wage-relationship. For here we see that fetishism is the general form of the contradictory interaction of the market relations of freedom and equality with the productive relations of inequality and exploitation. In *Wages, Price and Profit*[3] Marx spent much effort decoding the assertion of the classical economist that the value of labour is exactly represented by its price in the form of wages. Within the ideological framework of the bourgeois economic theories in which this 'law' had its origin, this statement is a tautology. For according to this law when the worker collects his Friday wage-packet he collects, in money form, the equivalent value or price of the work which he has done during the previous five days. From one point of view, then, this money represents his abstract power over commodities equivalent in value to his money wages. From another point of view, this money is supposed to represent the value of the labour performed during the week, its price which the capitalist who employs him pays for that labour. On this view of it, therefore, as a worker he is as much involved in a relationship of exchange with his employer as he is in purchasing commodities with his wages; both relationships are relationships in which the values exchanged are equivalents and are expressed in the form of the money he takes in wages. It is therefore a tautology, in so far as his relationship to the capitalist is an exchange relationship, that the worker gets the exact value, or price, of what he has sold to the capitalist, in the form of his weekly wage-packet.

But, for Marx, the relationship of worker to capitalist is not a relationship of exchange, or at least not merely. To view it simply as an exchange is to make a fundamental category mistake. What the worker sells to the capitalist is not the 'living active labour' which he performs during the hours of his work (what Marx calls simply 'labour'), but his *labour-power*, that is to say, his *capacity to work*, his power and skills, for a certain number of hours per week. What exchanges with wages is this capacity, for in so far as labour-power is really something which the worker owns he can sell it as a commodity at a price (wages) and the wages really will be the money equivalent of the value of his labour-power.

The exchange between the worker and the capitalist is a simple exchange; each obtains an equivalent; the one obtains money, the other a commodity whose *price* is exactly equal to the money paid for it.[4]

Hence the capitalist pays the worker for the use of his labour-power (*not* for his labour) at a value (price) which is determined, as all values are determined, 'by the quantity of labour necessary to produce it'.[5] The quantity in question is the quantity of labour required to produce and maintain in existence a worker (to feed, clothe and house him) *plus* what is required to educate him in the required skills, *plus* 'another amount of necessaries to bring up a certain quota of children that are to replace him on the labour market and to perpetuate the race of labourers'.[6]

But on both sides of this 'exchange' (of labour-power for wages) there is an anomaly. From the side of the worker, what he gets in return for his sale of labour-power is not, Marx argues, *wages*, strictly speaking, but wage *goods*. The worker receives no wealth, that is, money in its general form as wealth, since what he gets is determined in amount by what is required for his maintenance and the reproduction of his kind. Therefore, what he gets represents no general or abstract form of power over commodities in exchange, but only power over those commodities in particular which are needed to maintain him and reproduce other workers.

What he obtains from the exchange is therefore not exchange value, not wealth, but a means of subsistence, objects for the preservation of his life . . .[7]

Rather, then, than getting in return for his labour-power, power over commodities in exchange, he gets specific commodities in the form of money. It is, Marx adds, only in so far as he can save money, that is, personally abstain from consumption, that the worker acquires wealth properly speaking, in the form of the abstract power over commodities indifferently. And Marx is caustic about the hypocrisy of capitalists who preach this abstention to *their own* workers (since if they can save, they prove that their wages are above the average *necessary* level of wages) but abhor the prospect of workers as a class saving (since, among other things, this would drastically reduce levels of consumption).[8]

On the side of the capitalist, the anomaly is more striking. He who has bought a commodity in exchange has the right to consume it, which is exactly what the capitalist does with the labour-power which he has bought. But the consumption of labour-power by the capitalist is not the destruction of this capacity, but rather is its exercise, its being put to work, over the conditions of which the capitalist has legal control. The exercise of labour-power is *labour*, the worker's work activity during the week, his *productive* activity. Labour-power, namely as the capacity to work, *produces nothing*. It exchanges with values. Labour, the exercise of this capacity, is that which *produces* value. But the worker *has already been paid* for the availability of his capacity; that exchange is over, so to speak, *before* anything has been produced. Consequently, a proportion of the values which the worker produces by means of his labour are values over and above the values which he has received as equivalent to the availability of his labour-power. The capitalist, in consuming what he has paid for, receives a higher value than that which is represented in the wages paid — he receives a 'surplus value' which is created by the worker's labour.

At this latter level, then, there is no exchange at all. If the capitalist did not extract this surplus value, he would not be a capitalist. But if he does extract it, then the wages which he pays the worker are not the equivalent of his *labour*, that is, of his value-producing activity, at all.

On the other hand, the capitalist really does pay the market price of the worker's labour-power. Thus, what the worker perceives to be an equivalance — a 'fair exchange' — is not a fantasy, an appearance. What he perceives is the money equivalent of his labour-power in the form of the money equivalent of his labour. This is what explains the mistake in the bourgeois economists's dictum: the worker receives in wages the exact equivalent of the labour he sells. Thus Marx says:

Firstly. *The value or price of the labouring power* takes the semblance of the *price or value of labour itself*, although, strictly, value and price of labour are senseless terms.
Secondly. Although one part only of the workman's daily labour is *paid*, while the other part is *unpaid*, and while that unpaid or surplus labour constitutes exactly the fund out of which *surplus value* or *profit* is formed, it seems as if the aggregate labour was paid labour . . . On the basis of the wages system even the *unpaid* labour seems to be *paid* labour.[9]

It *seems* as if there is still an exchange going on, because when the worker receives his wage-packet at the end of the week, the perceived nexus is that between the money which it contains and what the worker has been doing during the previous five days. But this form in which the week's productive activity — labour — is expressed is in fact the expression *in the form of an exchange* between a commodity and its money equivalent of a relation of *surplus extraction* between the worker's wealth-creating activity and the capitalist. It is, in other words, a relation between persons existing in the form of relations between things. It is a relation of exploitation and therefore of inequality, existing in the form of a relation of exchange and therefore of equality.

It is, furthermore, a relation of 'fetishisation', since the worker, by means of his activity, creates the very power which exploits him, namely capital:

Thus the productivity of his labour, his labour in general, insofar as it is not a *capacity* but a motion, *real* labour, comes to confront the worker as an *alien power*; capital, inversely, realises itself through the *appropriation of alien labour*.[10]

Marx's discovery of this category confusion between labour and labour-power is, moreover, not merely the discovery of a confusion within economic theory. It is also the discovery of the real mechanisms of an actual social process. Not merely is that which is not an equal exchange *perceived* in the form of equality: that relation of exploitation actually *exists* in the form of its opposite, that is, in the social transaction of wages for work done as equivalents. But the complexities of the real mechanism whereby this process occurs can only be unravelled once the distinction between labour and labour-power has been discovered. For, in so far as labour is not and cannot be that which exchanges for wages, the use of the category 'labour' to describe that which is in an equal exchange with wages necessarily causes the relation of inequality to disappear from the worker's perception of the social process. It becomes impossible, without this distinction, to describe the relation as what it really is, as a relation of exploitation. For this the category of labour as a wealth-creating activity is needed. Yet if 'labour' is understood as and is not distinguished from labour-power, labour appears as what labour-power is, namely a commodity, a capacity to work which can be sold at its exchange value.

The appearance, then, of the relation of inequality in the form of equality exhibits a relation between a 'fetish' and what it fetishises; a relation which is, in its structure, precisely that which, in less technical terms, we have repeatedly discovered in non-economic ideologies — that of a social relation being lived through social perceptions which misrepresent that social relationship. If, therefore, we can find exact expression for the contrast between the ideological representation of the labour/capital relationship as an exchange of equivalents and the scientific representation of it as the extraction of surplus value, then we will be on the way to answering our question: what does the scientific critique of ideologies show them to be?

Once again the contrast between these 'representations' is not that between 'truth' and 'falsehood', since, as we have seen, *in reality* the worker gets the value of his *labour-power* in exchange. For the same reason, the contrast is not that between 'reality' and 'illusion'. Marx himself insists that the appearance of exploitation (inequality) in the form of an exchange of equivalents (equality) is the fetishised appearance of an exploitative relationship in a *really existent social form*.

None the less, although the appearance of the relationship of exploitation in the form of an equal exchange of a commodity for money is not an unreal appearance, it is not a true representation of it either. The two-sided truth, the contradictory reality of the capitalist mode of the production of wealth is *the fact itself of a relationship of exploitation socially existing in the form of an exchange of equivalents.* Scientific knowledge is that which is capable of explaining, because it has the concepts with which to do so, the mechanism whereby this process of fetishisation occurs. The claim of Marxism to be the science of capitalism rests on its having forged the necessary concepts, in particular on its capacity to employ in systematic explanations the distinction between 'labour-power' and 'labour'.

Within the confused conceptual framework of the misread category of 'labour' and the 'market price' of labour, the phenomena of fetishism cannot even be registered, never mind explained. For, looked on as a market relationship, the labour/wages relationship is one of equal exchange. The tautology of the bourgeois 'law' so far holds: it is true that the value of labour-power is represented by its price in the form of wages. But once the distinction between 'labour' and 'labour-power' is exhibited, the law ceases to be a tautology and becomes the overtly *false* statement that the value *produced by labour* is represented equivalently by wages. In short, a statement which, in its ideological confusion between labour and labour-power, is ambiguous between tautology and falsehood, when read as a statement about the value of the labourer's wealth-producing activity, is shown to be unambiguously false; and, when read as a statement about the value of labour-power, it is shown to be an unambiguously true tautology. In the absence of the distinction between labour and labour-power, the original tautology would appear to represent the simple truth. Given the distinction, it is possible to see the original law not as being straightforwardly false but as *systematically ambiguous as to truth value*. At one level it is true, since it truly represents the fetishised reality; at another level, it fails to represent the reality since it is impossible, within the terms of that category, to represent the reality *as fetishised*. The relationship, therefore, in which Marxist science stands to this apparent economic law is not merely that of greater to lesser explanatory power, but as the arbiter of the truth values of a systematically *opaque* proposition. For Marxism is able to assign to it the precise conditions under which, when it is true, it is true and, when it is false, it is false.

I propose to generalise from this instance and argue that it is in the character of all ideologies that, although they contain some unambiguously true and some unambiguously false utterances, the central case of an ideological utterance is that of a statement which, *within the ideology*, is ambiguous as between truth and falsity. In general, that is to say, what true assertions and what false assertions are made within an ideology cannot be know from within it but only within the science — Marxism — which has the key to their ideological character.

To denote more precisely this relationship between Marxist science and the systematic ambiguity of ideologies, I introduce the notion of a 'rescuable truth' — and correspondingly of a 'rescuable falsehood'. A 'rescuable truth' is an assertion whose truth or falsity cannot be decided within the ideological discourse in which it occurs, but is known to be true when appropriated within the scientific discourse which de-mystifies the categories of the ideology. Similarly, *mutatis mutandis*, it is the case with 'rescuable falsehoods'. Rescuable truths and falsehoods, therefore, in their pre-scientific, ideological form are neither true nor false, but are fetishised truths or falsehoods. Within the ideology their truth values cannot be decided, because the ideological discourse is incapable of reference to the conditions under which the truth or falsity, as the case may be, of the assertions in question is unambiguously decidable.

If this is correct, then it follows that the heart of any ideology consists in its rescuably true or false representations of the social mechanisms and that the heart of the appropriate science consists in its capacity to rescue just those true and just those false representations. We can say on the strength of this that Marxism is the 'rescued truth' of capitalism.

The claim to scientificity, then, which Marxism makes is one which rests on perfectly standard considerations of greater fundamentality. Relative to bourgeois economic ideology, Marxism is more scientific because it is more fundamental. It is more fundamental, first, because, it can explain just as successfully all that ideology can successfully explain: thus it explains the exchange relationship between labour-power and wages in terms of equivalence and exchange. Second, it can explain all that ideology cannot explain: thus, without the distinction between 'labour' and 'labour-power', bourgeois ideology can form no notion of the extraction of surplus value, whereas with the distinction Marxism can. Third, it can explain why it is that the ideology can explain what it does explain and why it is that it cannot explain what it fails to explain: for Marxism can determine under what conditions the bourgeois 'law' of the exchange of equivalents does hold and under what conditions it does not.

Finally, it is now possible to make clear in what way Marxism itself has no new alternative economic utopia or prescriptions to offer, beyond those which it knows 'heuristically' in and through its criticism of capitalism. We can also see what is wrong with that Marxism which we will have reasons to call later 'fideistic' Marxism. This is that arrogant, supposedly autonomous Marxist 'science' which amounts to the unfounded claim to a privileged access to 'Marxist' truths. This 'fideism' — so called because it is a Marxism of an entirely esoteric, self-referential sort, a self-supporting *faith* — is also a sort of perverted Platonism. It ignores all the gains won from Plato's argument in the last two chapters, above all the proposition that 'knowledge' wrests its objects, what it knows, only out of the anomalies and contradictions of its subject-matter. Correspondingly, it adopts all that is unacceptable in Platonism, for it sets itself up as a self-sufficient 'scientism' which knows only truths not to be found within the criticism of ideology.

By contrast, on my argument, Marxism's claim to scientificity rests uniquely upon the adequacy of its critical relationship with capitalism. Its knowledge is knowledge of capitalism, not of some alternative, better economic future beyond it, for it *is* the 'rescued truth' of capitalism. Of course, in another sense Marxism is radically innovative in its economic theory, for in order to expose the 'truth' of capitalism it has to forge entirely new concepts and categories of which bourgeois economic theory knows nothing. Marxism does not know capitalism as capitalism knows itself. Therefore, although it is true to say that Marxism is the science of what bourgeois ideology is the ideology of, namely capitalism, Marxism has to deconstruct the object which is given to it in bourgeois ideology (the processes of capitalist wealth production) and reconstruct its object in radically different, more fundamentally explanatory categories. We can say, therefore, that Marxism is scientific because of its adequacy to its own object and that this object is given to it by the ideological structures of capitalism. But in knowing that ideological object, it cannot know it as it is known in ideology but has to make a radical break with the ideological concepts and categories by means of which capitalism knows itself.

In a word, Marxism is the only valid knowledge of capitalism, for it is its rescued truth. Paradoxically, for that very reason it can never become the *self*-knowledge of capitalism. For capitalism cannot do without its ideology. It is structured on its ideological processes, that is, on the misappropriation of its own truth. Were Marxism to become the self-knowledge of the capitalist world, it would destroy its own object, namely that very capitalist world. To 'rescue the truth' of capitalism is to destroy it. It is therefore just in this sense that Marxist science is also a revolutionary *praxis*.

II

It is now possible to make clearer in what way morality is to be contingently, that is, historically, identified with Marxism. The formula for this identity can now be that Marxism is the 'rescued truth' of the moral ideology of bourgeois society. Marxism is the theory and revolutionary praxis whereby capitalism, in its moral dimensions as in its economic, is made to speak clearly the truth which it simultaneously generates and obscures. Again, Marxism as the science of morality no more has any independent moral truths of its own to impart (hence its apparent amoralism) than it has any esoteric economic truths to offer. Marxism is the praxis of requiring capitalist society to speak and practise unambiguously its own truths. And it will destroy capitalist society if it succeeds.

There is, therefore, a necessary ambiguity within Marxism towards the economic and moral achievements of capitalism. In illustration of this, consider the following passages from *The Communist Manifesto*:

> The bourgeois, historically, has played a most revolutionary part . . . It has been the first to show what man's activity can bring about. It has accomplished wonders far surpassing Egyptian pyramids, Roman aqueducts and Gothic cathedrals, it has conducted expeditions which put in the shade all former Exoduses of nations and crusades . . . The bourgeoisie, by the rapid improvement of all instruments of production, by the immensely facilitated means of communication, draws all, even the most barbarian, nations into civilisation . . . It compels all nations, on pain of extinction, to adopt the bourgeois mode of production . . . National one-sidedness and narrowmindedness become more and more impossible, and from the numerous national and local literatures, there arises a world literature.[11]

Compare this with a further passage from the same work:

> The modern bourgeois society that has sprouted from the ruins of feudal society has not done away with class antagonisms. It has but

established new classes, new conditions of oppression in place of old ones . . . The bourgeoisie . . . has pitilessly torn asunder the motley feudal ties that bound man to his 'natural superiors', and has left remaining no other nexus between man and man but naked self-interest, than callous 'cash-payment' . . . for exploitation veiled by religious and political illusions, it has established naked, shameless, direct, brutal exploitation.[12]

In a word, the bourgeoise is the first truly universal force in history (the claims of Christianity notwithstanding): it has created the first cosmopolis. But the principle which governs its universalising energies is exploitation and the creation of class antagonisms. Its 'one world' is a world of class conflict.

Throughout Marx's detailed dissections of the class mechanisms of the capitalist social order there is ever this sense of what one might call his 'systematic' or 'principled ambivalence'. On the one hand, capitalism has been a truly revolutionary and progressive force in history, unleashing theoretically unlimited productive potential, vastly extending man's capacity to control natural processes, breaking down national and cultural barriers, loosening relations of feudal servility and profaning the holiness of political and religious hierarchies. Historically, the bourgeoisie has been a liberating and liberalising force. Politically, it has put democracy, the rights of man, freedom of speech, thought and writing un-conditionally on the agenda. These are, for Marx, among the irreversible gains of the bourgeois revolution.

Simultaneously, however, and, as it were, in the same act whereby it furthered these revolutionary goals, capitalism produced and, in its development, intensified the class struggle. Capitalism rests in principle on and progressively heightens the antagonism between the owners of capital and those who own nothing but their labour. Furthermore, as it develops its productive potential, it becomes increasingly an unstable structure, since it is decreasingly able to absorb the wealth of production which it generates. In general the instability of capitalism derives from the fact that the ever more effective use it makes of the instruments of production — its technology and its capacity to exploit raw materials — cannot be contained within the relations of production — the private ownership of capital and the exploitation of labour. For the instruments

of production demand the socialisation and democratisation
of the relations of production: but capitalism *consists* in the
private ownership of capital.

Modern bourgeois society with its relations of production, of exchange
and of property, a society which has conjured up such gigantic means
of production and exchange, is like the sorcerer, who is no longer able
to control the powers of the nether world whom he has called up by
his spells. For many a decade past the history of industry and commerce
is but the history of the revolt of modern productive forces against
modern conditions of production, against the property relations that
are the conditions for the existence of the bourgeoisie and its rule . . .
Because there is too much civilisation, too much means of subsistence,
too much industry, too much commerce. The productive forces at the
disposal of society no longer tend to further the conditions of bourgeois
property; on the contrary they have become too powerful for these
conditions, by which they are fettered, and so soon as they overcome
these fetters, they bring disorder into the whole of bourgeois society,
endanger the existence of bourgeois property.[13]

This is not the place for the detailed discussion of the
economic analysis of the recurrent crises of capitalism. What
concerns us is a parallel movement of crises at the moral
level. I have remarked on the ambivalence which Marx displays
at all levels towards capitalism as a social phenomenon. But
this is not a strictly accurate way of putting it, since it is not
so much Marx's attitude to capitalism which is ambivalent as
capitalism itself. For Marx, capitalism is a systematically
ambivalent structure.

Just as capitalism is an economically contradictory process
whose social relations of production cannot contain the
development of its instruments of production, so morally it
is a contradictory system, and in a parallel way. Some account
of this contradictoriness was given in chapter 6, where I
argued, apropos of the bourgeois political morality of toleration, that whereas in its origins this bit of liberal political
morality had been a progressive, critical doctrine, it had
become part of an ideological response to the facts of class
oppression in which the nature of that oppression as class
oppression became obscured. So put, the Marxist argument
about toleration may seem to be unambiguously critical of

it as merely reactionary, as a value wholly to be swept aside in any social order which abolished class oppression. This, however, is far too simple an account of the form of Marxist criticism of bourgeois moral ideology. Marx's response to bourgeois moral ideology is neither that of the moralist, who has some alternative moral ideology to offer in its place, nor that of the pure amoralist, who displays no concern for such moral notions at all. The full complexity, the two-sided nature of Marx's response to bourgeois morality, both welcomes it as irreversible moral progress and denies that, under capitalism, it is possible to realise toleration in practice without ideologically betraying what it prescribes. This, although a complex response, is essentially but the positive face of the description of 'toleration' as ideological. It was the bourgeois revolution which brought about the economic, social and political conditions which made inevitable the demand for toleration as the appropriate moral response to them. And yet it is precisely those same conditions which prevent that morality of toleration from being fully realised. Positively, the Marxist response to the radical ambivalence of the bourgeois morality of toleration is to demand from capitalism that it establishes those conditions under which *its own* morality can be realised. This capitalism cannot do without ceasing to be itself: its own 'truth', at the moral as at the economic level, cannot be rescued without its destruction as capitalism.

The 'radical ambivalence' of bourgeois political morality is exhibited from the earliest days of its development. Historically, the rise of the bourgeois class to economic power first in Europe and then in America is not merely contingently connected, but is in some more intimate relationship with the development of radically new moral and political ideologies. In no way simple or even in its achievements, it is still possible at a relatively early period in the history of the bourgeois revolution to identify a fairly clear picture of the new political morality. Characterised by individualism, by a stress on autonomy, by a dominantly negative conception of freedom — as the freedom from constraints imposed by others — by a corresponding recognition of pluralism as an inevitable and welcome consequence, and by toleration as the necessary principle of pluralism, bourgeois political morality made an early appearance in the history of the revolutionary break of the bourgeoisie from feudalism. Marx summed up the contribution made to these moral and political developments by that most bourgeois of all early religious movements — Lutheranism — when he said that 'Luther restored the authority of faith by destroying faith in authority.'[14] 'Faith', in the sense of an authoritarian, theocratic Christendom — a regime — is destroyed, as is all belief in arbitrary authority, by the rise of 'faith', the personal response, in private, individual experience, to a personally encountered God. The secularisation of this implicitly liberal morality is a later, but predictable, bourgeois development. But what is historically significant is that the development of something like a mature liberal moral theory in a relatively pure form long *anticipates* the social development of the bourgeoisie as a fully-fledged recognisable class of any sort, let alone its eventual emergence as a *ruling* class. The historical significance is this: liberal political theorists, in the early days of the bourgeois revolution, could think out the moral principles of their revolutionary programmes with hardly a thought given to the social and economic conditions under which they would eventually be forced to implement them. More specifically, they could acknowledge explicitly the new economic, political and social conditions which required the new political morality without any consciousness of the fact that those new conditions would imply, in their later development, an increasingly bitter struggle between classes; a struggle in which, paradoxically, their liberal political morality would become a stick with which the ruling class — their own successors — would beat a class of industrial workers drafted from country to city in the biggest forced migration of peoples in world history. They could espouse so unambiguously their liberal moralities because the evidence of the essentially *class* character of the new conditions to which they responded was, at the time, hardly there to be seen. There was, even as late as in the seventeenth century, no visible industrial proletariat of any importance.

The evidence was there, none the less, and there were some who saw it. In the years 1648—53 Gerrard Winstanley wrote a series of pamphlets on behalf of the diminutive, but energetic

'Digger' movement, favouring a full-blooded anarcho-communism of a consistency and rigour which far outstrips that of the best minds in the near-related, but essentially 'liberal' and bourgeois Leveller movement. Winstanley, arguing in the name of the 'poor oppressed people of England', called for the total abolition of private property, of the wage-relationship, of public religion, of national law courts and of university education and for a relatively sophisticated theory of worker democracy. He foresaw clearly how a class of labourers working 'for hire' necessarily produce and reproduce the conditions of their own oppression and he must be the first representative of labour to call for something like a general strike:

This Declares likewise to all Laborers, or such as are called Poor people, that they shall not dare to work for Hire, for any Landlord, or for any that is lifted up above others; for by their labours they have lifted up Tyrants and Tyranny; and by denying to labour for Hire, they shall pull them down again . . .[15]

Not only does Winstanley have a clear-eyed view of economic exploitation and its class character, he has a clear picture also of the way in which all non-working class elements in society will congregate around the ruling class in a veritable complicity of ideological support. That power of oppression which he calls the 'Kingly power' is like some sort of sprawling social weed, the head of which was cut off with the execution of Charles I, but:

alas oppression is a great tree still, and keeps off the sun of freedome from the poor Commons still, he hath many branches and great roots which must be grub'd up, before everyone can sing Sions song in peace . . . there are three Branches more of Kinglie power greater then the former [i.e. King Charles] that oppresses this Land wonderfully; and these are the power of the Tithing Priests over the Tenths of our labours; and the power of the Lords of Mannors, holding the free use of the Commons, and wast land from the poor, and the intolerable oppression either of bad Laws, or of bad Judges corrupting good Laws . . .[16]

Winstanley's communism is unambiguous in its recognition

of the class character of political, economic, legal and religious oppression. But his capacity to identify the class character of the new social order which was emerging in the mid-seventeenth century owes more, one suspects, to the prophetical and the millenarian religiosity of his character than to any well-supported empirical analysis. It is unsurprising, in fact, that Winstanley's work disappears from English history for nearly 250 years, to be retrieved in this century in the work of two continental Marxists, Bernstein and Petegorsky.[17] It was written far in advance of its time.

If more equivocal about class, the Levellers were, on the whole, in no two minds about the purity of their political liberalism. In the heyday of English revolutionary fervour — in the period, roughly, from 1645 to 1650 — the writings of Lilburne, Overton and Walwyn exhibit a commitment to a liberal political morality far purer in its conception than any to be found subsequently in English political writers, certainly far purer than anything in Locke, still generally regarded as the founding father of English political liberalism. One has only to compare, for example, the unconditional support for the toleration of all beliefs and of none, which is found in William Walwyn's *The Power of Love*,[18] or in Roger William's *The Bloudy Tenent of Persecution*,[19] with the tentative and much qualified commitment of Locke's *Essay on Toleration*, with its restrictions of the toleration of atheists and Roman Catholics, or with his proposal in *The Reasonableness of Christianity* of a simplified eirenical Christian propaganda designed to keep the masses in order.

Thus, in the final manifesto of the Leveller party, the so-called third 'Agreement of the People', most of the familiar liberal freedoms are declared. The signatories 'Agree to ascertain our Government, to abolish all arbitrary Power, and to set bounds and limits both to our Supreme, and all Subordinate Authority . . .'[20] Thereafter follows a list of incontrovertibly 'liberal' demands: the accountability of public officers (III), the division of powers and office between the legislative and executive (IV), annual parliaments (VIII), the abolition of 'any Lawes, Oaths or Covenants, whereby to compel by penalties or otherwise any person to anything in or about matters of faith, Religion or Gods worship' (X), the rights of conscientious objection (XI), the right to remain silent without incrimination at a court of law (XVI), the abolition of capital punishment except for murder and like offences (XXI), the abolition of tithes (XXIII), the freedom of parishioners to choose their own ministers (XXIV), trial by jury (XXV) and others besides.

It will be said, and rightly, that the relative purity of Leveller liberalism as compared even with that of Locke is but the innocence of youth. The Levellers were writing in a revolutionary situation, a situation in which not only the incorrigibly alarmist (and inept) Presbyterians of the Long Parliament but also men of good sense and political insight were well aware that a sophisticated party organisation such as that of the Levellers in alliance with their sympathisers in the highly politicised New Model Army posed a real threat to the fragile establishment which the anti-royalist conservatives had imposed. But in that revolutionary situation they did not have to face the problems of establishing the new political order which they planned. They were considered at the time to be utopian thinkers, particularly by Cromwell, who had some sympathy with them, and by Ireton, who had none. And they were utopians, but for a much more fundamental reason than that they had only a revolutionary, but not post-revolutionary, programme. The consistency of their liberalism disguised the inconsistency it was in with their equivocal commitment to democracy.

Colonel Rainsborough, among the more politically radical of the Levellers, had indeed argued in a famous speech to the Army Council at Putney, that:

Really I think that the poorest he that is in England hath a life to live as the greatest he; and therefore . . . every man that is to live under a government ought first by his own consent to put himself under that government; and I do think that the poorest man in England is not at all bound in a strict sense to that government that he hath not had a voice to put himself under.[21]

But it was Ireton, that acute political analyst and operator, who pointed out, with rather more consistency, that if the Levellers argued *on grounds of natural law* for even a limited extension of the franchise (and that is all they ever argued for, Rainsborough's apparent inclusiveness notwithstanding), then on those same grounds there could be no logic to prevent an argument for *universal* franchise; and then, he adds (consciously touching on a raw Leveller nerve), 'Why may not those men vote against all property?'[22]

The Levellers had no answer to this. They argued for limited political democracy and full-scale liberalism on the basis of a free market in commodities and land, on the basis, that is to say, of the economic interest of their class. Politically, they were never more than verbally committed to full manhood suffrage (still less, as Winstanley was, to universal suffrage), and although there is much controversy about quite which classes they meant to exclude by the phrase,[23] the third *Agreement of the People* confines the franchise '(*according to natural right*) to all men of the age of one and twenty yeers and upwards (*not being servants, or receiving alms*) . . .'[24] Economically, the Supreme Authority is to conserve foreign trade (IX, 1) and the 'lives, limbes, liberties, properties and estates' of the people (IX, 2); it may not interfere with the rights of merchants to trade where they will and under what conditions they freely negotiate (XVIII), nor shall it be 'in the power of any Representative, in any wise, to render up or give, or take away any part of this Agreement, nor level mens Estates, destroy Propriety, or make all things Common . . .' (XXX). The problem for the Levellers was that they could argue against the established constitutional franchise only on the grounds that natural right was a more fundamental law than the constitution. But any argument from natural right would, as Ireton had pointed out, imply the radical democratic conclusion that *all* men (and, worse, all women) had that same right. But how could a differential right to property be made consistent with full political democracy? The moral and political liberalism, in terms of which the Levellers argued for their place in the political arena, was always more inclusive in its economic consequences than the Levellers were prepared to tolerate. It was Rainsborough, again, who drew the bitter conclusion from Ireton's reply to the Levellers: 'Sir I see, that it is impossible to have liberty but all property must be taken away.'[25] It was a conclusion which, although implicit in their own arguments, the Levellers were not prepared to draw.

Few were. Those who, like Winstanley, had the courage to follow such arguments out to their logical conclusions argued themselves out of the historical record. And yet history had argued them back in again by the nineteenth century, when Mill, in his *Essay on Representative Government* faces exactly the same problem all over again of how to reconcile liberalism with democracy, only now in the face of an actual mass working-class movement with its own organisation, a consciously alternative social and moral principle of solidarity and a militant leadership. Mill solves the problem in favour of liberal freedoms rather than full democracy, proposing a universal franchise but with differential voting rights weighted in favour of the 'educated classes'. Mill's argument refuses to confront not merely logic, but the facts as well: in particular the fact that that very bourgeois society which first demanded liberal freedoms as of right also gives birth to a social class which it cannot afford to incorporate into the political settlement in which those freedoms are institutionalised. The arguments between the Levellers and Winstanley anticipate in theory the history which they had little enough reason to predict.

Liberalism, it becomes clear, is in the normal case, consistent with the hegemony of the bourgeois class. But as MacPherson has pointed out,[26] full-scale democracy is ever a threat to that hegemony. The greater consistency of Winstanley is perceptible at this point, for political democracy is not consistent with private property, class exploitation and the wage-relationship. But liberalism is empty rhetoric without political and economic democracy. Consequently, the Leveller doctrines of the great liberal freedoms — of speech, of thought, of writing and from arbitrary arrest — its doctrine that each man is to count as one and no man as more than one, arising as they do out of a conception of society as a free market in property, are born out of an insoluble contradiction. The contradiction is simply this: the bourgeoisie needs liberal political morality as its natural moral rhetoric. Historically, it is responsible for the fact that it is now an indispensable part of our political and moral vocabulary, a fact which cannot be reversed. But the bourgeoisie *as a class* cannot produce the conditions — of economic democracy — which are the necessary condition of the realisation of its rhetoric. In brief, the bourgeoisie *cannot* practise what it *has to* preach.[27]

It is something very like this which Marx had to say about that far greater bourgeois revolution, the French Revolution. One way of reading Marx's relation to the French Revolution is as the attempt to define the political, social and, above all, economic conditions under which it would be possible to realise the French revolutionary morality — of liberty, equality and fraternity. For morally the French Revolution points beyond the very economic, social and political conditions which it established. Again, the bourgeois revolution makes compulsory moral notions which it cannot realise. It is in so far as Marxism can claim to be the science which defines the conditions inhibiting this realisation and to be the praxis of creating the conditions which would disambiguate bourgeois morality that Marxism can also be said to be the 'rescued truth' of that bourgeois morality.

In the meantime it is clear why Marxism has to be ambiguous about bourgeois morality. Marxism cannot simply reject it *as* 'bourgeois' or even *as* 'ideological'. Epistemologically, the form of words in which simple rejection is expressed is the description 'false'. But, as we have seen, this is precisely what one is not doing in describing a position as 'ideological'. Rather, in so describing a set of beliefs — or a form of society — one is characterising it as inherently ambiguous *between* truth and falsity. In addition, the claim is being made that the ambiguity in question is rooted in certain social conditions for which that ambiguity is functional. It is for this reason that the Marxist criticism of bourgeois society is not simply a matter of theoretically exposing its falsehoods. This criticism is essentially a praxis, a praxis of bringing about the conditions under which the ambiguities of capitalism can be resolved, a praxis which I designate, in general terms, as 'rescuing the truth of capitalism'.

We can now also see rather more clearly why Marxism has wrongly seemed, even to many Marxists, to be amoralistic. For it is true that Marxism does not offer any alternative morality. And just as there is a sort of Marxism which is a form of fideistic *scientism*, so there is a Marxism which is a form of fideistic *moralism* for which communist society is known as the absolute moral future of mankind. By contrast with this, it has to be said that Marxism cannot think morally beyond the conditions of capitalism except to the extent that those capitalist conditions themselves already point to further contingent possiblities. Which is exactly what capitalism does. The criticism of capitalism does not presuppose an alternative morality. The moral criticism of capitalism consists in the demand that it realise its own truth in practice; that it establish genuine equality before the law and genuine equality of access to it, that it adequately house, clothe and feed the whole population without discrimination, create equal access to equally good education for all and, above all, that it democratise at all levels, crucially in the social relations of production. Capitalism will not do this, because it cannot do so and survive as capitalism. And yet it is capitalism which makes compulsory the language in which it is possible to state these demands. Capitalism has to live its own morality ideologically, that is to say, it can sustain its moral convictions only as a way of not recognising the fact that it installs the very conditions under which those convictions are unrealisable. It cannot abandon the moral language it cannot live.

As a moral argument with bourgeois society, therefore, Marxism presents itself as the 'rescued truth' of bourgeois morality, that is to say, *not* as opposing bourgeois moral rhetoric with an alternative moral rhetoric. Marxist talk about 'communist society' is not talk about an alternative moral ideal. Marxism is the attempt to determine the conditions of the possibility of bourgeois morality itself. The role of the notion 'communist society' in that attempt is as the specification of the conditions under which the radical ambiguity of bourgeois moral language could be reduced to plain moral talk, the conditions under which bourgeois morality could be unambiguously lived by all men, when pluralism, toleration, democracy — and even love — could be accepted as imperatives to obey which is not simultaneously to be enmeshed in an ideological misperception of class exploitation.

In the meantime the apparent amoralism of Marxism simply

152 *Morality is Marxism*

consists in the well-judged refusal to speak a moral language, the conditions for the possibility of which do not yet exist: to speak morally under capitalism we must refuse to moralise. As Eagleton has succinctly put it, 'you don't engage in "moral" debate with men who can only conceive of morality moralistically. It is in the silence of those who refuse to speak "morally" that the true meaning of morality is articulated.'[28]

NOTES

1   Karl Marx, *Grundrisse*, translated by M. Nicolaus, Harmondsworth, 1973, pp. 86–7.
2   Karl Marx, *Capital*, I, part I, i, iv, translated by S. Moore and E. Aveling, London, 1970, p. 72.
3   Karl Marx, *Wages, Price and Profit* in *Marx and Engels, Selected Works*, (1 vol.), London, 1968.
4   Marx, *Grundrisse*, pp. 281–2.
5   Marx, *Wages, Price and Profit*, VII, in *Marx and Engels, Selected Works*, p. 210.
6   Ibid.
7   Marx, *Grundrisse*, p. 284.
8   Ibid., p. 287.
9   Marx, *Wages, Price and Profit*, IX, in *Marx and Engels, Selected Works*, p. 213.
10 Marx, *Grundrisse*, p. 307.
11 Karl, Marx, *The Communist Manifesto*, in *Marx and Engels, Selected Works*, pp. 37–9.
12 Ibid., pp. 36–8.
13 Ibid., pp. 40–1.
14 Karl, Marx, *Contribution to the Critique of Hegel's Philosophy of Right, Introduction*, edited and translated by T.B. Bottomore, in *Karl Marx: Early Writings*, London, 1963, p. 53.
15 Gerrard Winstanley, *The True Levellers Standard Advanced*, in *The Works of Gerrard Winstanley*, edited and introduced by G.H. Sabine, New York, 1941, p. 262.
16 Gerrard Winstanley, *A New Years Gift to the Parliament and the Armie*, in *The Works of Gerrard Winstanley*, p. 357.
17 E. Bernstein, *Socialism and Democracy in the Great English Revolution*, translated by H.J. Stenny, London, 1932; D.W. Petegorsky, *Left-Wing Democracy in the English Civil War*, London, 1941.

18 See W. Haller, *Tracts on Liberty in the Puritan Revolution*, Columbia, 1934, Vol. II, pp. 273–304.

19 Extracts from which are to be found in A.S.P. Woodhouse, *Puritanism and Liberty*, London, 1938.

20 *An Agreement of the Free People of England* (May 1, 1649), in *Leveller Manifestoes of the Puritan Revolution*, edited by Don M. Wolfe, London, 1944, p. 402.

21 *Putney Debates*, in Woodhouse, *Puritanism and Liberty*, p. 53.

22 Woodhouse, *Puritanism and Liberty*, p. 63.

23 Cf. C.B. MacPherson, *The Political Theory of Possessive Individualism*, Oxford, 1962, chapter 3.

24 *Leveller Manifestoes of the Puritan Revolution*, pp. 402–3.

25 Woodhouse, *Puritanism and Liberty*, p. 71.

26 MacPherson, *The Political Theory of Possessive Individualism*, pp. 273ff.

27 Note that this is a quite different strategy from that of attempting to force bourgeois society to live up to its own ideals *as if it could*, a strategy as misguided as that of trying to force capitalists to pay wages which are *fair*. Marx's comment is apt: he remarks on the 'foolishness of those socialists (namely the French, who want to depict socialism as the realisation of the ideals of *bourgeois* society) who demonstrate that exchange and exchange value etc., are *originally* (in time) or *essentially* (in their adequate form) a system of universal freedom and equality, but that they have been perverted by money, capital, etc.' (*Grundrisse*, p. 248). They differ, Marx adds, from the 'bourgeois apologists' only in their 'utopian inability to grasp the necessary difference between the real and the ideal form of bourgeois society, which is the cause of their desire to undertake the superfluous business of realising the ideal expression again, which is in fact only the inverted projection of this reality' (*Grundrisse*, p. 249).

28 T. Eagleton, 'Marxists and Christians: Answers for Brian Wicker', *New Blackfriars*, October 1975, p. 470.

10

The 'Strong-Compatibility' Thesis

I

Before raising new questions let us take stock. Morality under capitalism is Marxism, in so far as Marxism is able to specify the conditions of the retrieval of moral talk from bourgeois ideology. It may be objected that the conditions of the possibility of morality are not the thing itself. To which it may be replied that, in the absence of something made impossible by certain conditions, the struggle to overcome those conditions is all that can be made of that thing. And so with morality: which is why I said earlier that Marxism is all that we can make of morality under capitalism.

It should also be clear, therefore, that although Marxism is the moral struggle in the only form it can take under capitalism, it is not itself the moral voice which it is struggling to make heard. I do not believe that Marxism uniquely, or even in any way at all, knows what to say from the moral point of view. As I argued in the last chapter, Marx's rhetorical invocations of communist society are not invocations of a moral ideal, even if, on the scores both of vacuousness and tendentiousness, they may seem to bourgeois readers to have that character (for that is what they expect morality to sound like). These fragments and sketches are meant as no more than provisional and perhaps even as metaphorical indications of the sort of society in which, among other things, moral talk could have an unambiguous relation with the forms of social life which characterise it. They indicate the 'material bases' for adequate moral talk. As for that moral talk itself, there is, as it were, quite enough of it already on the agenda, much of it indeed put there by the bourgeois society which Marx opposes.

From the moral point of view itself, therefore, Marxism *invents* absolutely nothing.

Not all Marxists, however, acknowledge this, as I noted at the beginning of part II. Some Marxists do propose 'communist society' as an alternative moral ideal. They are the fideistic moralists. The majority, however, just as simple-mindedly suppose that Marxism *replaces* the enterprise of morality as such, the proposition of fideistic scientism. In this they share a view of morality with their bourgeois opponents that morality is the sort of thing which is replaceable. They hold this on the naive and fundamentally destructive grounds that, if morality is not thought of as replaceable, then you must conclude that a particular view of morality, namely that embodied in bourgeois notions of human solidarity, is irreplaceable, 'eternally true', 'part of the natural order of things', or whatever. I hope I have said enough in part II to undermine this inference.

But suppose the best possible outcome for my arguments so far, namely that they are, in point of logic, valid and, on the score of interpretation, the best way of reading Marxism; suppose it to be demonstrated that Marxism's relation to bourgeois morality is neither that of an amoral substitute for it nor that of a particularly radical and purist instance of it; and suppose my view of that relationship is accepted, namely that it is the relationship of 'rescuer' to 'rescued' moral truth; supposing all this, cannot this argument still be rejected on the grounds that, although its inferences support the conclusion, that conclusion itself is so unacceptably out of line with both the theories and practices of mainstream historical Marxism as to be a purely theoretical and esoteric doctrine?

To some this objection might not matter even if it were true. But to Marxists it does matter and must. For Marxism is essentially a movement and a praxis which says what it is by means of what it does. A 'one man's Marxism' is as absurd as I shall later argue is a 'one man's Christianity'. And a movement which is defined by the praxes of its relationships with history cannot ignore what the history of those relationships tells us. A heroic esotericism which, in a purely individualistic and eclectical way, plucks out of that empirical history those elements in it which can be theoretically reconstructed into an ideal programme, is neither honest nor Marxist. You *can* do this and not for a moment would I deny the necessity of the internal criticism of Marxism by Marxists. And if, on some point or other, no one else is doing it, then you must; there is nothing remotely 'bourgeois individualist' about that. But no Marxist, however much he or she may feel the need to redefine critically his or her relationships with the actual movements, can altogether eschew responsibility for their historical record.

And because of the nature of my argument, this responsibility is particularly acute. The moral record of Marxism is bleak. It confronts my argument with the charge, at worst, of intellectual dilettantism, of fiddling with 'Marxist concepts' while the real movements scorch history with their oppressions unconcerned.

But to see the real force of this objection, it is necessary to make a distinction. The charge which really matters to my argument is not that which is written in the Marxist history of genocide, its enslavement of millions in work camps, in the enforced psychiatric treatment of sane (if sometimes wrong-headed) 'dissidents', in its repression of minority cultures, in its anti-semitism . . . This is not because these things are not morally objectionable, but because it is not clear what objection it is to a movement's standards that the movement itself has failed to live by them, at any rate in the case where, as I hope I have shown, we need that movement in order to maintain any historical grip on those standards.

Nor is it any form of reply to such moral criticisms of the record that the criticisms are hypocritical when they come from bourgeois mouths, though they often are just that. Truly, it comes ill from the mouths of those who, without moral scruple, stockpile first-strike nuclear weapons in the name of peace that they should proclaim the inviolability of human rights, or the sanctity of life, or that good ends can never justify bad means. But, all the same, bourgeois hypocrisy does not relieve the bourgeois of the duty to condemn it. And what the bourgeoisie must condemn in its own world it does thereby condemn in anyone else's world, including the Marxist's. Either way standards are impartial or else they are not standards.

In any case, if the moral performance of Marxism were all that could be condemned, the moral language of condemnation would not itself be in question. The question which is raised, however, is whether Marxism has the moral resources from which to condemn its own moral record, for if it has not those resources, then it *cannot* condemn itself and can in no way escape identification with that record. Hence, the charge which matters to my argument as so far presented is that Marxism does not condemn its own record because it cannot with consistency do so; for it is essentially destructive of the moral language in which such condemnations could be framed.

The 'morality is Marxism' thesis could not withstand such a charge, were it made to stick, without retreating into a vacuum of privatised eclecticism. And if my reply to this objection is that Marxism does potentially have the moral-critical resources necessary, whereas bourgeois morality systematically lacks them, the emphasis will, in view of the record, have to be on the word 'potentially'. For in practice, as I have said frequently in this essay, Marxism has become so wedded to a view of itself as amoralistically replacing morality that it has come altogether to lack the moral resources needed of it — particularly by its victims.

A mere symptom of the moral collapse of Marxism is its now almost doctinaire espousal of the meta-moral principle that actions or courses of action need no further justification than that they are shown to be means effective of producing 'good' ends. Famous defences of this principle are, of course, to be found in Lenin, but if instances closer to home are needed of the effects on moral thought which some Marxists can have, the following quotation from a contemporary British Marxist will do very well. Francis Barker argues:

On the question of torture . . . In revolutionary situations it will be the revolutionary ideology that provides the answers to 'moral' questions, consisting partly of the transference and re-activation of the previous historical ideology (it would be impossible to have a revolution in this country without elements of Christianity unwittingly providing some of the stuff of revolutionary ideology), and partly of a series of negations of the ideology and practice of the class enemy. If, for example, the oppressor (who is materially and historically constrained to be less than scrupulous about these things) tortures, then it is likely that the slogan 'Down with torture' and its equivalent prohibition in revolutionary practice will have a quite practical and immediate relevance. I saw a poster recently that referred to Zimbabwe, advancing the slogan 'No more hangings'. This was not a 'moral' poster.[1]

I say that such thinking is symptomatic. It is symptomatic of the thinking, described and criticised earlier, which leads the Marxist to suppose that all morality is unrescuably ideological, or that, if it is rescuable at all, it is so only in the form of a *tactical* 'transference and re-activation of the previous historical ideology', justified when it 'will have a quite practical and immediate relevance' but otherwise lacking moral character. Such thinking supposes that that moral thought which becomes possible under future conditions (communist society) is altogether impossible now (under capitalism).

Now it may be thought that my own position within Marxism is still insufficiently differentiated from this amoralism, that according to my account, as for Barker's, all history before 'communist society' consists in a moral vacuum, occupied by the purely tactical, non-moral struggle to bring about a future possibility of morality. But this is not so, although this is the conclusion which would be forced upon us by a pure theory of Marxism which conceives of itself as the autonomous 'science' of society. But as I have argued in part II, this is not how Marxism is to be conceived. For Marxism is essentially dependent upon — and not merely tactically exploitative of — the moral advances which it retrieves from ideology, even it if is *only* in their retrieved form that it is dependent on those moral advances.

Consequently my argument has now come to the point where it faces genuine and real problems of a practical moral sort whose theoretical form can be expressed best in the words of my introduction to this book:

. . . in face of the moral vacuousness of capitalism it is necessary to impose what I call a *significant moral silence*, a silence relative to the vulgar garrulousness of bourgeois 'free moral choices', but a silence whose significance must also be interpreted as sharply distinguishing it from the crassness of Stalinist amoralism.

Probably rashly, I take it that the need for 'moral silence' relative to bourgeois 'moral garrulousness' has been sufficiently established. But if so, the *significance* of this silence has yet to be determined and, in particular, how this significance is to be distinguished from the amoralism of Stalinism. Hence, the problem which faces us in this last section is this: morality is, indeed, Marxism. None the less, a Marxism which simply dismisses morality to the future, which denies of the present strategy of achieving it any of the moral character of the goal itself, is a Marxism which has lapsed into an amoralistic barbarism from which one could predict, but never be in any position to condemn, its own record of repression; and so is to be judged as no better than its record.

When, therefore, I argue as I do in this section, that Christianity has a crucial role to play in the construction of the significance of this moral silence, it is important not to understand me as doing anything more than this. I make no claims for the 'truth' of Christianity and certainly none for the thesis that Christianity is the source of distinctive moral insights of which Marxism has need to take any account. I maintain only that Christianity is a praxis which is situated in the terrain of the same problematic as Marxism is, the problematic which requires both that they show how, on the one hand, the present historical activity lies under the moral constraints of a future which, on the other hand, cannot be realised in the present without ideological falsification.

To Marxists, of course, this parallel with Christianity will seem implausible in the extreme and in principle. They will say that what is part of the problem cannot form part of the solution. But I am sure that they are wrong in this, for, on the contrary, the force of Marx's rejection of utopian moralism lies in the proposition that *only* what is part of the problem can form part of the solution. Of course, this is not to say that, being part of the problem, Christianity is *necessarily* part of the solution, but only that it may be; and that whether or not it is is a matter to be decided *by* criticism, not one to be assumed as a premiss of it.

Hence, a good measure of my argument — it occupies this chapter and the next — will take up the typically Marxist claim that Christianity is inherently ideological. I make some concessions to this view, but argue that it is too one-sided a description of the relationships between Marxism and Christianity. In return I offer an unfamiliar thesis about this relationship — the second substantive thesis of this essay — but I offer it far more tentatively than the first and in any case, as I have said, only in its bearing on the 'morality is Marxism' thesis. This second thesis I call the 'strong-compatibility' thesis and, in broad terms, it claims a mutual dependence, from distinct points of view between Christianity and Marxism. In this chapter and the next I attend to the form of this dependence in which Christianity needs Marxism. In the final two chapters I examine the other side of this relationship. From the point of view of the dependence of Christianity on Marxism, the dependence can be described thus: it is both necessary for Christianity to incorporate theologically and in practice the Marxist criticism of religion and possible for it to survive that incorporation. This criticism states that Christianity is ideological in theory and in practice. I hope to show that it is possible for Christianity to incorporate this claim. That this incorporation is necessary is a proposition worth maintaining only on one set of grounds, namely that it is *true* that Christianity is ideological. And I do not try to go beyond an attempt to indicate to Christians in what way this accusation *might* be true and what follows for the Christian *if* the accusation is true. As I said in the introduction to this book, I do not try to *do* any theology in this book, but only to set theology a problem which it ignores at its peril.

II

There is at least one good reason for proposing the strong-compatibility thesis, in spite of my reservations about it, and that reason is to force an issue that too little progressive 'left' theology has confronted properly, namely, the question of the compatibility of Christianity with Marxism. Barker has rightly noted the tendencies to 'verbalism' which can be detected in the Christian left and that 'metaphorical eclectic-ism' which, for example, allows the identification of the biblical *anawim* with the contemporary industrial proletariat.[2] Terry Eagleton, once a leader in the 1960s Slant movement of revolutionary Christians, has himself since remarked how he, with others:

> in the good old days of . . . the Christian left . . . we consistently made a category mistake about Marxism and Christianity — we thought that they were more or less the same kind of thing, and dazzling homologies could be drawn between them.[3]

Eagleton himself no longer thinks this, but much liberation theology still apears to do so, with its ready and unproblematic movement from biblical metaphor to political category and back again.[4] But this avoids the issue, and at two levels. First, as Eagleton goes on to say, Marxism and Christianity:

> are not synchronous discourses, they can't be translated into one another without a great deal of merely idealist acrobatics. Marxism is a theory and practice of resolving the contradictions of class society; it isn't a humanism, or an anthropology, or an eschatology, and it thus doesn't situate itself on the same ground as the Christian Gospel.[5]

Second, they are not 'synchronous discourses', for a reason which Barker gives: Christianity is among the phenomena which Marxism purports to destroy in its self-constitution as a science.

> There is, therefore, something radically problematical about the idea of a science *debating* with what is potentially its object *as if* it were an epistemological equal. This is one of the reasons why this debate is perennial and *as a debate* cannot be resolved.[6]

The issue which needs to be forced is whether, if at all, Christianity can incorporate, without loss of integrity, the Marxist account of religion as essentially ideological. The reason why it needs to be forced is that it is the claim of most Marxists that essentially it cannot. Christianity, therefore, must settle accounts with this claim, one way or another, before beginning to negotiate terms, theoretically, or practically, with Marxism.

The question of the compatibility of Marxism and Christianity is, therefore, first and foremost not a question of whether two sets of *doctrines* are logically consistent or not, but of whether or not the one can explain the other away as being unrescuably ideological. And although I think that most Marxists have been wrong either in what they say about this or else in what conclusions they draw from what they say, and although correspondingly, I think that Christians are right to deny that Christianity is unrescuably ideological, I suspect that too often Christians are right for all the wrong reasons.

It is common, for example, to hear Christians conceding far too much to Marx's criticisms of nineteenth-century Christianity, but conceding far too little to Marxists' criticisms of twentieth-century Christianity. Such Christians seem only too happy to admit that nineteenth-century theism was excessively 'transcendentalist', to concede that it postulated too 'un-historical', too 'de-personalised' a God who was set apart from, over and against man and history, and to believe that Marx was rightly critical of such theistic notions. But, they will go on to say, theology (with a touch of its cap to Marx) has itself become critical of its past and is today blessed with an immanentist, historical, personalised and even — in a concession which can *only* be classed as 'theological' — a *dead* God, who is 'the ground of being', discovered, no doubt, in places like 'the depths of human relationships' or to be 'engaged in the dialectics of history'. Again, all contemporary theology has washed its hands of the theology of the Kingdom of Heaven, in which people are supposed to be rewarded for individual merit or compensated for the manifest inequalities of 'this life': now, theology is eschatological, politically committed, communitarian. It has responded well enough, it is thought, to Marxist criticism.

One reason why at least some formulations of this Christian reply will not do (I have admittedly caricatured it) is that they concede far too much about nineteenth-century Christianity to be consistent with the continuities they claim for twentieth-century Christianity. It is, of course, true that there have been significant theological developments since the nineteenth-century, but to say, in effect, that the God of nineteenth-century Christianity is not the same God as the God believed in in the twentieth-century is historically naive and theologically counter-productive. For it denies the historically continuous character of Christianity itself. If what Marx was denying when (in the nineteenth century) he said 'God does not exist' is not what Christians are asserting (in the twentieth century) when they say 'God exists', then what twentieth-century Christians are asserting is too radically discontinuous with what nineteenth-century Christians were asserting for it to make sense to say that they held the same beliefs.

Besides, this response concedes far too little about twentieth-century Christianity. Even supposing there to be so little continuity between the transcendentalism of some nineteenth-century theisms and the immanentism of contemporary theisms — they *are* opposed theisms, after all — there is still an essential continuity between them in what can be called the 'theological problematic' which they share, the problematic which supposes a disjunction between God and man. It is this problematic which really characterises nineteenth-century theism and is what Marx really objected to in it — the assumption that God and man are in a disjunctive relationship to one another. Masterson's thesis about atheism seems correct;[7] that the history of the relationship between theism and atheism in the nineteenth century turns on the problem of how man can be asserted if God is asserted, or, for the atheist, on how man can be asserted if God is not denied. It seems very clear that our twentieth-century problematic differs from this only from the point of view of the atheist. As Masterson points out,[8] contemporary atheism is no longer, in the normal case, humanist by the indirect route of the explicit *denial* of God, but is comfortably and unproblematically settled in the habit of not having to raise the question in the first place. For the contemporary atheist, by and large, there just is no question about man which can be put in the form of a disjunction between man and God.

This is by no means so for most contemporary theisms. Within theology immanentist theisms are still formulated in terms of this problematic: it is to safeguard the autonomy of the human that the externalised, reified and timeless 'God out there' is rejected. This can be illustrated from a curious

feature of an unlikely source, the contributions of Hick and
Cupitt in *The Myth of God Incarnate*.[9] Both Hick and Cupitt
agree on the impossibility of its being true of only one individual that he is both God and man. For Hick this is like
saying of a shape drawn on a piece of paper that it is both
a square and a circle: it is contradictory to say this.[10] Cupitt
is no less forthcoming. For him traditional Christology suggests
a synthesis and continuity between things divine and things
of this world',[11] whereas:

Christianity's proper subtlety and freedom depended upon Jesus's
ironical perception of *disjunction* between the things of God and the
things of men . . .[12]

For both Hick and Cupitt, then, the alternatives are either
the relationship of disjunction between God and man or else
that of relative position along a continuum between God and
man. For Cupitt the denial that Jesus, being man, could be
God follows from the premiss that the relationship between
them is disjunctive. One and the same being cannot be the
subject of *both* sets of predicates. For Hick, the purpose is to
deny to Christianity its claims to a unique incarnation of God
and to allow for the possibility of incarnations in other
religious traditions. To this end he denies that the 'divinity'
of Jesus could be that of a totally transcendent being; the
predicate of divinity must be one which falls on the same
continuum as that on which human predicates fall, even if a
bit further along the line. For Cupitt, then, the transcendence
of God excludes the incarnational form of immanence; for
Hick, the immanence of God excludes the Cupitt form of
his transcendence. But in either case immanence and transcendence are terms in polarity. God is either one or the
other, not both.

Marx's opposition to theism is based not on accepting this
disjunction, so that, in the name of man (or 'history' or
'worldliness' or science), he rejects God. If his rejection of
theism were of this common nineteenth-century breed, it
would follow that atheism, consisting in the denial of what
the theist holds, would be, for him, the last word necessary
on the subject. But it is not his last word on the subject, it is

at most his first. His position is far more complex than any mere negation. In one of the few passages in which he explicitly comments in a philosophical way on the question of the existence of God, he appears to say two quite inconsistent things.[13] First, that theism is false; second, that theism is incoherent. Clearly no proposition can be both. If a proposition is false, this can only be because it says something — something which is false. Its contradictory, in this case atheism, will then necessarily be true. But if a proposition is incoherent, then it does not say anything at all — as to say of a shape that it is both circular and square is not to say anything. Strictly, then, an incoherent sentence has no contradictory, although it may have a purely verbal contradictory — as to say that it is not true of this particular shape that it is both a circle and a square is the verbal contradictory of saying that it is both circular and square-shaped. But the contradiction is only in the sentence-form, for the contradictory of a sentence which states nothing states no more than the sentence it contradicts. Only sentences which state something can be false. So theism cannot be both false and incoherent.

What Marx in fact argues in the third Paris manuscript is first that theism is false, and that *both* theism *and* atheism are ideological. This is not quite the same thing as saying — absurdly — that neither is coherent, but one is true and the other false. Quite what Marx's position amounts to in detail is something which I shall be considering later. In the meantime we can confine ourselves to this general conclusion. At the simplest level Marx is just rejecting *the terms of the argument* between theism and atheism. Theism is rejected because it supposes an opposition between God and man; atheism because it accepts the terms which theism lays down and can speak of man only indirectly, that is, via the negation of theism. To the degree that both accept this disjunction as terms of the argument, they are caught up in the same problematic.

For Marx, though, the point is not to settle the argument one way or the other on those terms. The point is to reject those terms. The ideological character of theism does not consist in its affirmative and (for Marx) false answer to the question 'Is there a God?' for atheism is equally ideological, in so far as it gives the negative and true answer to the same question. What is ideological is the question itself. It is a question man will only ask if he lacks, as Marx puts it:

> the evident and irrefutable proof of his self-creation, of his own *origins*. Once the essence of man and of nature, man as a natural being and nature as a human reality, has become evident in practical life, in sense experience, the quest for an *alien* being, a being above man and nature (a quest which is an avowal of the unreality of man and nature) becomes impossible in practice. *Atheism*, as the denial of this unreality, is no longer meaningful, for atheism is a *negation of God* and seeks to assert by this negation *the existence of man*. Socialism no longer requires such a roundabout method; it begins from the *theoretical* and *practical sense perception* of man and nature as essential beings.[14]

From the point of view of the Marxist, then, contemporary immanentist theologies can be seen as little else than a partial regression to that negative atheism which was very well known to Marx, which asserted man via the demythologisation of God. It is simply not true that Marx had nothing to say about such forms of theism. He effectively predicted them. On the other hand, it cannot be thought to follow from the fact that Marx rejected negative atheism as a surpassable stage of thought that he was not himself an atheist. If it is an informal characteristic of a secularised society that the majority just could not care, one way or the other, whether God exists, Marxism could be said to be, relative to this informality, militantly atheist. Marx regarded it as being an objective of revolutionary practice to bring about that state of affairs in which the question of God *could not* have any relevance and would have to be abandoned in the same spirit as, for the proper-minded bourgeois, you would not answer either affirmatively or negatively the question 'do the planets have angelic powers?' — since you have created a world in which there is *no room* for the question in the first place.

There is a third reason, connected with this last, why it was not only the theologically and politically conservative Christianity of his day which Marx rejected as ideological. He, and more particularly Engels, also rejected explicitly politically radical Christianity, not as if it was in the *same* way ideological, but all the same for being just that. In *The*

Peasant War in Germany[15] Engels sees the struggles between Luther and the neo-Anabaptist peasant leader Thomas Münzer as essentially political class struggles misread in their eyes as theological struggles.

Although the class struggles of the day were carried on under religious shibboleths, and though the interests, requirements and demands of the various classes were concealed behind a religious screen, this changed nothing in the matter and is easily explained by the conditions of the time.[16]

The 'conditions of the time' most obviously, include the *de facto* pervasiveness of a religious culture such that 'all social and political, revolutionary doctrines were necessarily at the same time . . . theological heresies'.[17] It is only for this reason, according to Engels, that it seemed necessary to read the class struggles in Germany theologically, but this necessity had certain crucial effects on the way Münzer defined his revolutionary programme. His politics were incorrigibly eschatological and even chiliastic. Although a communist, his programme was less a platform of peasant demands related to actual historical possibilities in contemporary Germany than 'the anticipation of communism *by fantasy*'.[18] One is reminded of the later English Digger, Winstanley, about whom I said much the same in the last chapter. Münzer, Engels says, sought:

a society in which there would be no class differences or private property and no state authority independent of or foreign to the members of that society. All the existing authorities, insofar as they refused to submit and join the revolution, were to be overthrown, all work and all property shared in common, and complete equality introduced.[19]

Münzer, like Winstanley, anticipated, in the form of a communist *myth*, a stage of social development — communism — which would become possible only on the basis of the achievements of the bourgeois revolution to which they were in fact *opposed*. In the circumstances, then, their religious reading of the political struggles in which they were engaged caused them to misread the issues in a way which was, in effect, actually reactionary, although as revolutionary theorists, they were far more consistent than their bourgeois opponents.

The general thesis which Engels develops out of his study of the Peasant War is about what he identifies as a necessary connection between the 'religious way' of looking at the world and the failure to see that world realistically — specifically the failure to recognise theological struggles for what they really are, namely misleading ways of reading class struggles. But as Maguire puts it:

Marx and Engels put religion on trial before a rather Kafkaesque tribunal: insofar as religion is sincerely religion, it is a set of abstract platitudes, at best useless, at worst harmful to the advancement of humanity; insofar as it says anything about the social and political reality of its time, it has ceased to be religion.[20]

For Engels the theological differences between Luther and Münzer could somehow be left out of the final explanation of their opposed political praxes. But this, as Maguire says, simply begs the question against Christianity and on non-empirical, a priori grounds. Either, Engels holds, Christianity is empirically, socially, practically empty, a tissue of tautologies in an abstract 'religious language', or else if it becomes politically committed to the class struggle, it ceases to be Christianity, and becomes atheist. Of course as an empirical generalisation, derived from the historical evidence, this dilemma could serve as a very proper warning to Christians: they *are*, as the evidence shows, in danger either of fetishising Christianity into the special religious language of an inbred religious community or else of rejecting, in the name of revolutionary politics, just that Christianity. But, to be a warning, this has to be an empirical proposition. Engels buys his certainty about this at the price of evacuating it of content: he makes the empirical point *criterial*. Hence, for Engels, you haven't got Christianity at all unless you have this political vacuity. And that is why, in the end, he cannot in principle believe in the Christianity of any genuine revolutionary.

No Marxist ought to be committed to any such a priori doctrine. It is the sclerosis of explanatory theory. That Marx and Engels were committed to it accounts for a curious feature of their criticism of religion which marks it off from their criticism of any other form of ideology, namely their lazy view that, whereas there are ideological *forms* of politics, economics, law and so forth (thus allowing for the possibility of *post*-ideological forms of each), religion is essentially ideological, *pre*-socialist and *pre*-communist. And this is odd. For it is not as if they could — or ever did — claim that religion, or even Christianity, was necessarily *bourgeois*, as they might well have claimed that representative democracy is. Perhaps their proposition is that there is no evidence of religions prior to the earliest emergence of class society, but even supposing that to be half-plausible, at best it would show that Christianity has never in fact been able to transcend the class struggle in the way it has often claimed to be able to transcend it. It would show nothing to cast doubt on the potential of Christianity to make a revolutionary and significant contribution *to* the class struggle.

As an empirical proposition, however, Engels's thesis does contain a genuine warning for 'left' Christians. This disjunctive thinking which revolves around the poles either of an evaporated religiosity (Edward Norman)[21] or else a sacralised utopian politics (Bonino)[22] can catch 'liberation' theologians trying to have it both ways at once, as in the work of Alfredo Fierro, *The Militant Gospel*.[23] Caught on the horns of this dilemma, he is impaled by both. Religious language, in so far as it is *religious*, is purely negative, critical, metaphorical and 'non-cognitive': it is metaphor *for* the politics of liberation, but has no cognitive relation with religious objects of the sort we would expect of knowledge. In so far as it *is* truth-functional and cognitive, religious language is the 'scientific' (Marxist) critique of religious language at a second-order level. It too says nothing of religious objects, for in so far as it says anything, it says something *about* religious language. In short, like Engels, Fierro holds that, as knowledge-generating, religious language has no religious content and in so far as it has any religious content it is not knowledge-generating, it is but metaphor. To all of which the Marxist will very properly retort: why should anyone be bothered with religious metaphors for revolutionary politics, if the religious metaphors say nothing that the revolutionary politics cannot already say for itself?

III

It seems, then, that any Christian response to Marxism which proposes a more positive theoretical relationship than simple rejection must come to terms with the fact that Marxism suspends over the head of *all* contemporary forms of religious belief and practice the potential charge that they are ideological beliefs and practices: that it is for *Marxism*, not for Christianity, to judge when Christianity is, or has been, guilty as charged. For there is no defence against this charge which can be given in theological language alone — or, to be more precise about it, there is no defence against this charge which can be given in that theological language which constructs its religious character in terms of the denial of its own materiality as a concrete, historical praxis. Conceived of as expressive of a pure religiosity, that language cannot know itself in respect of those social relationships between belief and social reality with reference to which the judgement of its ideological character is made. And as it cannot know itself in these relationships, it can make no claim even to know its own, religious, objects.

If Engels (and, with him, so many contemporary Western Christians) are right in this view of religious language, then it must follow that Christianity is *inherently* ideological. For on the model of 'knowledge' developed in the preceding chapters, it is a mark of what will count as knowledge that it not only 'knows' its own object according to criteria appropriate for the sort of object known, but that it knows also the material conditions which govern that relationship to its own objects. But if Christianity is to be understood as a form of 'knowing' which cannot in principle know its own relation to those material conditions, if its character as 'religious' excludes a priori its having such knowledge, then Christianity is on its own account inherently ideological.

But, we may ask, what could such a distilled essence of Christianity possibly be, which consists in nothing but the sum total of propositions, beliefs and practices which are distinctively 'religious' and as such excludes all dependence upon, or even reference to, other non-religious propositions, beliefs and practices? What could be known within such a discourse except a world of purely religious objects which it would 'know' only in the Pickwickian sense that it tautologously defined them into existence for the empty purpose of 'knowing' them? And what account of 'faith' would it be, according to which faith has no objects except those which it creates for itself by means of so vacuous a fiat? In fact, Fierro is right, such a discourse could make no genuine claims to speak of anything at all, not even of its supposedly religious objects. It would be but a tautologous circle of self-reference. At best it would be but metaphor and at its more redundant.

It is no use denying that many contemporary accounts of religious language are ridden with this 'fideism', whether of a Barthian or of a neo-Wittgensteinian sort. Characteristic of this fideism is the conviction that religious discourse is 'autonomous',[24] a conviction which amounts to the rejection of my central proposition about knowledge and is the view that religious language has no business seeking to satisfy any conditions on knowledge other than those which it can itself autonomously lay down. In one version, the neo-Wittgensteinian, religious discourse is a 'language game', an autonomous and exclusive set of rules governing talk of religious objects, such talk making sense, it is thought, only in and for that language game. It does not make sense in terms of any other form of discourse or language game, but it is not for that reason nonsense. For if religious language cannot be made sense of, say, by reference to historical evidence, it cannot be made nonsense of by reference to historical evidence either. Historical — for that matter sociological, scientific, psychological — evidence is neither here nor there from the religious point of view.[25] Hence, in another version of fideism — Bultmann's — belief in the resurrection of Jesus is neither confirmed by the evidence for nor falsified by the evidence against the occurrence of a *historical* resuscitation of the body of Jesus.[26] A religious belief neither is a belief in any historical facts nor is it related to any in respect of its meaning or truth. Only what is itself a religious experience can enter into relation with a religious utterance by way of its confirmation or denial.

It is little wonder that critics of contemporary fideism in

the analytical tradition of philosophy have no time for it. If religious discourse is of the sort that it cannot in principle be falsified by reference to evidence of whatsoever non-religious provenance, then it is not a form of discourse at all.[27] It is vacuous noise, the 'abstract religious platitude' of Engels. But the Marxist goes further than this, for the purely analytical point ignores — at any rate gives no account of — what is most significant about this vacuousness, namely that it is a vacuousness which is organised in and routinised by widespread social practices, in and by means of which people interact in terms of this vacuousness, and interact not merely with each other, but individually and collectively with society as a whole. Moreover, for the Marxist, this socially lived vacuousness is also socially functional. For whether or not a fideistically defined religious language can make any justified claims to know its own, *sui generis*, religious objects, the fact that the perceived relation to those objects is such as to *exclude* reference to the materiality of the praxes of those perceptions means that religious language is a way of not-knowing, of misrecognizing that materiality. Religious language is not just vacuous, it is *ideologically* vacuous. It is, then, materially one of the ways there are for not-knowing the social forces which govern our material world; it is a way of living out a contradictory relationship with reality.

It is little wonder, therefore, that the Marxist should conclude that Christians are fated, by the demands of their own discourse, to live out a permanently uncertain and ambiguous relation with the demands of the material social world. For in so far as they cannot know the materiality of their own discourse, they cannot control their own relationship with it. And this is why, for Marx and Engels, even revolutionary forms of Christianity seem like accidents, are always, within the record of Christian history, anomalies and short-lived: the religious perception of the world, being utterly at the mercy of the prevailing ideological wind, is but the spirit breathing at the world's will.

And so for the Marxist, the supposed autonomy of religious discourse as religious is but the reverse face of its heteronomy as material. Its vacuousness as religious is but its manipulability as political. In chapter 3 I gave one instance of how this uncertainty of its relation with its own materiality can be lived in religious practice.[28] Further instances could be multiplied indefinitely. Listening on a recent occasion to the 'bidding prayers' at a Eucharistic service, the prayers said 'for the unemployed' seemed to me to inhabit a twilight world somewhere between the feeling that 'we ought to be doing something about unemployment' and the belief that to pray thus *was* to be doing what the Christian should do about it. It was as if this ambiguity was the very form of the Christian relationship with 'the unemployed', which at once makes them present within the act of worship only to dematerialise them on arrival.

If Christianity is nothing but this fideism, then Marx and Engels are right, Christianity is unrescuably ideological. The proposition which I shall be defending, in face of this fideism, is that, on the contrary, Marxism is related to Christianity as the necessary condition of its 'rescued truth'. It is the proposition that if Christianity is to make any claims at all to knowledge, then it must satisfy the conditions for that form of self-knowledge which consists in the capacity to internalise the knowledge of its own relationship with the material social world and to be transformed by that knowledge. Hence this proposition entails a programme for Christianity: that it reconstruct its belief-claims, its social organisation and its relationship with the social world on the basis of this self-knowledge. This is the 'criticism of religion' which is the process of 'rescuing its own truth'. In this task Marxism has a decisive role. It is only in so far as it incorporates, theoretically and practically, the Marxist criticism of religion, that Christianity can recover from the emptiness of its fideism the capacity to speak its own truth without that ambiguity, epistemological and moral, which we have seen to characterise ideological systems of belief.

At this point the second half of the equation of 'strong compatibility' comes to the fore in the form of a question: as it lives through the exigencies of this relationship with Marxism, will Christianity have anything of itself to say which Marxism does not already say? Does this proposition of 'strong compatibility' not amount to a simple reductionism? The second part of the thesis is the answer to this question, that it may have something to say specifically to Marxism, although the argument for this is not presented until the last chapter. But to summarise in advance: *within* the revolutionary class struggle it is possible for Christianity to recover an authentic language in terms of which it can construct a necessary criticism of Marxism, at least in its claim to be morality. For although Christianity can and must allow Marxism to be the necessary condition for morality, it must deny any claim for it as the sufficient condition. Marxism is both necessary to and deficient as the moral praxis of capitalism. And Christianity, through its typical and central beliefs, can show why.

The second part of the 'strong-compatibility' thesis thus refers back to the 'morality is Marxism' thesis as a necessary qualification on it. But, in turn, that criticism of Marxism cannot be understood except in relation to the first part of the 'strong-compatibility' thesis, for no pre-critical Christianity has anything to say to Marxism which Marxism cannot either show to be inherently ideological or else something which it can say for itself non-ideologically. In this chapter and the next I take up the question of the Marxist critique of Christianity as ideological, and in the last two the question of the Christian critique of Marxism as morality.

IV

But we must begin with the obvious and major objections to the 'strong-compatibility' thesis, those which would seem to question its propositions a priori. In the course of this we will, in this chapter, for the most part be discussing some false moves in the argument which are commonly made either by Marxists, or else by Christians or, in some cases, by both.

The obvious objections seem to fall generally into two categories. First, there are objections to the Christian belief-system itself. Second, there are objections to the social and historical role of the institutions which have espoused, defended and promulgated that belief-system.

To the belief-system of Christianity, defenders of the incompatibility view have a form of objection which I shall call 'ontological'. This objection, taken on its own, is both the most widely canvassed and the weakest. It is roughly this: Christians believe that the universe is peopled with agencies and entities and activities and events — a God, an act of creation, an act of redemption, souls, grace, post-mortem survival and all the rest — all of which the Marxist, as a Marxist, is committed to deny. Christians are, thus, ontological theists and mentalists; Marxists, on the other hand, are ontological materialists. Since ontological im-materialism and ontological materialism cannot both be true, one cannot consistently hold both. So a Christian cannot consistently be a Marxist. In my view this is not a very serious objection when taken by itself, because although most Marxists are, indeed, ontological materialists, there is nothing in Marxism (that is, in the science) which requires these onto-logical commitments. However, it does become a serious difficulty when taken in conjunction with the second form of objection, so I will go on to consider this immediately return-ing to the ontological objection later.

The second form of objection to the compatibility thesis has to be taken rather more seriously. This set of objections can be generally designated 'historical', although this is really just a term of convenience covering two quite different sorts of objection. The first sort of historical objection is simply to the empirical record of Christian Churches in their relations with nearly every progressive movement in our Western history. That record is sometimes said to have been wholly reactionary. This, however, is to oversimplify the matter, although the charge is not much weakened by the fact that it should be more accurately described as 'diplomatic' or just plainly Machiavellian. The objection, so stated, is that Christian Churches have opposed all revolutionary movements in the last two thousand years of our history until they have proved successful and then, once established, have joined them; but that, in addition, those Churches have sometimes crucially thrown their weight on the side of the successful repression of revolutionary movements. Either way, it is said, the Churches have an appallingly reactionary record and, further-more, show every sign of continuing to display diplomatically acrobatic proclivities in the present day towards any prospect of a socialist revolution. The old instincts are still there. There are already signs, in fact, that the Christian Churches are preparing themselves *theologically* for the possibility of socialist revolution, while simultaneously in practice committing themselves to its frustration in nearly every part of the world.

Now the reason why this charge must be taken more seriously than the ontological objection is that it may seem to some Marxists — as it did apparently to Connolly — to be irrelevant to the Marxist what *private* beliefs Marxists hold so long as they do commit themselves to the struggle for socialist programmes. This, as an answer to the question of whether or not a Christian can be a Marxist, may be satisfactory to some Marxists, although it is a foolish Marxist who finds it so, but it certainly will not satisfy any Christian. But let us see, first of all, what there is in this contention, for it is important to be clear that it is not any such proposition as this which I am defending.

First, some Marxists are prepared to say that they see no reason why a Christian should not be a Marxist for just so long as he is genuinely a Marxist. Whether, when he is genuinely a Marxist, he has problems defining his Christianity as a result, is a matter for him, his conscience or his Church: but it is irrelevant to the great issues to the solution of which, as a Marxist, he is committed. If he is committed to them, it cannot matter what his reasons are. Marxists have no need to be concerned with bourgeois ideals of private motivational purity. All that is needed is correct *praxis*, a unity of verifiable analysis and strategically well-directed action. The consistency, or otherwise, of his private beliefs with his Marxism is quite beside the point.

Second, some Marxists are prepared to admit that some Christians have, personally, become Marxists precisely on account of their Christian beliefs — not that is, in spite of them, but because of them. Thus, for example, Camilo Torres, Paulo Freire, the Slant Catholics in the 1960s in England and many others. There is a minority of Christians who have come to believe that fidelity to their Christian beliefs entails and not merely permits that they accept a revolutionary socialist stance. And some of these people make very good Marxists indeed. No Marxist, it seems, can have any good reason for spurning the assistance of such comrades in the revolutionary struggle just because, again as a matter of private motivation, they view that struggle in the light of an immaterialist ontology.

Third, there are culturally specific reasons of a tactical nature why Marxists might not at all mind the mix of Christianity with Marxism. Connolly is reported to have answered to the question how he could reconcile membership of the Church of Rome with the materialist conception of history as follows:

> Well, it is like this. In Ireland all the Protestants are Orangemen and howling jingoes. If the children go to the Protestant schools they get taught to wave the Union Jack and worship the English king. If they go to the Catholic Church they become rebels. Which would you sooner have . . .?[29]

Of course, this will hardly do as an answer but there are, obviously, circumstances, societies and cultures in which Christian beliefs are the only, or at least the most favourable, soil for the cultivation of socialist ideas. There are obvious reasons why this has been so spectacularly the case among Roman Catholics in Latin America. In Britain, however, Catholics have no very strong socialist tradition on which to draw. On the other hand, in Britain the low-church dissenting brand of Christianity has a long history of association with the spread of socialism, if also, on some views, with the containment of its revolutionary potential. In any case, at least contingently, if not necessarily, it may be true that, in some conjunctures of ideologies and social conditions, it is via their Christianity that converts to socialism have been made.

None of this, however, will do as a defence of the proposition that a Christian can consistently be a Marxist. The fact that some Christians have been Marxists, and even the fact that some Christians have been Marxists just because of their Christianity, does not show that any of them have been consistent in being both. Nor can the Christian accept, and the Marxist is foolish to imply, that the Christian commitment to an immaterialist ontology is a private matter separable at all fundamentally from the commitment to a historical, empirical institution, a 'visible Church', as it used to be called. It would be quite wrong for the Marxist to drop his guard on this matter: for if the 'criticism of religion' is not the main preoccupation of the Marxist in a country like Britain today, it is important that the Marxist should not ignore what the implications of Marxism are for that criticism. Marxism cannot treat Christian beliefs as somehow incidental and private, which, as it happens, some of the population hold and some Marxists might hold too, if they can put up with the banter from their comrades. For this criticism is the criticism of a nexus which there appears to be between an ontology and a praxis which are jointly embodied in historical institutions with self-defined material commitments. More simply, the Christian either believes his ontology as a member of a Christian Church or else he is not a Christian. The idea of a 'private Christianity' is as absurd as is the idea of a 'private Marxist'. Christianity is either a praxis, in which case a serious problem about its historic relation with Marxism and about its potential for revolutionary commitment is raised, or else it is not a praxis. But if it is not, it is probably compatible with anything whatever.

That being so, it becomes impossible to separate the Marxist critique of the ontology of Christianity from the Marxist critique of the historical role of institutional Christianity. And this brings us to the second and more fundamental form of the 'historical' objection to the 'strong-compatibility' thesis: not, that is, the objection derived from the evidence of the empirical record, but that which is derived from the nature of the Christian commitments to history which are entailed by its ontology. The reason why no separation can be made between the criticism of the ontology and the criticism of the historical commitments is, in fact, the same both for Marxists and Christians.

It is true, perhaps, that the Marxist has no ontological commitments, as a Marxist, which have any bearing on what entities do and what entities do not actually people the universe. It is extremely dubious whether Marxism, represented in the materialist conception of history, involves any *ontology* of a materialist sort whatever. Indeed Marx himself was notoriously hostile to just those materialist ontologies which do provide the standard arguments against Christian theism and immaterialism. What the materialist conception of history does assert, however, is that all belief-systems, the Christian by no means excluded, have a 'materiality' about them, a materiality which derives from the fact that they are social effects as well as being systems of belief; and that, in virtue of their materiality, the question of what socially causal relationships they are caught up in is a matter not of the inner laws which are proper to them as 'ideas', but of the material relations those beliefs are in with the mechanisms of social causes and effects. The Marxist, therefore, cannot on his own account be allowed to say that the Christian universe of God, grace, redemption and after-life is a private illusion of private minds, existing in some world apart from the social world of interacting social causes and effects. For the belief in this universe is necessarily a praxis of historical and political engagement. And the Marxist wants to know whether those ontological commitments do not necessarily entail that the Christian must misrecognise and so live out in distorted form its relation with the praxis of revolution.

Nor can the Christian consistently deny, as the fideist does, that this is a question which challenges the character of his beliefs. The beliefs of the Christian are not just the beliefs of the members of an *ad hoc* community, whose nature as a community and whose historical mission is a matter extrinsic to the character of the beliefs themselves. The material, social relations in which they stand are constitutive of the belief-structure itself. All Christian beliefs are material praxes; all Christian ritual and sacramental acts are embodiments of material relations between belief and the social world. The question for the Marxist is whether those beliefs and practices of Christianity do not necessarily situate the Christian in mystified, contradictory relations with that social world, whether Christianity is not materially ideological, with whatever revolutionary intent it may wish to construe itself.

This question, when addressed by the Christian to himself, is not a question simply of whether he can believe a set of immaterialist doctrines simultaneously and consistently with the commitment to revolutionary socialism, but whether he can accept, simultaneously and consistently, the criticism of the religious enterprise as such which that revolutionary commitment both presupposes and entails. And so our discussion has brought us back to the question already raised in this chapter: has a Christianity which has lived through its critical relationship with Marxism anything left to say which is distinctively Christian? If Christianity were to come to 'know itself' as a revolutionary praxis, would not that self-knowledge be the destruction of its identity as Christian?

V

We are not yet in a position to answer this question. First, we must consider yet another false move designed to guarantee the Christian a distinct, non-Marxist identity. This false move is worth mentioning here, if only for the reason that it is one which I once made myself and now wish to disown. In an earlier article[30] I argued as if Marxism were nothing but a form of the sociology of knowledge, that it offered no more than an account of the social origins of ideologies and of their class character. If this were all that there is to the Marxist criticism of ideology, nothing would be easier than to show that the question of the *truth or falsity* of Christian belief-claims is independent of what Marxism shows of them. For, of course, from the fact that you can explain *why* a certain belief is held by a group of people in terms of material social conditions, it does not at all follow that the proposition they believe is *false*. It does not follow that $1 + 1 = 2$ is a false proposition just because most people seem to have all the wrong reasons for believing it to be true, or even because, when asked, they seem to not have the slightest idea why it is true. In just the same way, I argued, just because most Christians are unaware of the fact that their belief-system is, to put it somewhat crudely, determined by material social conditions, or even because most Christians to whom the idea has been put have denied it, it does not at all follow that the belief-system itself is a system of false beliefs. If the materialist conception of history merely explained *why* Christians assert and believe what they do, then as such it could have nothing to say on the question of whether the beliefs are true or false. Thus I saw not the slightest reason why the belief in immaterial entities is shown to be false, just because one can account on materialistic lines for the facts of belief itself. And, on the assumptions made about the materialist conception of history, this conclusion is correct.

But it is the assumptions about the materialist conception of history which are incorrect. Historical materialism, as we have seen, is very much more than merely an explanation of the historical bases of ideologies. It is a substantive critique of ideologies which is premised on the denial of that ideological separation of ideas *as ideas* from the relation of ideas to their materiality as social praxes. But even if Marxism made no further explanatory and critical claims than that of determining the social origins of belief, it still might be thought that Christianity is inconsistent with such materialist explanations. For, it may be said,[31] it is part of the *substantive content* of Christianity to believe that faith itself — the subjective act of adherence to God and the mental disposition to believe in revealed truths — is the result of a unique, unconstrained, extra-historical intervention of God. If this is accepted, then part of the content of Christian belief involves a belief about the origins of faith which is inconsistent with any account of those origins which might be given in materialist terms.

This, however, appears to mis-state the problem, although admittedly in a complex matter. There is nothing inconsistent in Christians granting that Christianity itself is 'historically determined', at any rate in that sense of the expression which appears to be properly Marxist. For Marx the determinism which man's social existence imposes upon his ideas and beliefs is not, as much Marxist rhetoric can misleadingly suggest, a form of causal determinism of the mental by the material, as if it were being said that somehow social and economic conditions uniquely, or even at all, cause ideas, as mental events, to happen. That proposition is just incoherent. And Marx held no view even like it.

Nor is it at all clear that Marx thought the *contents* of man's ideas and beliefs are 'determined' by their social existence. But there are some clear indications about what he did not hold.[32] First, historical materialism is perfectly at home with the notion that a wide variety of kinds of ideas — even opposed ideas — should flourish in even quite precisely defined and historically specific social and economic conditions. As we have seen, at one level bourgeois society expresses itself morally in a commitment to pluralism of ideas. Second, historical materialism is quite as happy with the notion of similar ideas flourishing unconstrained in historically very different social and economic conditions. Marx himself notes how, in his own time, German philosophy was far more 'progressive' than English or French philosophy, yet German society was economically, socially and politically hardly out of the Middle Ages.[33] None of this suggests a causally determinist picture either of the origin of ideas as mental events or of the objective contents of ideas: the first not at all and the second at least not in any straightforward way.

In fact historical materialism is not really a theory about the *origin* of men's ideas at all, either in psychology or history. It is a theory not about how men get their ideas, but about what determines the degree and character of their causality *as social events*. The famous Marxist hostility to 'idealism' consists not in denying that ideas have their origins as ideas in the mental, nor even in denying that ideas are real historical causes, but in denying that the historical efficacity of ideas, their historical agency, is determined by their character *as ideas*. Engels, we saw, did not doubt the genuine communism of Münzer's programme any more than we had any reason to doubt that of Winstanley: in fact, as *ideas*, they were considerably more consistent than those of their political opponents. Yet, as historical events, those 'ideas' of Münzer and Winstanley fell stillborn from the womb, because they had not come historically to term. They were, in Münzer's case at least, positively reactionary *as events*, although *as ideas* they were as 'revolutionary' as may be: which goes to show that their character as events (whether revolutionary or reactionary) is not determined by their character as ideas.

The materialist theory of history, therefore, is needed in the determination of the conditions which govern the social character, the social *materiality*, of the mental. To put it in the terminology developed in chapter 3, there may be all the difference in the world between what is meant by what is said and what is done by the act of saying it. The very fact that similar ideas can flourish under widely differing historical conditions and are revolutionary in some of these conditions, reactionary in others is, for Marx, the evidence that it is not in their character as ideas merely, not in their contents, abstractly defined, that their revolutionary or reactionary significance lies. Rather, that significance lies in the relation of those ideas as social (i.e. 'material') events to the complex social (i.e. material) structures of society — in particular in the relation of those ideas to the balance of forces in the 'class struggles of the day'. But in all events, the relationship is that of the material to the material. It may, therefore, be expressed as a causal relationship, without this implying that the material causes ideas *as mental*.

It therefore seems perfectly consistent for Christians, holding, if they do, that faith has its origins in an unconstrained act of God, also to accept what historical materialism says about *all* ideas, whatever their origins; namely, that their historical significance is determined not by what is 'said' by an idea, taken by itself, but in the complex relations between what is said and what what is said socially does — a matter determined by concrete material utterance-conditions. Since this is merely to accept that Christian beliefs do not autonomously control their historical significance — their relation to the class struggle — it is not at all obvious why Christians should have any reason to reject historical materialism in the name of beliefs about the historically unconstrained origins of the act of faith.

Nor, for that matter, do Marxists have any reason, on these grounds, to reject any such Christian account of the origins of faith. But since this is in both cases mainly because historical materialism is not an account of the origins of ideas at all, it may be thought that the supposed inconsistency between Christianity and historical materialism has its sources elsewhere. And this supposition is, in fact, correct.

Before considering more serious Marxist objections to Christianity, let us close the circle of the argument so far. We have noted the a priori character of Engels's 'Kafkaesque tribunal' in *The Peasant War in Germany*. Religion is *in principle* ideological. This is no better as a Marxist analysis of religion than is the typically evangelical Christian retort that prayer is *in principle* revolutionary. For historical materialism is precisely the doctrine that there is no set of ideas which is in principle revolutionary. Equally, just because ideology consists in a certain sort of *relation* of ideas and beliefs to a social structure, there is no way in which ideas, considered simply in themselves — or 'inherently' — and as abstracted from all such relationships, can be regarded as reactionary. It cannot be *inherently* ideological to believe in God. Any assertion of the form 'Christianity is ideological' must be the conclusion of an empirical demonstration that such and such religious ideas, within a given articulation of forces in the class struggle, have the tendency of misrepresenting that struggle, of diverting energies from their revolutionary objects, or whatever. As an empirical assertion in its most hostile form, such a conclusion could be at best (or worst) a *de facto* exceptionless generalisation. But as an empirical assertion, it would still be in principle defeasible.

This is why it remains important to distinguish within Marxism the criticism of religion based upon a priori commitments to ontological materialism and that criticism of religion which is based on empirical results within the theory of historical materialism. For historical materialism appears to be fully consistent with the refutation of ontological materialism and, in turn, ontological immaterialism appears to be consistent with historical materialism. The classical Marxist doctrine that religion is inherently ideological seems to get these lines crossed. For it is based, so far as the texts of Marx and Engels show, on the a priori commitment to ontological materialism. This is not only a philosophically contentious doctrine; not only is its denial fully consistent with historical materialism, that is, Marxism; the rejection of Christianity as *ideological* on the grounds of ontological materialism involves a misconception of what it is to show that a set of beliefs is ideological. You do not show this by way of an argument that such ideas and beliefs are philosophically, that is, a priori, *false*.

Although the argument of Marx and Engels which we have

considered in this chapter therefore misfires, there is a more recent Marxist polemic against religion which is not vulnerable to this rebuttal. Louis Althusser has constructed an argument derived, if not directly from Marx, then at least from a sophisticated reading of Marxism, on which Christianity turns out to be not merely always ideological, but inherently and paradigmatically so. This argument does not appear to rest on any a priori commitments to ontological materialism — in any case it can be stated independently of any such commitments — and is otherwise so special an argument that it requires separate treatment in a distinct chapter.

NOTES

1 Francis Barker, 'The Morality of Knowledge and the Disappearance of God', *New Blackfriars*, September 1976, p. 413, n. 10.
2 Ibid., p. 410.
3 Terry Eagleton, 'Marx, Freud and Morality', *New Blackfriars*, January 1977, p. 22.
4 Compare, for example, with Gustavo Gutierrez, *The Theology of Liberation*, London, 1974.
5 Eagleton, 'Marx, Freud and Morality', p. 23.
6 Barker, 'The Morality of Knowledge and the Disappearance of God', p. 404.
7 P. Masterson, *Atheism and Alienation*, Harmondsworth, 1973, p. 10.
8 Ibid., p. 155.
9 J. Hick and D. Cupitt, *The Myth of God Incarnate*, edited by John Hick, London, 1977.
10 Ibid., p. 178.
11 Ibid., p. 140.
12 Ibid.
13 Karl Marx, *Economic and Philosophical Manuscripts*, edited and translated by T.B. Bottomore, in *Karl Marx: Early Writings*, London, 1963, pp. 165–7.
14 Ibid., pp. 166–7.
15 F. Engels, *The Peasant War in Germany*, in *Marx and Engels on Religion*, Moscow, 1972, pp. 97–118.
16 Ibid., p. 98.
17 Ibid., p. 99.
18 Ibid., p. 103.

19   Ibid., pp. 112–13.
20   J. Maguire, 'Gospel or Religious Language: Engels on the Peasant War', *New Blackfriars*, August 1973, p. 350.
21   E.R. Norman, *Christianity and the World Order*, Oxford, 1979.
22   J. Miguez Bonino, *Christians and Marxists*, London, 1976.
23   A. Fierro, *The Militant Gospel*, London, 1977, chapter 5.
24   D. Cupitt, *Taking Leave of God*, London, 1980, especially chapter 1.
25   See, for example, D.Z. Phillips, *The Concept of Prayer*, London 1965; or his *Death and Immortality*, London, 1970, chapter 4.
26   'For the resurrection, of course, simply cannot be a visible fact in the realm of human history'. R. Bultmann, *Theology of the New Testament*, translated by Kendrick Grobel, London, 1959, Vol. I, p. 295. Cf. also, W. Marxsen, *The Resurrection of Jesus of Nazareth*, translated by Margaret Kohl, London, 1970.
27   Cf. A. Flew, 'Theology and Falsification', in B. Mitchell (ed.), *The Philosophy of Religion*, Oxford, 1971, pp. 13–15.
28   See chapter 3, pp. 30–1.
29   In the course of conversation with William Bell, reported in *The Workers' Republic, Selection from the Writings of James Connolly*, edited by D. Ryan, Dublin, 1951, p. 61, n. 2.
30   Denys Turner, 'Can a Christian be a Marxist?', *New Blackfriars*, July 1975, p. 248.
31   A comment made to me by my colleague at the University of Bristol, Dr C.J.F. Williams.
32   Cf. W.A. Suchting, 'Marx, Popper and Historicism', *Inquiry*, 15, (1972) pp. 235–66.
33   Karl Marx, *Contribution to the Critique of Hegel's Philosophy of Right, Introduction*, edited and translated by T.B. Bottomore, in *Karl Marx: Early Writings*, London, 1963, p. 49.

11

Christianity and the Ideology of 'the Subject'

I

Althusser's is a renewed and distinctive Marxist polemic against Christianity. It is significant at least of the political pluralism of twentieth-century Christianity — and perhaps also of its declining importance in terms of direct political influence — that Althusser regards Christianity as being no longer a decisive force in contemporary political ideology. That is not to say, though, that for Althusser Christianity is politically unimportant, but rather that it is not at the level of direct political intervention that Christianity matters politically. It is at the more fundamental level of the possibility of ideology generally that Christianity has its importance. For Christianity, as Althusser sees it, historically provided and continues to endorse and make absolute the terms under which — as a necessary condition — ideology of any sort can flourish at all.

Decisive here is the notion of 'the subject' — although not so much the notion itself as found in philosophical theory as the fact that the individual's everyday social experience of himself as being a 'subject' is given absolute and authoritative endorsement in Christianity. To understand this we need to go back to the notion of ideology itself. On my view, as much as on Althusser's, ideology is that framework or structured set of experiences whereby the individual is incorporated into the social world which he inhabits, so as to find it intelligible and valuable. Mrs Holt was able to recover her sense of being herself through the routinised perception of her relation to the class system of her social world. She 'places' herself in and through the cross-connections of descriptive and evaluative elements in her social language. It is just as true to say, moreover, that Mrs Holt *is placed* in what is to her an intelligible relation to her social world *by* the sentence she utters, as it is to say that she *places herself* in that relation by means of it. Indeed, in one crucial sense the former way of putting it is more precise, since the materials of her sentence were, so to speak, already there to hand, an available, in fact, an inevitable instrument, existing prior to her speaking it. In this way some value can be seen in that (otherwise very misleading) metaphor of the neo-structuralist Marxists,[1] according to which it is more appropriate to say: 'The sentence speaks Mrs Holt' than to say 'Mrs Holt speaks the sentence'. Of course, it is true that that individual, Mrs Holt, spoke the sentence. But her identity, her being meaningfully present as an individual speaking at a point of intersection of certain social events and relationships is a fact which is also constituted by the sentence which she utters. She is 'summoned' into personal and social existence by her language.

This 'being summoned into personal and social existence' by the social language which we speak is what Althusser inelegantly calls 'interpellation'[2] and is the fundamental act of ideology. But the condition on which ideology can enact this function is that social agents already recognise themselves to be 'subjects' capable of being personally called by social language into social and personal existence. Barker summarises Althusser's position neatly.

There is (Althusser writes) 'no ideology except by and for subjects', and its function is to constitute individuals as subjects in order that they recognise 'their' place in the social formation. 'Hailed', in Althusser's word, by ideology the always-ready constituted subject responds 'Yes, it really is me . . . I am here, a worker, a boss, a soldier!' Caught in a multiple system of interpellation, of universal recognition (of one's place, of one's subjectivity, and of others as subjects) and of absolute guarantee (of one's unique, irreplaceable subjecthood) the individuals within a social formation then 'work', 'they "work by themselves" in the vast majority of cases, with the exception of the "bad subjects" who on occasion provoke the intervention of the (repressive) State apparatus'.[3]

An ideology, therefore, is but a form of social discourse — whether political, legal, economic, moral or religious — by means of which social agents are called upon in a specific way to occupy a position, status or role in the social system. The conjunction of these ideologies constitutes what Barker calls a 'multiple system of interpellations'. But *ideology-in-general*, in Althusser's terminology, is what creates the possibility of any such act of interpellation in the first place. Ideology-in-general accounts for the fact that I, who recognise myself in my relation to the economic system as a 'worker', already exist as a self-aware subject-who-can-be-called into social existence by that name. We have to see ourselves as free, conscious subjects, if we are to be able to respond in a spontaneous, autonomous way to the call of ideologies in particular. Althusser, as I have remarked, appears to attach very little importance to the role of religion as *an* ideology among others. But he restates in a new form the classical Marxist doctrine, rejected in its old form in the last chapter, that Christianity is essentially ideological. This, for Althusser, is because the decisive intervention of Christianity is at the level of ideology-in-general, that is to say at the level of the conditions for the possibility of any ideologies in particular. The contribution of Christianity is that of absolutising the category of the subject itself, it makes available and endorses independently of any particular ideological conditions the sense of the individual's unique and self-conscious selfhood, constituted by his freedom and autonomy.

But to secure the basic conditions for ideology Christianity has to be, and is, capable of more than this. If all that were needed epistemologically for ideology to get off the ground were the category of the autonomous, free subject, it would be very doubtful as a matter of history, if Christianity could be held to court for the prevalence of ideologies. Christianity is in fact ill placed for the unqualified defence of the philosophy of absolute subjectivity, freedom and autonomy: existentialism surely has a far better claim to this role today. What is needed for Althusser's role of endorser of basic ideological conditions is a form of systematic equivocation between prima-facie contradictories, freedom *and* subjection, in an ideological simulacrum of harmony. And it is this which he thinks Christianity is uniquely well placed to provide.

The reason why this ideological conflation of 'freedom' and 'subjection' is a necessary precondition of all ideology is that some account is needed of the spontaneity, the freedom with which individuals respond, in ideology, to the *summons to subjection* which ideologies impose. People autonomously respond to the call of ideology — they 'work by themselves' — and yet that call is a demand that they subject themselves to the constraints of role and relationship which are imposed upon them independently of their wills.

By exploiting a mere linguistic accident Althusser is able then to persuade himself that Christianity is the main dealer in the requisite category confusion. He writes:

> The whole mystery of this (ideological) effect lies . . . in the ambiguity of the term *subject*. In the ordinary use of the term, subject in fact means: (1) a free subjectivity, a centre of initiatives, author of and responsible for its actions; (2) a subjected being, who submits to a higher authority, and therefore is stripped of all freedom except that of accepting freely his submission. This last note gives us the meaning of this ambiguity, which is merely a reflection of the effect that produces it: the individual *is interpellated as a (free) subject in order that he shall submit freely to the commandments of the Subject, i.e. in order that he shall (freely) accept his subjection*, i.e. in order that he shall make the gestures and actions of his subjection 'all by himself.' *There are no subjects except by and for their subjection.* That is why they 'work all by themselves'.[4]

The relevance of Christianity to this ideology of the subject is that the ambiguity between the triad 'subject—freedom—subjectivity' on the one hand and 'subject—subjection' on the other is given, as it were, a theory and a system in Christian theology by means of its reconciliation of freedom and obedience in the notion of the 'Absolute Subject' (God), subjection to whom is, for the Christian, his freedom and subjectivity. There is here a striking parallel between the analysis which Althusser gives of this systematised ambiguity and of its exploitation in Christianity and the analysis which I gave of the expression 'your betters' in the speech of Mrs Holt. Just as class ideology exploits the two-facedness of 'your betters' so as to achieve a spontaneous, but unexplicated (and illegitimate) influence from facts to values, so, for Althusser, the ambiguity of the 'subject' — between its bearings on autonomy and freedom and its bearings on subjection — achieves an illegitimate fusion of the ambiguity in the synthesised proposition that 'true' freedom, autonomy, subjectivity lies in subjection to the Absolute Subject, 'God'. Christianity, therefore, authorises and vindicates in the form of the 'mystery' of this fusion what is, in fact, the fundamental *mystification* on which all ideology depends: the mystification whereby in every form of ideology the individual freely and spontaneously accepts his subjection to the imperatives of the social structure.

II

The notion that we are free autonomous 'subjects' is, then, for Althusser, the fiction which makes all the other fictions of ideology possible. Its fictional character, furthermore, displays with particular clarity the structural features of ideology itself and, in the main, those features are for Althusser just those with which my own analysis of ideology has made us familiar. That structure is of a peculiar type of performative contradiction whereby ideological thought denies the origins which its very denials at the same time exhibit. Marx himself gives a particularly graphic illustration of this mechanism on the very first page of the *Grundrisse*.[5]

The individual and isolated hunter and fisherman, with whom Smith and Ricardo begin, belongs among the unimaginative conceits of the eighteenth-century Robinsonades, which in no way express merely a reaction against over-sophistication and a return to a misunderstood natural life, as cultural historians imagine. As little as Rousseau's *contrat social*, which brings naturally independent, autonomous subjects into relation and connection by contract, rests on such naturalism. This is the semblance, the merely aesthetic semblance, of the Robinsonades, great and small. It is, rather, the anticipation of 'civil society', in preparation since the sixteenth century and making giant strides towards maturity in the eighteenth. In this society of free competition, the individual appears detached from the natural bonds, etc. which in earlier historical periods make him the accessory of a definite and limited human conglomerate. Smith and Ricardo will stand with both feet on the shoulders of the eighteenth-century prophets, in whose imaginations this eighteenth-century individual — the product on the one side of the dissolution of the feudal forms of society, on the other side of the new forces of production developed since the sixteenth century — appears as an ideal, whose existence they project into the past. Not as a historic result but as history's point of departure.

On the social model of the classical economists, social and economic theory begins with the isolated, pre-social 'individual'. For that is how, in a free market society, man seems, as an individual 'detached from social bonds'. But in fact, Marx's argument goes on, that conception of the isolated pre-social man as *natural* is given rise to precisely by social conditions in which the individual role in the productive processes is *more* dependent on society than ever before.

The epoch which produces this standpoint, that of the isolated individual, is also precisely that of the hitherto most developed social relations.[6]

Capitalism, in which the socialisation of production has been carried further than ever before, gives rise to the notion, as its natural ideology, which denies this. The mechanism of ideology is exactly that which I have described so often by the formula: ideology obscures in what it says just that which gives rise to its saying it.

For Althusser this mechanism also dominates the processes whereby ideology-in-general is produced. The notion of 'the subject' — and the fact of our necessary self-ascriptions of subjecthood — exhibits this mechanism. Here the influence on Althusser of a certain reading of Freud is paramount. For both Althusser and Freud, my self-recognition as a subject, as an ego, as an agent and receiver of meanings, is caught up into this mechanism. To be a person — a self-aware ego — I necessarily perceive myself as a subject, as autonomous and free, as an agent both of meanings (language) and of values (actions). Yet my being a self-aware ego depends upon the repression in the unconscious of the very factors which determine my consciousness for what it is. To be *me*, that conscious and self-conscious self, I have *not* to know the constituents of my making; to be able to act freely and at will I must necessarily repress that which determines my acting. Consequently:

. . . when, in a sentence, I refer to myself as 'I', when I make use of the personal pronoun, the 'I' I refer to is the coherent subject (N); but the I which speaks that 'I', that coherent subject, has no such coherence: it is, in effect, merely a function, self-divided and distraught, of the unconscious which speaks me, but which allows me the comforting illusion that it is 'I' who speak.[7]

As the Freudian sources of this Althusserianism suggest, we are not here meant to be considering the effect of any particular ideology. Terry Eagleton is referring to the very constitution, the natural history, of subjectivity itself. The shocking paradox of this Freudianism lies in the fact that according to it the most basic phenomena of our world — the very possibility of experience at all — are said to be caught up in the contradictory machinery of ideology. Our being ourselves is premised on a contradiction.

Moreover, this analysis is carried further into the account of ideology. A neat parallelism is presented between the contradictory processes of personality construction and the equally contradictory processes of ideology construction.

The ideological is . . . this process of *misrecognition*, whereby individual historical agents, who are no more than the replaceable bearers of determinate functions within a mode of production, are mystified into that belief in their own 'centredness', into that imaginary relation with the world where the world is seen to exist for them and they for the world, which precisely ensures that they will carry out those objective functions which are deeply unconscious to them. The social formation has its reasons of which the subject knows nothing. The subject can't *know* the discourses which produce him . . . because the very process of being *constituted* as a subject involves the *repression* of that discourse, the misrecognition of those laws of the mode of production.[8]

The polemic against the subject is remorseless. In my view it is unsuccessful, which is as well for my argument, since, were it to succeed, it would destroy at one blow the two theses which are central to the argument of this essay. First, let us examine the bearing of the Althusserian polemic on the 'morality is Marxism' thesis, leaving to the final section of this chapter consideration of its bearing on the 'strong-compatibility' thesis.

III

The 'morality is Marxism' thesis appears vulnerable to this Althusserianism in the following way. That thesis identifies morality with Marxism on condition that through the Marxist critique of moral ideologies men are enabled to determine the circumstances in which they could, without the systematic distortions imposed by class society, discover their 'true' needs. I have already made it clear that nothing in this claim entails that Marxism is somehow in possession of superior esoteric knowledge of 'true' human needs. For the identity of morality with Marxism is based *both* on the fact that moral knowledge would be, if it were possible at all, knowledge of man's true human needs *and* that such knowledge is not possible except under social conditions which are realisable only in a post-capitalist society. Marxism is morality in the sense that Marxism is the condition of the possibility of morality (i.e. of that knowledge) and is at the same time the denial of that possibility under capitalism.

The vulnerability of the identity thesis lies in the fact that according to it the category of the 'subject' must survive in communist society. It must survive in the individuated bearer of needs, in the form of the individuated potential knower of what man's true needs are, in the form, that is to say, of the individuated, morally responsible human agent. If we can know now what the conditions for the possibility of such moral knowledge are, and can know that our being 'subjects' in this minimal sense is among those conditions, this is only because we can now distinguish conceptually between the subject of bourgeois ideology — Marx's 'isolated individual hunter and fisherman' — and that minimal notion of the subject — Marx's 'social individual'[9] — who is the potential bearer of fully socialised needs and the possessor of the knowledge of their realisation.

The Althusserian polemic against the subject forbids this distinction. The category of the subject and the necessity of our perceiving ourselves as centres of social agency are merely products of ideology, not, as it must be on my argument, epistemological necessities, if there is to be any distinction at all between science and ideology and therefore if there is to be any such thing as morality. In the long run to deny any scientific status within Marxism to the category of the subject — as opposed to an ideological conception of it — is to undermine the possibility of epistemology itself.[10]

For there is the greatest difficulty in conceiving how any epistemological distinctions whatever can be made without reference to some notion of the subject. What notion of the subject is entailed is, of course, a contentious matter, and depends, partly at least, on which epistemological distinctions it is thought fit to make. But at a minimum, if there is to be any epistemology at all which a Marxist could accept, it is impossible to do without this much ontology: there exist social agents which are individual parcels of highly organised matter (bodies) of which it can be said (a) that their individuation is that by which occurrent sets of psychological phenomena are individuated; and (b) that they are agents (i.e. efficient causes) of such individuated psychological phenomena.

That only such individuated parcels of matter speak, lie, deceive, are deceived, judge and act — or, for that matter, are socialised ideologically or non-ideologically — and that the noun 'person' is the general term standing for the kinds of bits of matter which can do and undergo these things is undoubtedly true. But it is not trivially true (any longer), since the Althusserians want to eliminate (or have got themselves into the position of being unable to fail to eliminate) 'the subject' as a category of scientific discourse in the name of what is, relative to this truism, a sheer *metaphor* about 'subjects *being spoken by* discourses . . .'.[11]

This metaphor is, if only a metaphor, at the very least misleading. It must be a metaphor unless the truism is denied that only human persons (subjects) can be said, in any literal sense, to speak; and is misleading because, being a metaphor presumably meant to help out the difficult neo-Freudian analysis of ideology, it undoes all the work of the analysis it is meant to illustrate. For it suggests (given the truism that only subjects speak) that discourses are (somehow) at least analogous to subjects, that is, agents, which is, in fact, among the propositions which the analysis is supposed to refute. It is easy to admit that 'discourses' are limitations on what can be said; that they license some and prohibit other general classes of factual claims and the inferences which can be made from them; that they are, in a word, 'paradigmatic', definitive for a science or for an ideology of a range of problems and a range of acceptable-in-principle solutions to them. But the notion that discourses can be said in any useful (even metaphorical) sense to be capable of 'speaking' is either nonsense, if it is denied that they are 'subjects', or else, if it is allowed that they are subjects in any literal sense at all, is plainly false.[12]

What is wrong with Althusser's metaphor is that it is being asked to do two jobs which it cannot simultaneously and consistently do. One point of the metaphor is to dramatise the ideological character of the belief that the 'autonomous' subject is the unique, self-possessed centre of social agency. We imagine our relation to the social structure to be that of an autonomous, free agent, a chooser of role, of meaning and of value within it. We imagine, in a word, that we are 'speakers' of our relations to the social structure, fully in command of the social language which we employ and that we determine, by our employment of that language, the nature of those social relations. This belief, however, is, in the strictest sense, an ideological belief, because the very fact that we imagine our relations to the social structure to be of this sort is itself an *effect* of that social structure upon us. The social structure is such that necessarily we must relate with it *as if* our relations with it were those of autonomous agents. Consequently the very belief in our autonomous agency is a product of what the belief denies; for all the while that we imagine ourselves to be 'speaking' our relations with the social structure, that social structure is 'speaking' its relations with us. It 'speaks us' in our ideological mis-perception of our relations with it.

The second point of the metaphor (which is inconsistent with the first) is that, although it denies any reality to the imagined autonomy of our social agency, it implies that *structures themselves are agents*, i.e. subjects. But 'structures' cannot 'speak', even *through* individual speakers. They can determine what it is possible to *say*, if they are linguistic structures; or what it is possible to *think*, if they are concep-tual structures; or what it is possible to *explain*, if they are theoretical structures; and even what it is possible to *choose and do*, if they are material social structures. But they cannot speak, think, explain, choose or do anything at all.

Up to a point Althusser recognises this. He speaks of what he calls 'structural causality',[13] the causality not of an agent in a relation of productive or efficient causality to effects distinct from that agent, but rather the causality which a structure exercises over what it structures. And this distinc-tion is exactly right. There is such a causality as 'structural causality', but a structural cause is not an agent, just because a structure is *nothing* over and above its effects: it is nothing more than what determines a structured complex *to be* a structured complex. Consequently, the causality which a structure exercises over its effects must be what Aristotle called *formal*, not what he called *efficient*, causality. For if (a) structures can cause, but (b) are not distinct events from their effects, then they are formal principles determining structured complexes for *what* they are, and cannot be efficient causes, bringing it about *that* effects, in just those structured complexes, occur at all. A formal cause determines *what* happens; an efficient cause determines *that* something happens (namely, what the formal cause determines will happen if anything happens). A formal cause is a specifying principle, an efficient cause is an agency. Hence the metaphor of 'discourses speaking . . .' is systematically misleading because what can only be a formal cause (a discourse) is made, in the metaphor, to do the work of an efficient cause ('speak'), as if a structure were not merely that which deter-mines *what* can be said but also that which brings it about that what *can* be said *is* said.

You cannot, however, have it both ways, even in metaphor. Efficient causes are agents and agents are, where human, subjects. Some notion of 'subject' is required by that of agency; and some notion of agency by that of praxis. So, either discourses are not subjects (which is what Althusserian theory says), in which case there is no category within Althusserian science capable of explaining agency, or else 'structural causality' is a form of efficient causality, in which case structures are agents and therefore subjects — the efficient causes of social phenomena. Therefore, either discourses are agents and subjects, which is false, or else the category of agency is itself undermined and with it that of social causality. But without the category of social agency Marxism collapses as a revolutionary doctrine. For, among other things, the very contrast between the speculatively passive and the revolutionary active forms of knowing disappears.

We are, then, brought back to the notion of 'the subject' itself. There is at least this much work which is usefully done by the metaphor of 'discourses speaking': it usefully eliminates a category which, because of their Cartesianism, it is perfectly understandable that some philosophers cannot distinguish from the category of the subject, namely that of the Cartesian 'self' or 'ego' which is defined by its self-consciousness.[14] But the subjects or social agents required in Marxist theory are not Cartesian psychological selves. They are, as I argued in chapter 2, language-bearing material organisms, *bodies*, and are the sources of the individuation *of* conscious activities. Subjects in the Cartesian sense are conscious substances and are individuated *by* their conscious activities. The existence of conscious, perceiving subjects who are social agents is presupposed, as I have said, to there being any conscious social activity or praxes at all. Cartesian selves are the supposed objects of a supposed subset of conscious experiences, that is, of a special sort of direct intuition of this conscious subject or 'self'. It appears to be thought by some Cartesians (and evidently some Marxists) that whatever there is to be said about the Cartesian self (that it is a product of ideology) can be said, via the conflation of the concepts, about 'subjects' in principle.

But any non-Cartesian — and certainly any Marxist — ought to be able to see through this confusion; indeed it is evidence of your Cartesianism, if you cannot. Aquinas,[15] Hume,[16] and Kant[17] all agreed in rejecting any notion of 'the person' or 'the self' or 'the ego', according to which the self would be something of which you would expect to have any *direct* experiences: for all of these, there simply are not any such experiences as those of which 'the self' is a direct object. Of course, agreed on that these philosophers differ on everything else. If, like Hume, you presuppose with Descartes that were there any 'self' you would have direct experience of it *and* deny that we do have any such experiences, then you end up without 'subjects' of any sort. But, as Kant argued, in fact that admission undermines any possibility of a realist epistemology and is fraught with idealist implications, so that although philosophers like Hume go on making epistemological distinctions — such as that between speculative and practical knowledge — they do so without any right. This is much the same complaint as mine with Althusser.

Of course, this reference to Kant should not mislead. The minimal notion of 'the subject' needed for an epistemology of Marxism is not so minimal as Kant's 'transcendental ego', existing, but not the object of sense (or of any other sort of direct) knowledge, known only as a postulate required for the possibility of objective knowledge of the world. Human subjects are material, perceptible, linguistic individuals, in short, *bodies*. Being linguistic they are capable of self-reflection. They *are* self-conscious, but they are not constituted as 'selves' by their self-consciousness. It is perfectly consistent with this non-Cartesian notion of the human subject that their self-consciousness should be constituted by conditions which lie, repressed, outside the range of that consciousness itself. And if this is true, then that self-consciousness which is not only not aware of, but is constituted by the repression of the knowledge of, its own self-constitution, is implicated in a structure of misrecognition which is, for Althusser, paradigmatically ideological. But just where are those Althusserian 'subjects' to be found (outside of Cartesian theory) who, in real life, are unable to perceive at least *that* they are constituted as 'selves' by more than their self-consciousness? Of course subjects are determined as subjects by more than their subjectivity. Who but philosophers with an interest in a theory deny this? That none of us know exactly *what* makes us be the subjects that we are; that all of us need *not* know this in order to be the subjects that we are may very well be true; and, no doubt, the theory which not only elucidates the mechanisms of this repression but is capable of describing the content repressed has to be of vital significance within the general theory of ideology itself. But the suggestion that the very perception of the self as a subject is implicated in the Cartesian identification of 'subject' with the self-constituting ego flies in the face of the facts with Aquinas, Hume and Kant found it easy to acknowledge because they, like the run of mortals, could identify no experience which corresponds with the ego of Cartesian theory. The fact is that we do not, in ordinary everyday ideology, so construe ourselves.

Althusser is, of course, right that ideology in the more general sense functions at the level of that primary obviousness with which a person is incorporated, socialised or 'interpellated' into the daily round of social role and routine and that to be 'summonable' a person has to be aware of himself as a subject under certain 'obviously true' descriptions. This is true for the reason which I have already given. That he recognise that he is a *subject* is a necessary condition on anyone's part of his being aware of himself as a possible social *agent*. But this recognition as such cannot be what makes his capacity to be 'summoned' ideological; what is ideological is the fact that he recognises himself *only* in those 'obviously true' (ideological) descriptions. It is the *descriptions in which* he recognises himself that are ideological, not the mere fact of self-recognition all on its own. And this is for the reason, among others, that there is no such thing as the 'mere recognition of oneself as a subject'. I can only be aware of myself *under some description*. I cannot be aware *just* 'of myself'. It is because of this that it is possible for a person to *mis*recognise himself, misconstrue the true nature of his social agency, for he can perceive himself via descriptions which are false or ideological. The question, therefore, whether a person's self-description as a subject is ideological or not is a question about whether the descriptions under which he is summoned by the social system are ideological or not. And that is a question about the social structure itself, not about the abstract 'capacity to be summoned' of social agents.

The trouble, then, with Althusser's account of the primary processes of ideological insertion — of 'ideology-in-general' — is that it presupposes the quite unwarranted assumption that people normally perceive themselves as subjects under the Cartesian description of autonomous self-consciousness. No one needs to think of himself as a pure subjectivity in order to think of himself as a subject, even in bourgeois ideology. But everyone has to think of himself as a subject whenever he forms any notion of himself as an agent, whether in an ideological conception of his agency or a scientific conception of his agency. The primary notion of a subject — as the minimum condition of any agency whatsoever, that is, as an efficient cause — is, therefore, a notion required equally by any ideology and by the scientific account of an ideology's origin and persistence.

The primary notion of the 'subject' which is required in a Marxist epistemology is characterised by at least the following two properties. First, as we saw in chapter 2, at a very general level, there have to be individuals that are bodies and language-bearers (or rather, to follow Aquinas on this, bits of matter which are language-bearing, that is, bodies). There have to be such bodily identities, if only for the reason that there have to be individuated entities for the Freudian theory of ego-constitution *to hold true*. Even if Freud is right, there must be the subject who is that individual of which it can be said that its constitution as a self-conscious ego is premised on the repression of the conditions which constitute it as such. But second, and more specifically, there are subjects which are not merely the subject-terms of the sort of assertions neo-structuralist Freudians make about ego-constitution and ideology production, but are also sensuous, material (and *therefore*) individual, but above all, *practical* agents, the individuated loci of needs and wants. These subjects are self-conscious, but, as I have said, are not constituted in general as individuals by their being self-conscious nor, in particular, are they constituted as the individuals they are by the peculiarities of the contents of their consciousnesses. On the contrary, they are, in general, individuals and, in particular, the individuals they are because of their bodies, that is, in virtue of their materiality. And it is just because of this materiality that their consciousness of themselves is not in that relation of immediacy to themselves that they cannot fail of self-knowledge. Thus, because of their materiality, because their constitution as subjects is contingent upon material conditions which are external to their *subjectivity* and because, therefore, their needs are knowable only mediately through knowledge of the external social conditions which generate them, they need the science of society in order even to know themselves. It is, therefore, as practical, needing subjects that they need this knowledge: as I put it in chapter 8, if we have any needs at all, we have at least one meta-need, the need to know what our needs are. We need knowledge precisely because our materiality as subjects puts our needs outside the range of immediate awareness and within the scope only of adequate science.

Viewed as such, it is pretty clear why the minimal notion of the subject actually appealed to by the 'morality is Marxism' thesis has nothing in common with Althusser's subjects, which are Cartesian egos. Mine are language-bearing lumps of sensuous matter. As sensuous matter they have needs. As language-bearers they are capable of misdescribing their needs. As material social individuals (bodies) they necessarily construct their misdescriptions in the form of a social order — or, more accurately, their misdescriptions come in the form of a social order in the first place.

Therefore, it is just as material-needing beings that the scientific knowledge of society is necessary to humans and the criterion of scientificity (by contrast with ideology) is the adequacy of the grasp of that total social mechanism whereby needs are simultaneously generated and deformed, that is, generated *in* distorted form — the heuristic model for this mechanism being, as I argued in chapter 9, what Marx describes as the 'fetishism of commodities': it is the model for it because it is its primary instance.

Furthermore, it is because scientific knowledge is what

answers to need that that knowledge can be construed as practical, indeed as *moral*, knowledge. But it can be construed as such only if we can allow as a category of science that of the conscious subject who is the bearer of needs; for without that notion we can form no concept of an agent, and without the concept of an agent it is not possible to ground any distinction between the epistemology of Cartesian subjectivities and the epistemology of revolutionary social praxis.

IV

I return finally (and very briefly) to the accusation of a special Christian complicity in the construction of the 'ideological subject'. Althusser locates this complicity, as we saw, in the mystified Christian fusion of 'subjectivity' with 'subjection' in the Absolute Subject, God, thus absolutising relations of spurious inference from freedom to obedience and from obedience to freedom. 'True' freedom becomes spontaneous subjection; in spontaneous subjection lies our true freedom.

Admittedly there are Christian theodicies of which this account is not a caricature and not all of them are on the lunatic fringe of Christianity. But it is significant — in view of the argument of the last section — that the best-known tradition (and perhaps the only one known to Althusser) in which these spurious conceptual linkages are made is, once again, the Cartesian. Certainly in Descartes[18] the route to God is through human subjectivity, for the argument for the existence of God in Descartes's philosophy derives its conclusiveness from the supposed certainty of its premiss — the Cartesian 'I think' with which the 'self' or 'subject' is identified. Further, in a reverse movement of epistemology, all our certainties other than that of the self's existence as a pure consciousness, including that of our bodies and of an 'external world', are derived from the guarantee which God provides of the veracity of human consciousness. We can be sure in principle of our knowledge of the external world because the God who created our organs of perception would not have simultaneously condemned them to systematic error. Here, then, we find replicated the duality which Althusser identifies. Our existence as pure 'consciousnesses' ('subjects') poses the necessity of the Absolute Subject, who, in turn, guarantees our status as knowers of and agents in the real world.

This dialectic is exhibited in even sharper form if we accept the Sartrean reading of it. Sartre argues[19] that the primacy in Descartes of the 'cogito' has an inner tendency to atheistic conclusions which lends his arguments for God an air of interested spuriousness. Logically, the philosophy of absolute consciousness is a philosophy of total subjective freedom. The absolute centre of meaning and agency ought logically to be the 'subjective self' to the exclusion of all other centres of meaning outside the self, including God. In fact, for reasons which, in Sartre's view, say more for Descartes's piety than for his rigour, this freedom which properly belongs to the human subject is transposed from the human will and projected in its entirety upon the divine will. God becomes absolute and omnipotent freedom, a freedom which, of necessity, must exclude all other freedoms. Consequently, the very human subjectivity which calls for God is annulled by the God which it calls into existence. Typically, then, the contradiction within Cartesian thought, between the intrinsic freedom of the human subject and the necessity of subjection to an alien, voluntaristic Subject (subjectivity calls for God, God calls for subjection) is itself annulled in a purely ideological reading of that most Christian formula 'subjection is freedom'.

By contrast with this, Sartre's own existentialism brings out how Cartesian subjectivism cannot be reconciled with theism. The formula in which the contradiction between the human and the divine subjectivities is spuriously reconciled becomes, in Sartre, the name of the impossibility of God's existence. God has to be the would-be identity of subjectivity and objectivity, of freedom and determination, of the 'pour-soi' and the 'en-soi' — an identity which, being unachievable in man, is achieved in 'bad faith' in God.

And so we come back to the complaint of fideism made against so much contemporary Christianity in the last chapter. There is a connection, which Althusser's writing supposes to be definitive of Christianity, between the doctrine of the autonomy of religious language (considered in the last chapter) and the doctrine of the autonomous, Cartesian subject. For it seems that as the discourse of Christianity is said to be autonomous, so is the 'religious subject', the speaker of that discourse, said to be autonomous. For within the fideistic account of religious language a structurally central place is found for the autonomous human subject. So to say, just as the discourse spoken is epistemologically autonomous, so what the discourse 'speaks' is the autonomous subject as speaker of it.

Now just as the Marxist criticism of religion dethrones — 'de-centres' — the discourse, so it dethrones the illusions of the Cartesian and subsequently existentialist human subject. It therefore undermines the very foundations of this fideistic Christianity, although it is not as if it were not itself riddled with enough theological contradictions of its own making. It is the fundamental illusion of so much Christianity today that it can, first of all, fix the centre of the universe in its own interest, on God, and then speak authoritatively from that centre in the language of God. The theologian, for all the self-criticism in which he has belatedly engaged, is still committed to the privilege of his own discourse. It is as if the theologian is compelled to believe that there must be an autonomous being somewhere and that his language is the language in which to speak of it, invulnerable to political (or for that matter, psychological) criticism. But it is just this compulsion which lands us with the most intractable of today's theological problems. For although there can be only one autonomous being at the centre, unfortunately there are two candidates for the position God and man. Necessarily, then, they compete for the privileged position, in relations of mutual exclusion. In so far as God is centred, man is de-centred; in so far as man is centred, God is de-centred. Consequently, as is to be predicted, havoc is wreaked above all with the traditional doctrine of the Incarnation. The very notion becomes incoherent, as Cupitt maintained in *The Myth of God Incarnate*. There cannot be two autonomous beings at the centre, they must be 'over —

against' each other. Hence, if Christ is at the centre, he cannot be both God and man.

It is evident, then, that fideistic theodicy and Sartrean atheism alike are implicated in that theological 'problematic' which I discussed in the last chapter, according to which the affirmation of man is set in disjunctive relationship with the affirmation of God. They cannot both be free. This disjunction is inherent in Cartesianism and is not resolvable in the terms in which it is stated. That is why its spurious resolution in the pious Christian formula is the merest rhetoric, even if it is the routinised, practised rhetoric of an ideology. It outdoes 'your betters' as a way of resolving a contradiction into an interested two-facedness.

But if fideism and Sartrean existentialism are implicated in this problematic, so, in a different way, is Althusser. For Althusser, the problematic of God, whether settled in the direction of theism or atheism, is that problematic within which the question of God is raised disjunctively with the question of man. Althusser proposes neither to affirm one in terms of the other, nor to affirm either in terms of the denial of the other, and concludes that he must deny both God and man, or rather the whole problematic within which man and God appear in opposed relation to each other. His atheism, therefore, takes the form of the attempt to think outside the terms of this problematic, on the assumption that in the absence of these terms of reference there is no question of God to be raised — or, for that matter, of man. But so long as the question of God which he proposes to abandon is one which is determined by this Cartesian and fideist problematic, atheism *tout court* is a long way off. Not for a minute should Christians concede that such disjunctive theodicies are intrinsically Christian. Indeed, were this the place to do so, it would be possible to show exactly the contrary, namely that what is distinctive about Christian theodicy is precisely its rejection as pagan of any attempt to say either what man is or what God is in terms of some contrast between them. For the Christian view of the transcendence of God is such that it simply cannot make sense to ask in what this contrast consists. As McCabe has argued:

Circles and squares and triangles and such occupy their mutually exclusive territories in the common logical world of shapes. It is part of the *meaning* of a circle that it is not a square or any other shape; hence to say that something is both a circle and a square is to say both that it is and is not a circle, and this . . . is to say nothing at all. Similarly being human and being, say, a sheep, occupy mutually exclusive territories in the common logical world of animals. It is part of the meaning of being human that one is not a sheep. And so on. But just what or where is the common logical world that is occupied in mutual exclusion by God and man? A circle and a square make two shapes. A man and a sheep make two animals: God and man make two what? It may be part of the meaning of man that he is not any other creature; it cannot be part of the *meaning* of man that he is not God. *God is not one of the items in the universe which have to be excluded if it is just man that you are talking about. God could not be an item in any universe.*[20]

At this point the theologians will be nodding their heads in gestures of familiarity. For we are back with the old chestnut of the relation between the 'immanence' and 'transcendence' of God. About this question all I have been able to say is that they are *not* terms of contrast, such that one has to be traded off against the other, as if, as McCabe puts it, there were some one common 'reality', bits of which God occupies in exclusion of all else, other bits being occupied by man to the exclusion of God. And as another theologian, Schillebeeckx, puts it:

The creature does not need to give way to God when he approaches as water has to give way to a piece of wood that is plunged into it . . . God is not a fellow creature who occupies his own space beside me and to whom I have to yield if he wants to occupy my space as well. He is, even when he confers grace, transcendent through interiority.[21]

It is not convincing if Marxists suppose that theism can be swept away simply by denying what Christians have no very good reason to affirm in the first place. But, equally, it is not convincing if Christians suppose that they can unproblemati- cally live out their relationship with the world via concepts of God which are *at once* ideological and theologically un- justified. In short they cannot count on even their own best prayers when their theology renders them self-contradictory and the practices entailed by them are demonstrably ideological.

But if the theologians will recognise here the familiar face of a professional problem, perhaps also they will recognise here that the central remaining question about the 'strong-compatibility' thesis is but a version of it. If the Marxist criticism of religion is the necessary condition of its 'rescued truth', we want to know whether, in the upshot of that criticism, the Christian is left with anything to say which the Marxist is not already saying in his revolutionary theory and practice. We want to know if anything in post-critical Christianity 'transcends' that which is made immanant in that revolutionary practice. This, then, is the question to which the final two chapters must address the makings of an answer. But at least, perhaps, we will know in advance better than to suppose that this 'immanence' and this 'transcendence' are terms in polarity; and certainly we will find in the relation between these terms no basis for the view that they generate the polarity between 'religion' and 'politics' which is the common ground shared by 'fideistic' Christians and 'scientistic' Marxists.

NOTES

1　But see my discussion later in this chapter, pp. 195—8.
2　L. Althusser, 'Ideology and the Ideological State Apparatuses', in his *Lenin and Philosophy and other Essays*, London, 1971, p. 162.
3　Francis Barker, 'Science and Ideology', *New Blackfriars*, October 1977, p. 481.
4　Althusser, in *Lenin and Philosophy*, p. 169.
5　Karl Marx, *Grundrisse*, translated by M. Nicholaus, Harmondsworth, 1973, p. 83.
6　Ibid., p. 84.
7　Terry Eagleton, 'Marx, Freud and Morality', *New Blackfriars*, January 1977, p. 27.
8　Ibid., p. 24.
9　Karl Marx and Friedrich Engels, *The German Ideology*, edited and translated by C.J. Arthur, London, 1970, part I, p. 42.
10　A point ironically illustrated by the work of Hindess and Hirst, whose 'Marxist' elimination of all epistemological categories as

'ideological' represents the ultimate *reductio ad absurdum* of Althusserianism. See Barry Hindess and Paul Hirst, *Mode of Production and Social Formation*, London, 1977, chapter 1.

11 Cf. Eagleton, 'Marx, Freud and Morality', p. 21.

12 This is a radical inconsistency in Althusserianism which Hindess and Hirst do not fail to exploit, but in a tendency whose political consequences are disastrous.

13 Cf. L. Althusser, 'Marx's Immense Theoretical Revolution', in L. Althusser and E. Balibar, *Reading Capital*, London, 1970.

14 Cf. R. Descartes, *Meditations*, II.

15 T. Aquinas, *Summa Theologiae*, Ia, q. 87 al.

16 D. Hume, *Treatise* I, IV, vi.

17 I. Kant, *The Critique of Pure Reason*, B 157–9.

18 Descartes, *Meditations*, III.

19 Cf. J.-P. Sartre, 'La Liberté Cartesienne', *Situations*, I, Paris, 1947, pp. 314–34.

20 H. McCabe, 'The Myth of God Incarnate', *New Blackfriars*, August 1977, p. 353.

21 E. Schillebeeckx, *The Eucharist*, translated by N.D. Smith, London, 1968, p. 80.

12

Significant Amoralism

In chapter 10 I outlined in quite general terms the main claims of the 'strong-compatibility' thesis. The first is that Christianity must and can incorporate into its theology and practice the Marxist criticism of religion; the penalty attached to the failure to do this is that Christianity lapses into fideism and becomes unrescuably ideological. The question which remains, however, is whether, in the outcome of this criticism, Christianity is left with any resources from which to construct an equally fundamental criticism of the Marxist pretension to be morality. In my view that criticism of Marxism is urgent. It matters that the Christian be in a position to make it.

I

As a first step in the argument, a distinction needs to be drawn and a relation defined between 'strong' and 'weak' compatibility.

On a 'weak-compatibility' thesis it would be maintained that there are no formal inconsistencies between the theories of Marxism and the doctrines of Christianity; the assertion that there are no propositions in either which entail the denial of assertions held to be true in the other. It is clearly impossible to demonstrate that there cannot be any such inconsistencies, and nothing which I have argued so far (or will argue) pre-supposes that this can be done. So far I have argued only that *theism* is not weakly incompatible with Marxism, since it is consistent with the materialist theory of history and both Marxism and Christianity are consistent with the denial of ontological materialism. Of course, weak compatibility is a high-risk thesis taken by itself. For, although it is impossible to demonstrate, it is vulnerable to refutation by any significant counter-instance. At best I hope to have shown only that theism is not a counter-instance of this sort.

However, even if full consistency of doctrine is not demonstrable, it is possible to remain untroubled, because the strong-compatibility thesis does not actually require consistency of doctrine in the sense just defined — for the question of compatibility is 'dialectical', not, like that of formal consistency, logical. By this I mean that there is a possibility of genuine debate between Marxism and Christianity, because there are things which it is crucial to be able to say and realities with which it is crucial to be in cognitive contact, some of which it is possible to say or be in cognitive contact with only within Christianity and others only within Marxism. There are things to be said and done of which only Christianity makes sense, and things to be said and done of which only Marxism makes sense. The problem of compatibility arises because at crucial points Marxism makes nonsense of some of the things of which Christianity makes sense, and Christianity nonsense of some of those things of which Marxism makes sense. The need to think this tension out dialectically derives from the fact that it cannot be concluded simplistically that one of them must be wrong — as the logician, concerned with consistency, is tempted to do — without losing the capacity thereby to say some of the things which it seemed important to be able to say in the first place. Nor can you appeal to any third position of height at which the divergences are reconciled in a grand synthesis. There is no hope of any coherent synthesis between Marxist theory and Christian doctrines, and if I provide no arguments here, perhaps we can make do with the lower-grade evidence which is provided by some of the better-known attempts to create such syntheses, exemplified, again, by some of the Latin American 'theologies of liberation'. Persuasive as rhetoric, there is no substance in those happy-sounding metaphors stretched across biblical and Marxist categories, in which the *anawim* become the proletariat, liberation becomes redemption politicised, alienation is original sin, and even, I have heard, the priesthood is metamorphosed into Leninist revolutionary leadership.

The theological justification for raising the question of compatibility lies, therefore, not in the fact that at an utterly abstract level it is possible to construct such rhetorical homologies, but that, on the one hand, at every other level nothing of the sort is attainable, since Marxism and Christianity seem to be radically incommensurable languages, and, on the other hand, both ways of situating man in his world seem to be necessary on pain of reducing whole sectors of human experience to unintelligibility. The problem, then, is that we fail to understand how to relate to our world without either, and yet it is hard to see how to make sense of the conjunction.

Nonetheless there is one area of seeming doctrinal convergence between Christianity and Marxism to which a great deal of attention has been paid in the writings of 'liberation' theologians. This is in the notion that Christianity is, in some sense, 'essentially historical'. If Christianity can consistently accept the materialist theory of history, and if the Christian belief-system is not to be understood as merely the set of propositions which, *de facto*, are those held by individual members of the empirical institutions of Christianity — if, in other words, Christianity is essentially the *praxis* of those beliefs — then it can be seen, as Marxism itself must be seen, to be a praxis *of history*. This is to say that it is a historically conditioned action-system, defined by its relations with historical contingencies, and which could not, any more than Marxism can, have anticipated its historical origins, nor will it, any more than Marxism will, survive the completion of its historical tasks. Both, then, are historically contingent praxes, the praxes of particular, historically defined conditions. It is clear enough what these 'historical conditions' are for Marxism. They are those which we collectively call by the name 'capitalism'. Marxism, the scientific critique of capitalism, realises itself as this critique by abolishing the conditions which require it. Consequently, with the realisation of a universal and fully socialist society, Marxism, as the revolutionary praxis of capitalism, *eo ipso* eliminates itself.

It is all too easy for Christians to seize upon a strong analogy here, for Christianity too has its 'time'. There is an 'age' which Christianity will not survive. Awkwardly, however, for those much given to stressing the historicity of Christianity, the 'age' upon which it is supposed to be contingent is history *as such*. It thus is also given to claiming that Christianity 'transcends' any *particular* historical conditions, even if it does not claim to transcend historicity. The tensions here are difficult to define, let alone to maintain. On one side, Christianity is thoroughly 'historical': it is the historical form of the life of God. As Christianity it will not survive with whatever will survive history — if anything does. What, if anything, does survive history Christians call, variously, 'the Kingdom', 'eternal life', even 'heaven'. But in the Kingdom there will be no churches, no Church, no priests, no sacraments, no faith, no hope, only love, a fully socialised humanity and a fully humanised society — the life of God not any longer in the form of the 'sacred', but in the form of the life of *man*. In short, Christianity will realise itself only at the cost of its abolition *as Christianity*. It will realise itself as a fully human reality only by abolishing itself as a sacred reality, that is, as a Church, as a sphere of life apart.

But just for the reason that the historical life of God is necessarily expressed in the form of an 'apartness' from, a non-identity with, the contingencies of any particular historical epoch, Christianity cannot be identified with even that response to those conditions which, in a particular historical period, is demonstrably the scientifically warranted response. Christianity, under capitalism, cannot be identified with Marxism, even if it follows from the fact that Marxism is the scientifically justified response to capitalism that Christianity can know itself and the nature of its praxis only through the Marxist criticism of it. Marx often reflected on how pointless it was to attack religion simply as such without directing the attack at those conditions which, in ideology, seem to require it — as we saw in chapter 1. Christianity itself points to a similar strategy in its own critique of itself: it seeks to abolish itself by seeking to abolish those conditions which, in a particular period, require it to represent, to *symbolise* the depths of what it is to be human in the form of a sacredness, in the form of the refusal to admit that what is most fully human could be compatible with the conditions of alienation and exploitation which historically obtain. Thus the dynamic of Christianity consists in this refusal, expressed theologically in its witness to the fact that the Kingdom *cannot now be present*, that the human race cannot be fully human, that man's full humanity must exist partly in the form of those symbolic anticipations of it which cannot be yet realised in practice. Christianity needs Marxism under capitalism because Marxism is the knowledge of what those conditions are, under capitalism, which, in preventing man from being human, require that humanity to be expressed in the form of the sacred.

Those conditions are, under capitalism, the structures of domination and oppression, of exploitation, the structures of lies, mystification and hate, the machinery of war, of imperialism, of racism and of sexism. These structures are such that it can be only ideological to speak of loving[1] within them, just as it can be only ideological to speak of toleration on these terms. Consequently, one side of Christianity − a sorely understressed side of it − shares a parallel conviction with the Marxist, that it is in the business not of *loving*, but rather of securing the conditions of the possibility of loving. Christianity recognises that in the sense in which to love − to be fully human − is the point of its praxis, it is possible only to symbolise love, to anticipate it *in its absence*, and that it is ideological to claim any more for love in the conditions of bourgeois society.

In view of this, and anticipating important clarifications which I will be making in the last chapter, I introduce the formula that for the Christian love is 'present' within history *only in the form of its absence*. By this I mean, for the time being, that that presence is of that sort alone which love can have in a world whose governing structures are, in the last instance, structures of exploitation; that kind of existence alone which fully socialised humanity can have in a world of irrational competition over the resources of production and exchange; that kind of presence alone which Christ can have in a world of dehumanised, alienated social relationships.

And so it is necessary to say that Christ, or love, or community may be 'present' — indeed may be said to be 'really' present — in the world, but that they are present only in the form of their absence.

No doubt this formula is somewhat obscure (and I shall have something to say by way of explanation shortly), but in it lies the chief parallel with the Marxist argument about the possibility of morality. To see this, it is necessary to recall the structure of the whole of the preceding argument of this essay, involving, regrettably, a good deal of repetition. Morality, I have argued, is Marxism. It is so because morality consists in our knowledge of what to do, given the 'facts'. The overwhelmingly dominating fact of our age, which governs our reading of all other facts and simultaneously all inferences about what to do, is capitalism. But exactly as capitalism is the dominating moral fact, so it is the dominating scientific fact. Indeed it would not be the dominating moral fact were it not the dominating scientific fact, and what shows morality to be Marxism is whatever shows Marxism to be the fundamental science of capitalism.

Paradoxically, however, what Marxism shows about capitalism is that it is a set of conditions in which morality is ideological. This paradox I proposed to resolve by saying that although Marxism is, in a sense, 'amoral', since it argues the impossibility of moral knowledge in capitalist conditions, none the less it is all that morality can be under those conditions, since it is the theory and the practice of realising the conditions of the possibility of morality. What that theory determines in the way of strategic imperatives for the practice is the challenging of capitalism to realise its own truth, to practise the morality it cannot but preach, which it can never do without destroying itself. For capitalism cannot realise the moral imperatives which it generates. This practice of forcing capitalism to conform to the truth of itself is therefore a revolutionary practice. For since conformity is structurally impossible for capitalism, its moral imperatives can be realised only on the condition of its destructuring.

It is possible, therefore, and right, to speak of what I shall call the 'significant absence' of morality from Marxism. 'Absence', because Marxism does show that morality, as a project, cannot be realised under capitalism; but a 'significant' absence, because Marxism also locates the precise conditions and mechanisms whereby morality is forced, on pain of mystification, to be silent. This absence of morality from Marxism is thus no mere negation, no *mere* amoralism. Indeed, what Marxism exposes is the amoralism of capitalism which, to revert to a term introduced in chapter 3, 'cynically' perverts the very language which it generates. In the negative sense, therefore, it is capitalism, not Marxism, which is amoralistic. Marxism does not 'deny' morality. On the contrary, it is precisely in order to rescue it from cynical betrayals that it denies the possibility of its presence — imposes moral silence — in an inherently ideological moral world.

In an analogous way I have stressed a much neglected dimension of Christian thought which puts it alongside Marxism in this respect. 'Love', 'brotherhood', 'community' are, as I have said, 'present' for the Christian 'only in the form of their absence'. By this I mean, in part, what I am now calling 'significant absence'. Christianity sets the astringency of this assertion, its irony, in opposition to that real cynicism which must result from the platitudinous imperatives, so forthcoming from Christians, to 'love' *within* conditions of gross and systematic exploitation.

So much can be conceded by way of a parallelism between Christianity and Marxism. The argument has them converging upon a common strategy, not just incidentally, but by virtue of certain inner necessities of the life of each. First of all, there is a common relationship, within each praxis, between the conditions which require it as a praxis and the praxis itself of abolishing those conditions. In this lies what can be called their common 'historicity'. Both are committed to the elimination of themselves by means of the revolutionary elimination of the contingent conditions which require them to be what they are. Second, both praxes are governed by the overriding recognition of the need to exploit the field of what I have called the 'significant absence' and by a scepticism about the possibility of morality itself within capitalist conditions.

The problem with this argument, however, is that most

Christians today seem disinclined to accept it. In fact most Christians would probably wish to reject, as being too paradoxical, any such formula as that 'love is present only in the form of its absence' and, more particularly, my contention that love is not possible under the conditions of capitalism. For they will want to deny that the conditions of the possibility of love are in principle historical at all. For most Christians, Christianity is essentially the assertion, which to Marxists is essentially ideological, that *love is always possible*; that whatever the historical conditions, whatever else may be impossible (for example, justice) and for whomsoever else love may be impossible, for the Christian it is always possible to love.

Such Christians, moreover, do not hold this view just by the way. It appears to be a central claim of Christianity, one which Christians are impelled to maintain as a consequence of some of their more fundamental doctrines, in particular by the belief that in the historical person of Jesus, God intervened decisively just in order to alter human calculations of the possibilities. For in the risen Christ, it is held, God is present in a body which is uniquely and always *present*, ever available at *any* point in history. Here, again, the Marxist will detect the signs of Christian transhistorical pretentiousness. For if the risen Christ is the presence of God within history at any and every point, then clearly his being present is not dependent on any particular set of historical conditions. Equally, then, with morality: if Christ is ever-present to history, irrespective of particular historical conditions, then morality — love — is a possibility in any historical conditions. Why, then, should it matter to the Christian what at any particular historical juncture are the political, economic or social conditions of the time, if it is possible to love equally in any of those conditions? Newman exposes very graphically the theological roots of this dimension of Christianity:

When once Christ had come . . . nothing remained but to gather in his saints. No higher Priest could come, no truer doctrine. The light and life of men had appeared and had suffered and had risen again; and nothing more was left to do. Earth had had its most solemn event and seen its most august sight; and therefore it was the last time. And hence, though time intervene between Christ's first and second coming, it is not *recognised* . . . in the Gospel scheme, but is, as it were, an accident . . . When he says that he will come soon, 'soon' is not a word of time but of natural order. This present state of things, 'the present distress', as St Paul calls it, is ever close upon the next world and resolves itself into it.[2]

If, therefore, every point in time is equidistant from eternity, every point in time is as good and as bad as any other for loving. Whatever the conditions of the possibility of love are, they are realised by the resurrection of Jesus for all time. They are not, therefore, historically contingent conditions.

II

There is no doubt that today this emphasis on the transcendent presence and immediacy of God has become a platitude among those Christians (probably a majority at least in Europe) who are opposed to what they see as the 'politicisation' of theology — it is a sort of stock response, worth, none the less, a Reith lecture or two. For such people my formula will appear hopelessly negative and sceptical and, if one-sided, quite on the wrong side. Everything else may witness to the absence of God; Christianity, however, is alone in witnessing to his presence.

But I am inclined to regard this response as yet another phenomenon of that Christian fideism, according to which the relation of faith to its objects is autonomous and internal, in no way dependent on conditions which are not themselves matters of faith. Christianity, it is said, witnesses to the 'transcendent', where the 'transcendent' is understood as a realm of objects and agencies and events other than and apart from the historical, the political, the economic, indeed, the human. This realm — let us call it collectively 'the Kingdom' — is present within the secular, but not as being in any way dependent, for our relation to it, on any of those 'secular' conditions.

I suggested earlier that there is a version of Marxism which can be called a 'fideistic moralism', for it makes its supposed 'knowledge' of communist society into a kind of moral absolute, into a *given moral standard* against which the moral deficiencies of capitalism can be read off, as bad copy against its model. Likewise, there is a fideistic Christianity, which appeals to texts about the Kingdom being 'within you'[3] as if, to return to an analogy used earlier, the history which Christians are struggling to write is governed by some higher text *which has already been written* and to which they have privileged access — leaving only the i's to be dotted and the t's crossed, or, as Newman put it, leaving only 'the gathering in of the saints'.

But this will not do. So far as it goes the analogy is as exact for the Christian case as for the Marxist's. Indeed the as yet unwritten text *is* present in the struggle to write it, is present as a real norm governing even the fine detail of the creative struggle. But it is present, *really* present, not as already written, but as *absent*, not as that completed knowledge which finally reveals the significance of each fragment of the draft, but in the form of the fragments themselves, in so far as they both create the final outcome and derive their significance from the outcome they are making.

In this way my formula does not emphasise the absence of the 'Kingdom' *at the expense of* its presence: that is no better than, because it is no different from, any emphasis on the transcendence of God at the expense of his immanence, or vice versa. Rather, this formula emphasises what I take to be the fundamental meaning of Christianity itself, namely the fact that the presence of God, paradoxically, *takes the form of* his absence.

Of course, this formula needs the kind of explanation which I could give only if I were to say a great deal more than I have the space, or theological knowledge, to say in this programmatic essay, about the notion of a symbol. For to say that Christ is 'present in the form of his absence' is to say the same as that he is present in a sign, or symbol.[4] A 'symbol', in the sense in which I shall be using the term, is precisely the form of presence which a thing, person or event has in its absence. Indeed it *is* the presence of something in the form of its absence.

However paradoxical this formula may seem, it refers to a perfectly familiar and general feature of our experience. We speak unproblematically about 'Jones not being present' at a party at which he was, or might have been, expected. When we do so we refer to something about the party which people miss *in* it, and what they are noticing, in missing Jones, is Jones-in-the-form-of-his-absence. His absence is, in the context of the party, significant, a commentary on it and, in the sense of the word which I am employing here, his absence from the party is a symbol of him, or, to speak a little more precisely, those features of the party which derive from his not being at it are symbols of Jones, for they are his presence in the form of his not being there.

To say, therefore (somewhat cumbersomely) that Jones is present at the party 'symbolically' is indeed to contrast the mode of his presence with that which it would have taken had he turned up (that is, if he had been 'really' there), but that is by no means to say that symbolic presence is not a *real presence*. For it is one of the real features of the party that Jones is absent from it, his not being there has a real significance for the party and is capable of realising genuine effects, for example, on how the party goes: the better or worse for his absence.

Of course, there are an indefinite number of people who are not at the party whose absence is in no way significant. They are all the people who were not and could not have been expected to be there. The absence of such people has no 'reality' at all, for it consists merely in the non-realisation of an abstract and purely logical possibility. Such people are not, therefore, 'present in the form of their absence' but are *merely* not there.

It is important, therefore, not to make the mistake of supposing that the 'symbolic presence' of something is to be contrasted *tout court* with its 'real presence'. For although in one sense the symbolic presence of X necessarily implies the absence of X, in another it implies the real presence of its absence. But there is another mistake which it is just as important to avoid: that of supposing that a symbol of X is some other reality, Y, which is the 'symbol of' X. A symbol is not an empirical reality, plus a significance. The symbol is the significance itself. Jones's absence from the party is not some quasi-event or entity which is *given* the significance of his not being there, for his not being there is only 'real' via its significance, is only perceptible via its significance and only affects the party via its significance. Hence, if Jones's not being there is in some way 'real', its reality is nothing other than the reality of its significance.

In view of this it is possible to see why it is wrong for Christians to insist on some mode of the presence of Christ (or love) over and above that defined by the formula that he is present in the form of his absence; and equally why they would be wrong to press for some account of the possibility of morality over and above the possibility of a praxis concerned to realise the significance of the absence of morality. I shall leave the moral question for further consideration in the last chapter, but on the theological question it is true that Christians want to say both that the risen Christ is present to and that he is absent from history. But it would be quite wrong to suggest that this 'presence' of Christ to history takes any form other than that of his absence. It is not that Christians believe Christ to be present in the form of his absence (that is, symbolically) and that they also believe him to be in some other way 'really' present as well. For *that* form of the contrast between 'symbolic' and 'real' presence cannot be made. The sense in which Christ's presence is a form of absence is by contrast with two modes of presence which are now impossible for the risen Christ, namely the historical presence which was his before his death and his eschatological presence in the realised post-historical Kingdom. It is only in relation to these modes of presence that Christ is absent from history: but it is also *specifically as not being present in these ways* that Christ's presence within history is defined. There is no word in ordinary language which serves to describe the precise mode of this presence, but only a technical theological term. When Christians want to describe the mode of Christ's presence within history, they say, or traditionally have said, that it is 'sacramental', by which they have traditionally meant that it is his presence in the form of his absence, a symbolic, but none the less real, presence.

In so describing this mode of presence the Christian designates the only form of it which is possible within history. It is because of the structure of our social world as historical that no other presence is possible. Christians should not find this difficult to accept, for the author of John's Gospel knew it well enough; he has Jesus insisting on the very same paradox, that if he is to remain with his disciples after the resurrection he *must* go away:[5] (indeed we can say that Jesus' departure, the so-called 'ascension', is not so much a separate event from the resurrection, as part of its *meaning*). In the same way, therefore, as Jones's absence from the party is present in the party in the significance of this absence, so too the necessary absence of Jesus from history is understood in what we can make of its significance for history. That significance is discoverable only by reference to what it is in human history which requires that absence. Jesus is precisely *not* the ever-present 'centre of history'. His significance for history lies in his absence from it.

But, finally, we can only know those historical conditions historically, as they are found contingently in its actual course. We do not know 'historicity' as such, but only concrete historical conditions. It is for each age to discover its own history as a structure of concrete conditions requiring the absence of Christ, those structures which we have seen to be determinative of the impossibility − the 'presence in the form of its absence' − of morality. Here, then, the convergence becomes a full identity of praxes, for today it is the structures of the capitalist world which condemn our moral and religious language to that systematic ambiguity which chiefly characterises the ideological. It is those structures which demand that we do not claim, as Christians so cheerfully do, that, for example, the Church *is* a community or people. At any rate, if Christians are going to make this claim, it is one which has to be set beside the criticism of the language of communitarianism which Marxism provides.

The Church can never be a community under the conditions of capitalism, because the Church means by 'community' what it means by love, and what it means by 'love' is Christ. Everything which the Church claims about the reality and presence of Christ within history is shot through with its ironic perception of the necessary absence of Christ from history, an absence whose significance for history is exhibited by the necessary ambiguity of love and community — and of morality generally — and in the criticism of the conditions which require that absence. The Church itself is in this way a symbol or 'sacrament' of Christ. It *is* not community: it is the promise of community, the promise of the world as community and is the praxis of realising the conditions for the possibility of that outcome. It is for this reason that, as the Marxian formula puts it, the Church realises itself by abolishing itself — as it is in the general nature of promises to do. The material social conditions under which community is an unambiguous possibility for all men are just those under which the Church eliminates itself. The Church becomes a community just when mankind becomes a community. But *just* then the Church ceases to exist; which is why, for the Christian, the beginning of all criticism is the criticism of religion.

The idea, then, that the Church is *now* a community is but the fetishised, reified idea of a concrete historical future for mankind, expressed in the form of a reified ontology. As such the Church is, and unfortunately often has been, exactly what Marx said that it was. It is, however, theologically pretentious to say that the Church is a community. The Church is, in fact, either false to its historical mission, or else is a revolutionary movement. Of course, it is unfortunately true that the Christian Churches have often preferred, and continue to prefer pretending, to be communities — indeed just now they would seem to prefer being just one big happy 'ecumenical' community — to being a revolutionary movement. The Church has shown a constant proclivity to be a community concerned about itself rather than a praxis about the world. None the less this record of betrayal is but one half of the story; in response to the charge that historically speaking its role has been entirely reactionary, it must first of all be said that whatever about the facts of the matter the theological essence of Christianity is a commitment to just that praxis of emancipation to which the Marxist is committed: this, if only for the sake of rescuing any truth of its own.

Hence, in any historical epoch the most fundamental question the Christian is constrained to ask is how, in the material social conditions of that epoch, its revolutionary praxis is to be defined. Certainly the fideist is in this sense right: Christianity, unlike Marxism, is not *itself* a political doctrine; it does not out of its own resources alone pull out the appropriate revolutionary strategy, correct for any, let alone every, age, as it were like a rabbit out of a hat. On the contrary, the Christian Church has had constantly to redefine its historical mission — and therefore its ontology and belief-system as a whole — for every age and in terms of the revolutionary issues of that age. Thus if Christianity is not *itself* a political doctrine, it is of the nature of its own inner energies that it must set itself in relation to one; that, whichever it is, which in mediating the relations of the beliefs to the historical tasks of the age, will set them on a footing in that historical reality.

And is not this in fact what the empirical history of Christianity consists in: its pursuit of that analysis of contemporary conditions which will define its historical mission in the form of a contemporary praxis? And is it not just over the question of what analysis to back — or where agreed on analysis, what side to back — that Christianity has constantly divided itself? Is not this, after all, the true lesson which can be learned from the Peasant War in Germany, from the English Civil War, from the French Revolution, from the Industrial Revolution, even from the Russian Revolution? It is simply false that Christianity has always adopted a counter-revolutionary stance. What is true, however, is that it has always fragmented itself over the question of revolution or reaction. The Roman Catholic faction did, certainly, set its teeth officially against the bourgeois revolution, theologically in the sixteenth century, in an openly political way in the nineteenth, and not in the name of more advanced ideas, but in the name of neo-feudal reaction. On the other hand, some factions of the Protestant churches maintained a tradition of continuity with the bourgeois revolution, precisely by backing — in often exceptionally purist, if also sometimes wildly utopian ways — the implicitly democratic, anti-authoritarian freedoms of the bourgeois revolution. As we saw in chapter 9, long before the political theorists of the bourgeois revolution had set about containing its most radical implications, many Protestant groups had set out those implications in theological form: those Anabaptist, Levelling and Digging groups were already embodying ideas of democracy, freedom of conscience and consent far in advance of the bourgeois political theory, let alone the bourgeois political reality. Now, perhaps, when the bourgeois establishment has by and large exhausted its revolutionary potential, the Protestant churches lie by and large exhausted as Protestant, abolished as Protestant by their own realisation as bourgeois.

Now, too, it may be necessary, indeed it seems increasingly likely, that just when the official churches are drawing together in vertical ecumenical solidarity with one another — a movement which, in effect, amounts to the effort fully to bourgeoisify a still remarkably feudal Roman church — they will have to split horizontally over the question of the socialist revolution. If, on the basis of their domestic experience, British Christians might wish to doubt this prospect, they should reflect on the fact that by the end of this century more than half of all Roman Catholics will be living in Latin America alone and that there, but not only there, many signs are evident of an *alternative* ecumenism of socialist Christians in uneasy tension with the official ecumenism of the established churches. Not much can be safely predicted about what or how it will happen. But what does seem to be clear is that at least a new crisis of theology and praxis, pregnant with the possibility of schism, is being created for Christianity by the crises of capitalism itself, particularly by its failures in the Third World.

Theologically speaking Western Christians seem ill-equipped to cope with such a prospect. The force of my central proposition about compatibility is that if the Christian is to retain orthodox continuity with his own beliefs, the Christian must take up the historical tasks of revolutionary socialism. And we should be clear about why this is. This Christian commitment to Marxism derives not from some absurd general proposition that Christians should be in favour of revolutions. Christians are not revolutionary *on principle*.

To be a revolutionary on principle is to be an utterly un-principled revolutionary. And it is fair to say that as there are absurd Christians who are reactionary on principle, so there is an absurd kind of Christian who is a mere adventurist, in a permanent mental attitude of hostility to something called 'the world'. The Christian must now be a Marxist, if and only if the Marxist is right that the only way to be engaged with our own historical reality is through the praxes of the socialist revolution. For just so long as the 'world' is 'capitalism', Marxism is what defines the praxis of the Christian.[6]

It is, of course, no consequence of this argument that the completion of the tasks of revolutionary socialism necessarily spells the end of 'pre-history', nor that there cannot be any post-Marxist Christianity. There is no more reason to believe this than there is to believe that the world will necessarily survive long enough for the socialist revolution to replace capitalism at all. After all, it is technically possible to destroy the world in a day, and increasingly likely that we will. Furthermore, there are not and could not be any conclusive guarantees that, even if the world survives long enough for this to be possible, the socialist revolution will be necessarily successful. Marxists are not historicists. They do not maintain that there is one inevitable destiny of the human race. The Marxist holds only — and he must submit this proposition to the court of evidence — that for just so long as capitalism extends its grip on the world, and for just so long as capitalism thereby intensifies its own irrationalities and contradictions, revolutionary socialism is increasingly made to be the only rational response to it. There is reason to accept this, not because Marxism is endowed with gnostic powers of prophecy, nor because Christians are compelled to believe that love will necessarily conquer exploitation and hate. On the contrary, the normal Christian expectation is that if you love you will be killed. (The evidence for this proposition is hardly overwhelming in post-war Western Europe, but accumulates daily in that world the West impoverishes — another fact which Christians have always had reason to predict.) Rather, it is a question of what the technical, economic, political and social realities of capitalism allow the options to be, and they are, on the Marxist account of them, either that of living out the irrationalities of ideology or else of engaging in the class struggle simultaneously in the name of and in the hope of discovering what it is to love. A *Christian* has no such analysis. But he may be convinced that unless Marxism's anlaysis is just false, it, and it alone, defines those conditions under which the imperative to love may be freed from the *present* sources of its ideological, mystified ambiguities.

I emphasise the word 'present'. Who knows what further problems the future may have in store? And yet fear of the future is no grounds for failing to respond to the imperatives of love in the present. The Christian may believe that there is a 'final solution', but who is he to offer answers to questions which have not yet been asked? More particularly, is there not some basis for the Marxist suspicion that the Christian concern for *ultimate* solutions is often but a way of not coming to terms with Marxist questions about the present, is a symptom of that 'transhistorical pretentiousness' which is but a form of living in bad faith with history. Bad faith with history is, for the Christian, bad faith in God. One of the chief lessons from the theology of 'liberation' is its theological demonstration that, for the Christian, *ideology* and *idolatry* are synonyms. That is not another, theological, story. It is the story of this book.

NOTES

1   I do not attach here, or elsewhere in this essay, any specific meaning to the word 'love' beyond that sense of the term in which, for a Christian, it is equivalent to morality and morality equivalent to it. I mean by 'love', in brief, 'the moral life'. If this vagueness seems to be symptomatic of the general 'abstractness' of the argument as a whole, I can only re-emphasise the point that the moral life is not a set of results which are given to us unambiguously by history, nor a set of prophecies which will be given to us in the future. 'Morality' is both what we wrest from ideology in the present struggle with it and the struggle itself to wrest what we can from ideology. How and when that struggle acquires the name of 'love' is what this and the next chapter are about.

2 J.H. Newman, *Parochial and Plain Sermons* (1868), VI, xvii.

3 Luke, 17:21. Actually, the translation of the phrase is uncertain. RSV translates 'is in the midst of you' giving 'is within you' as an alternative, less favoured by the context. The Jerusalem Bible gives 'is among you'. My thanks are due to Dr Margaret Pamment for pointing this out to me.

4 I use the terms 'sign' and 'symbol' interchangeably and in ways unrelated to the various ways there are of distinguishing between them, which in any case vary between philosophical, anthropological and theological uses.

5 John, 16:7.

6 Peter Hebblethwaite (in *The Christian Marxist Dialogue and Beyond*, London, 1977, pp. 106–7) once took me to task for saying that capitalism is wholly evil itself and the cause of all the evil there is. I do not maintain this and never did. In fact I think that capitalism does cause a great deal of evil, but I have been at great pains not to make my case rest on this fact, to the point, perhaps, of protest from the many millions in the world who quite straightforwardly starve to death or get killed in the direct interests of capital. My case is, to repeat, that what capitalism causes — more strictly, 'structures' — is an *ambiguity between* good and evil, an ideological blurring of moral judgement itself. It is, therefore, inextricably bound up with that evil which it does directly cause, since it is structured upon the misperception of that evil. It cannot, that is to say, survive the revolutionary recognition of its evil *as evil*. But what is more significant, it cannot even survive the revolutionary realisation of what is good in it — see chapter 9.

13

The Possibility of Morality

I freely admit that I end this book with a question to which I do not give any satisfactory answer. Unfortunately that question is the main question to which this work has been addressed — is morality possible? My argument has taken us a short way along the route to an answer, but only so far as to get us to another, more technical, version of the same question. For so far all the answers given have been by way of reflection on the question of what morality, if it is possible, would be like. We have, as it were, some account of the shape of what morality must be, and I have presented the case that bourgeois morality does not have it, for what imperatives do seem to be derivable from within the bourgeois social world derive from its ideological misperception of that world. It therefore seemed to me that whatever theory and praxis had the shape of an adequate criticism of that ideological morality would have the shape of morality; that the shape of that criticism is defined by the strategy of 'rescuing the truth' from ideology; and that Marxism has that shape. Consequently, morality is Marxism.

None the less the 'Marxism' in question is an ambiguous phenomenon and in two distinct, though related, ways. First, 'Marxism' *the theory* is ambiguous between that which is equipped conceptually to acknowledge its role as bearer of the moral task and that which, in its 'scientistic' positivist form, is not. Second, Marxism in many of its *institutionalised* forms seems altogether to be disqualified for this moral role by its record. The two ambiguities are, however, crucially related in the fact that what has actually happened is that the 'Marxism' institutionalised, for example, in Soviet Russia, is precisely that scientistic, positivist theory which evacuates the criticism of ideology of any moral reference. This Marxism has projected its 'science' beyond the present constraints of the very morality it avows and so, filled with the strength of its 'science', happily plays power-games over the graves of its victims in a supposed moral vacuum of history. Its 'moral silence' is the silence of the *moral* graveyard too.

It seemed, therefore, that a Marxism which would be adequate to the proposition which its moral task imposes on it would be a Marxism which is capable of demonstrating both how the 'present' bourgeois morality has no future which is not within the socialism which destroys it and how the commitment to that future none the less lays the activity of bringing it about under the moral constraints, not of bourgeois morality, but of that future itself. In formal terms, that Marxism would have to be capable of demonstrating how that morality is both 'absent' and 'present', or, more precisely, is 'present in the form of its absence'.

It was for this reason that Christianity was entertained in the argument. For at least it has the language of the problem, in theory it too has the shape of an adequately defined morality, that shape which we need in view of the tasks which the world sets for us morally. But it too is an ambiguous phenomenon, if, in theory part of the solution, too often it is in fact part of the problem. The second major proposition of this book has, therefore, been that only a Christianity which has freed itself both theologically and politically from its complicity with bourgeois morality is in any position to speak to Marxism with moral authority; that it is in the dialectics of what I have called 'strong compatibility' that the shape of morality, in theory and practice, is to be found.

But if that is what morality is, what shows that it is possible? What shows that the question has an answer? More particularly what shows that there is future which lays the present under its constraints? This, I say, is the question to which I do not, in this book, give any answer; at any rate I do not attempt to show that there *is* an answer to this question, even if I cannot leave my argument altogether unsecured in any view as to what would count as an answer to it. In this book I do not take the justification of morality beyond the following propositions: if morality is to be justified, it will be by whatever shows that there really is a future state of affairs which governs and shapes our present historical action of achieving it; and this will be so, even if the actual achievement of that future *within history* is not to be counted upon, even if, in other words, the achievement of that outcome in its final form must, as the Christian believes, be ultimately in the character of a gift, a 'resurrection'. And I should want to say only this about the possibility of there being such a future, and so of the possibility of morality: whatever it is, if anything, which would give us grounds for believing that there is such a future outcome is what we would have to call by the name 'God'. And so I will take leave of the argument of this book with the agenda outlined for another, which is a necessary complement to the first.

I

But there is some mopping up to be done in the meantime. I have distinguished, broadly, between a Marxism which is equipped and a Marxism which is not equipped to be the bearer, under capitalism, of the historical role of morality. More needs to be said about this distinction, if we are to see in what way the two Marxisms differ in their capacity to generate substantive moral judgements about the conduct of the revolutionary-critical struggle.

The paradox of Marxism is that only it can claim to be morality, and yet what it shows about morality is its impossibility under capitalism. It was for this reason that since chapter 9 I have preferred the formula that Marxism is all that morality can be under capitalism and that its relation to morality is as the revolutionary movement, the practice, of achieving the conditions of the possibility of morality. It secures its credentials as such in so far as it has correctly identified within the structures of capitalism the lines of social causality leading to a revolutionary break with capitalism and therefore with class antagonisms and their basis in private property; and it secures those credentials only in so far as it can credibly be represented as the praxis of achieving that revolutionary break, a praxis which is governed by the moral constraints of its heuristic knowledge of the goal of emancipation.

It should be noted, however, that for 'scientistic' Marxism the relationship of this revolutionary struggle to the result which it is meant to secure — communist society — is a purely *causal* relationship. And this is the fundamental reason why, in the end, such Marxisms fail to satisfy the conditions for morality in the sense required, the reason why, in other words, for these Marxisms the present struggle does not itself lie under the constraints of that future morality for which it purports to struggle — if it genuinely sees itself as doing even that. For in a full account of morality we need not only the knowledge of what actions are such as to bring about, causally, the possibility of morality, but also, within that class of actions, the knowledge of which of them are such as to disclose *now* that reality of which they are the causally antecedent conditions.

Put a little more plainly, the relationship between action and goal of action — the relationship of 'means' to 'end' — has, within moral thought, a dual aspect, a causal dimension and what I shall call a 'symbolic' dimension, these in relations of extreme complexity to one another. 'Scientistic' Marxism, however, fails to do justice to this complexity because, in its positivistic conception of 'science', it can do justice only to the causal dimension at the expense of the symbolic.

'Scientistic' Marxism has appropriated from true Marxism — and has then reified it — the capacity to do justice to the nature of, and the laws governing, the socially causal relations between means and end. Certainly, for any adequate account of morality we need knowledge of such laws. We need to know of an action X whether it is such as to contribute causally to the bringing about of the state of affairs which is its goal. And to do this we need all the apparatus of classical Marxism, in particular we need an account of the 'initial' or 'boundary' conditions, as they are called, within which any causal agency operates. It is this knowledge which Marxism claims to provide. What our actions succeed in bringing about socially and historically is determined by the structure of society and by the historical possibilities which that structure allows for, as we saw in the cases of Münzer and Winstanley.

These, the 'initial' conditions, are what Marx refers to in a famous phrase: 'Men make their own history . . . but under circumstances directly encountered, given and transmitted by the past'.[1]

Marx employs a wide variety of terms and expressions to denote the social mechanisms of capitalism which are, in this sense, the 'initial conditions' determining causal chains between social action and social effect. Central to this vocabulary are three groups of terms which are linked together within the theory of historical materialism as a whole in systematic relations and in degrees of fundamentality: the economic, the political and the ideological. The basic description of the initial conditions is economic and consists in that most complex part of the theory which describes the mechanisms of exploitation — of the extraction of surplus value by capitalists from the unpaid labour of workers. The economic analysis is presupposed by the political description of capitalist society as a construction out of the conflict between two broad classes — roughly between the social and political organs constructed on the economic roles of extracting surplus value or having surplus value extracted. In turn, as we have seen, the theory of ideology presupposes this class conflict, since the mechanism which that theory describes is that by which ideas generated by class conflict serve only to obscure the class conflict from which they arise.

Now there are two common forms of objection to the Marxian causal theory, implying as it does a form of social determinism. The first, which is quite general and directed at the determinism itself, is that it is inconsistent with the so-called 'freedom of the will'. The second is directed specifically at the theory of ideology which, by placing 'ideas' within the context of material causes, appears to deny that ideas themselves can be causally efficacious, which, it is sometimes said, is internally inconsistent. For is not Marxism itself a system of ideas which are supposed to cause social, indeed, revolutionary results?

As regards the first of these objections, it is nothing but the confusion of the truistical with the false to interpret Marx's talk about the determinism of 'initial conditions' as having any bearing on the psychological question of 'free will'. Marx's determinism is full-blown and is not susceptible to queasy revisionisms. But it has no bearing on the matter of the freedom of the will, any answer to which question is consistent with the determinism of Marx. The question of whether men's wills are free or not is a question about whether men are free or not to choose which action to do in any situation in which doing alternative actions is a logical or physical possibility. So far as I know Marx is utterly silent on this question and with good reason, since his determinism is not intended as an answer to the question 'on what conditions of freedom or otherwise do men choose to do what they do?' but to the question 'what determines what their actions *count as*, socially and historically?' I may or may not determine freely what I do. But I do not determine autonomously what that which I do *means*. I may freely, or otherwise, decide what to buy in the supermarket out of the range of commodities on the shelves. But what makes my exchanging of metal tokens for those commodities at the check-out *to be an act of buying* is no decision or intention of mine either to buy or to call what I am doing 'buying', but the mechanisms of the social institutions of exchange and money. If I choose, even freely, to make these transactions under those 'initial conditions', then *necessarily I buy*.

It may perhaps be conceded that Marx's determinism is compatible with the freedom of the will. But it may not be so readily conceded that the theory of ideas (theory of ideology) can be appropriately couched in causal terms. In view of this it is important to remember that, as I argued earlier,[2] Marx never denied that ideas are socially efficacious. He denied merely that ideas, precisely in their character as ideas (that is, *as mental*) could have material, social effects. It is in their 'materiality' as social events that ideas are caught up into that web of causally interacting social phenomena which the determinist theory explains. What the social occurrence of an 'idea' says is, according to Marx, a function of what its occurrence *does*, and what it does is a matter governed by entirely different laws than those which govern the relationships between ideas *as ideas*. Laws of the latter sort are laws appropriate within the 'interpretative' disciplines — logic, hermeneutics, literary criticism and so forth. And I know of no evidence of a tendency in Marx to deny the autonomy of these disciplines in themselves. What Marx does reject, and quite rightly, is any attempt to ascribe a social causality to ideas just in virtue of their content taken by itself, or, alternatively, any view, for example, of literature which, in the name of purely 'literary' criteria, explicitly or in effect, denies their reality as effects within an overall complex of social (that is, material) causation.

Given these distinctions, it is now possible to introduce a new, more abstract, but only verbally distinct formula for the mechanism of ideology. I shall now say that an ideology is *a system of signs which are both social effects and social causes. But they are signs which, on the one hand, mis-signify what causes them and, on the other, cause that which, as signs, they deny.* Cumbersome as this formula may be, it is none the less precise. Furthermore, it brings out what is fundamental in the structure of all ideology, namely that ideology is a disease in the relationship within a sign between *causal* and *symbolic* efficacy. The morality of toleration is in this way a system of 'signs' which is needed for (caused by) a class society. Yet, on the one hand, it mis-signifies the class society which causes it by representing it as an *order* and, on the other hand, by means of this mis-signification plays an efficacious role (as repressive tolerance) in the very class oppression which, in what it signifies, it denies.

Marxism has at its disposal the causal theory equipped to unravel the complex contradictions between sign and effect out of which ideology is built. It is in a position theoretically to predict what 'signs' will have what effects. And it is in a position to do this because it is not misled by the idealistic illusion that 'signs' necessarily bring about as effects that which they signify. All the same, the technical apparatus of historical knowledge of the contingent laws of capitalism at best give only a causal theory of the relations between signs and their social causes and effects.

If, as in 'scientistic' Marxism, this were all that Marxism had to offer, then it would follow that morality could not, in the meantime, be identified with Marxism. If ideology, as social cause, brings about that which, as sign, it denies, 'scientistic' Marxism, on the contrary, is a causal agency which is without that symbolic reference to what it causes which is required as a credential for morality. Supposing, then, that we could plausibly construe Stalinist (or Brezhnevian) Russia as a means necessary to a final moral outcome of which we could approve (and this is to suppose a great deal), still in no way can those Stalinist conditions be taken to represent anything much of the moral form of that outcome, to be *saying* anything about what that outcome is like. It thus utterly fails to symbolise what it (dubiously) is a means of achieving.

And in so far as Soviet Russia is a product of this 'scientistic' Marxism,[3] this is exactly what we should have expected. For that Marxism eschews all reference within the revolutionary struggle with capitalism to that moral order which it seeks to bring about, other than to the causal conditions of its possibility. On this account it may be possible, although I doubt it, to construe that Marxism as the revolutionary *agency* of the possibility of morality. But it can in no way make 'present' the demands which the goals of that struggle make upon the conduct of it.

II

To be absolutely clear about the exact nature of this morally deficient Marxism, we can compare its position with that of authentic Marxism on the interconnected questions of toleration and violence. Authentic Marxism, we saw, treats toleration as a 'systematically ambiguous' requirement of the capitalist social order. The historical demand for toleration has to be regarded as an irreversible advance in civilisation, and yet it also has to be seen, under capitalism, as ideological. The logic of the Marxist strategy towards the demand for toleration is to push capitalism to meet the conditions under which toleration could be universalised. To push capitalism so far is to push capitalism over the brink, since ultimately those conditions can be met only in a classless society. This strategy does, it seems to me, bring together successfully, in the required measure of unity, a symbol — toleration — and the socially causal action of realising the conditions of the possibility of toleration. It thus represents paradigmatically revolutionary socialist morality. The strategy is *symbolically* adequate because toleration, its principle, is *part of* what would be essential to that state of affairs — communist society — which it causally brings about: the strategy of 'rescuing the truth' of toleration signifies, anticipates symbolically, what it effects.

If, however, Marxism is the necessary form of the criticism of morality — necessary from the point of view of its realisation — it has, of itself, *no* power to originate moral concepts of itself. There are, in fact, absolutely no moral insights for which Marxism has been responsible. It cannot even pretend to be the morality of the future. Rather, it is the science and the strategy directed towards the future in which what will count as morality is a matter to be settled by men acting under relatively, though decisively, freer conditions than they can under capitalism. What Marxism 'knows' of that morality it derives wholly from other sources: in the case of toleration from bourgeois moral thinking. The point can be made more generally: Marxism is not a visionary humanism, it is not a new ethic of universal brotherhood, or sisterhood, or of love, or even of a 'disalienated' future for mankind. There would in any case be nothing new about such age-old ideals. In so far as it 'knows' its own teleological imperative of 'emancipation', it knows it only within the critique of the capitalist conditions which themselves demand that goal, even if, at the same time, they inherently frustrate it. Marxism is both less and more than a new morality. Less, because it has no moral notions of its own to offer; more, because it is the science and the practice of the possibility of morality itself.

The contribution of authentic Marxism to what I have argued is both a symbolically and a causally adequate moral strategy is, therefore, that it can specify the causally necessary conditions for the symbolic adequacy of moral action *in the present*. For its goal of emancipation is not wholly absent, it is also present in the actions of achieving it. It can show this because what it does seek knowledge of are those mechanisms of the capitalist social formation whereby are generated moral symbols and imperatives, which both distort what they signify and cause what their signification denies. It is only in the light of an understanding of these mechanisms that it will be possible to disclose the technical principles for the required moral casuistry of a revolutionary socialist ethic.

It is just here, though, that the paradoxes come through to the surface. One of these is that the Marxist is often constrained to conclude that *it is not necessarily only by means of tolerating that the truth of toleration can be rescued.* It would be an idealistic misreading of the dialectics of this strategy if it were thought, in neo-Kantian spirit, that only such actions are justified whose principles we can envisage as a constituent of some moral utopia. For this would be to escape the clutches of an amoralist scientism only to fall into those of a fideistic moralism which, as we have seen, would have all actions to be performed in the name of some already written historical text which is their norm. On the contrary, Marxism recognises that it may be perfectly consistent with the strategy of rescuing the truth of toleration that one does not tolerate in particular instances. All Marxists would agree that it is necessary to be intolerant towards those claims and interests whose satisfaction can be shown merely to ensure the hegemony of the ruling class in capitalist society. And Marxists are surely right in taking this view. For toleration would be reduced to an ideological banality, if invoked to require the toleration of such interests and claims, since it would be simply to employ the principle of toleration in the reproduction of the conditions which frustrate its realisation. In clear-cut cases there is no theoretical problem about this, since such toleration would be neither causally nor symbolically efficacious. Not only would such action frustrate the goal of bringing about a genuinely tolerant society; it would also miscall what toleration *means.* No one could learn what toleration is from its abuse in such cases: indeed they could only mislearn what it meant to be tolerant if they took them to be instances of tolerant behaviour.

In any case there is a further point, not perhaps sufficiently emphasised in my argument so far. We cannot assume that toleration, in the form of the bourgeois moral imperative, will turn out to mean in socialist conditions what it means in bourgeois conditions. If this is not taken into account, the notion of 'rescuing the truth' of bourgeois morality is easily misunderstood as implying that bourgeois toleration is 'bourgeois' and ideological only in its *effects* within a class society, as being part of a mechanism reproductive of class dominance; and that it is possible to disentangle the 'true meaning' of toleration from its involvement with this mechanism of social reproduction within bourgeois society. But it is not possible to do this, for the reason given earlier: within bourgeois society bourgeois morality is ideological, which means that within bourgeois society morality is *inherently* ambiguous between truth and falsity. To revert to the analogy used earlier,[4] when a writer discovers the right words to 'fit his thoughts' he *discovers* what he wanted to say and that the words he has discarded were not saying it. He does not already know what he wants to say and then fits words to it. Likewise, we do not know from bourgeois morality what morality is and then seek to find the conditions of its possibility. Rather, in seeking to unbind bourgeois toleration from the constraints of bourgeois society we are setting in motion the processes of learning what toleration *means*: and that is also what we mean by moral action.

For both these reasons it is quite wrong to understand the strategy of 'rescuing the truth' of bourgeois morality as a simple rule-governed activity of, as it were, forcing bourgeois society to live by its own moral code as it is understood in bourgeois conditions. The strategy has to be more complex than that and, among other things, that strategy must allow for the principled refusal to tolerate, in certain circumstances, for the sake of toleration itself. I therefore introduce the important meta-moral principle of the 'inclusion of counter-instances under a rule'. To illustrate what I mean by it, I adduce the (to English ears) disreputable example of the defensive tactics of Italian football teams. Clearly the point of playing football is to win and therefore to score more goals than the opposing team scores. This means at least sometimes taking the ball into the opposing team's half of the field. It is equally clear that only an observer wholly ignorant of football would conclude from the fact that a player passed the ball back, away from the opposing team's goal, that he was thereby somehow contributing to the advantage of his opponents. Sometimes to get the ball intelligently forward it is necessary to pass back. Of course, if none of the players in a team ever passed the ball forward outside his own half, the team could not be said to be trying to score at all and therefore could not be said to be trying to win, but at best to be trying not to lose. But short of such an exceptionless rule there is no precise minimum number, or even proportion of moves of an attacking sort which is required of a team which can be said to be trying to win.

The tactics of Italian football teams approximated, it was once thought, to an ideal minimum. It was possible to wonder sometimes how you would convince a Martian observer that the point of the game was to score goals. But even in the heyday of their boringness, Italian teams did not in fact lose or even draw more often than they won. Just when observers (and more to the point, the opposing side) had been lulled by sheer frustration into carelessness, the Italians would score on the break. Suddenly the whole strategy is illuminated by one carefully timed move. The defensiveness, which had seemed to be mere spoiling, a refusal to play the game, is illuminated as the refusal to play *the opponent's game* — or, more strictly, the refusal to let the opponents play their own game — all as part of a strategy of winning. Had they not scored, we should not have seen this. But when they do, we can re-read all their defensiveness as being part of a pattern of play the only point of which was, in the end, to win.

This granted, Italian football was, of course, unattractive to watch. To suggest this as a criticism is to suggest that the entertainment value of football matches requires that teams should try to win by attacking more often than they defend. But on the supposition that to adopt an attacking policy is to put yourself at a disadvantage relative to the other team — your team lacks their strength and stamina, say — then the requirement to be entertaining would amount to the requirement that you adopt tactics with which you are less likely to win than with the defensive tactics which come naturally to your team. Your team will have every right to complain if the point of playing the game — its entertainment value — is defined in such terms that your opponent's strategy is given the advantage, so that, in not playing *their* game, you are said not to be playing *the* game.

This analogy can be partially extended to explain the moral strategy of the 'inclusion of counter-instances under a rule'. Although clearly non-tolerating cannot itself be justified as a *rule* of the social game, none the less it would be just as insane to suppose that no act of non-tolerating can ever be justified as it would be to suppose that passing back is never justified in football. Furthermore, just as there is no fixed minimum proportion of forward moves which is criterial for trying to win at football, so the justification for non-tolerating in the social game does not depend on any fixed ratio of acts of toleration to acts of non-toleration. It is perfectly intelligible to envisage a form of the social game of tolerating in which most moves are non-tolerating moves, so long as some moves are tolerating moves and they are crucial ones, that is, moves which establish that the game being played is that of tolerating. This, in the end, is what counts, in tolerating as in football. It is only as forming a part of a pattern of game-winning play that defensive play is justified. Likewise, it is only as part of a pattern of tolerating activity that non-tolerating behaviour is justified.

In what way must non-tolerating behaviour be 'part of' a pattern of tolerating behaviour? The initial, but insufficient answer is that it must be a *necessary* part of such a pattern, that is to say, it must be required by that pattern as a condition of its being precisely that — namely, a pattern of tolerating behaviour. But this reply is insufficient, because the notion of 'tolerating behaviour' is ambiguous between that activity which is merely designed to bring about a state of affairs in which actual tolerating is made a universal and non-ideological possibility and that activity which is able symbolically to represent what it would *mean* to be tolerating in that state of affairs. The necessity, therefore, of the non-tolerating activity depends for its character on whether what is in question is symbolic or causal necessity. It is in the latter sense that Marxism provides the analysis on the basis of which we can judge the necessity of non-tolerating activity. The Marxist theory of ideology enables us to see under what conditions positively tolerating activity would be morally counter-productive; counter-productive because it would causally contribute to the frustration of the goal of bringing about conditions in which genuine and non-ideological toleration would be possible. Marxism, then, enables us to see when, by contributing to the frustration of what it signifies, tolerant activity would be merely ideological.

This point can be made more clearly if we compare this 'casuistry' of non-toleration with that of violence. Toleration is a value or symbol which can in itself represent what the moral strategy of toleration is designed to bring about, because we can see toleration as being a constituent part of that state of affairs. Class violence, violence in the conduct of the class struggle cannot, on the other hand, be so regarded. Marxism is perfectly capable of establishing this, since it is the science and practice of the elimination of class itself. There will be no classes in communist society and, *a fortiori*, no class violence. There is, therefore, no form of violent action between classes, from whichever side it comes, which can, *of itself*, symbolise an alternative future for the human race; none which can, of itself, *say* anything to signify a rupture with the present necessities of class society. There is, as a result, nothing to be said for any sort of violence in itself, because violence, in itself, has nothing whatever to say: except, perhaps, something about what appears to make it necessary.

None the less, a clear-cut distinction can be made in principle within the class of violent actions, all of which are in themselves excluded from a symbolic role, between those which are *excluded by* whatever does symbolise communist society and those which are *necessary* if those symbols are not to fail in their capacity to symbolise it. Here again, Marxism can supply the required casuistry. Violence in the cause of oppression, or (and this comes to the same thing in most cases) violence in the cause of the maintenance of the capitalist hegemony, not only fails to signify in itself, but is part of a pattern of behaviour which is *excluded by* whatever does symbolise a society which is rid of class violence. On the other hand, violence directed against class oppression in such cases where non-violent action would undermine the capacity to symbolise peace becomes necessary — necessary, that is to say, as part of a pattern of symbolically adequate pacifist behaviour.

Consequently, the authentic Marxist strategy condemns,

and rightly, any insane suggestion that only positively tolerant or pacific behaviour is justified in the waging of the class struggle. In view of the way in which, in a class society, the odds are so heavily stacked in favour of ruling-class interests, the suggestion that only positively tolerating or pacifist behaviour is justified is analogous to the requirement on Italian football teams that they should play only entertaining, attacking moves.

The suggestion parades as the requirement that Italians 'play the game'. It is in fact the requirement that they play to their own disadvantage, that they play their opponents' game, one which they can only lose. In chapter 6 we saw how bourgeois toleration is ideologically tied in with bourgeois preconceptions about capitalism as a social order. From the point of view of those whose real interests can never be secured or even transparently identified within that 'order', to play the game of toleration is to play into the hands of those who control the rules of it — the bourgeoisie itself. It is for this reason that bourgeois toleration fails even to symbolise what a genuinely tolerant social order would be like. To say 'I must tolerate the class enemy in order to represent the possibility of the classless society against which he violently struggles' is, normally, an utterly self-defeating policy. For not only will this normally be to hold back the revolutionary struggle in real effect, it even fails to signify any genuine notion of toleration at all. Both causally and symbolically it spells nothing but defeat.

Causally non-reactionary efficacy is therefore a necessary condition of symbolic adequacy. Marxism is the causal theory required for any judgement on that adequacy. But a causal theory is not a sufficient condition. For just as the negative, defensive play of the football team is illuminated as part of a strategy of winning by the flash of attacking brilliance — and is justified only thereby — so non-tolerating has the capacity to say something positive about what the revolutionary means by an alternative society, only as illuminated by acts of positive toleration which are both their point and their justification. This is, in fact, the nature of revolutionary activity — to refuse to tolerate or love where the bourgeoisie require these forms of behaviour in the interests of their spurious order and then to offer toleration and love just at that point where the bourgeoisie have to refuse it or else abandon their class interest — at the point where to offer love represents the demand for a new order of things, where to love and to tolerate is to begin to say something entirely *new*.

The appropriate moment for such acts of positive love and toleration is incredibly difficult to judge. Getting the occasion right, however, is of the greatest importance, for on our capacity to do so depends any hope of our rescuing an ordered moral language from the disordered shipwreck visited upon it by our bourgeois ideologies. It is the condition of this possibility that we restore the language of love, of toleration and of peace and justice to that context in which alone it can make unambiguous demands on us, to its proper place within the revolutionary struggle to emancipate society from the contradictions to which advanced capitalism has condemned it. It is a mere intimation of what the effects of such a moral restoration would be like that Marx himself, the self-appointed epigone of amoralism, can quite unselfconsciously and without a trace of humbug employ the whole armoury of conventional moral appraisal in straightforwardly moral condemnations of capitalism for its brutalisation of children, women, men, mind and matter in the factory system.[5] Marx has no need to be afraid of such language because he has it firmly entrenched within the revolutionary theory and practice, where it has an ordered relation to its object. Outside that theory and practice, however, the language of morals is humbug.

If, by contrast with the case of Marx himself, scientistic Marxism insists on its autonomy and self-sufficiency in respect of morality, then there will be no conclusion to be drawn but that the structure of revolutionary theory and practice is that of a dramatic, but still shoddy expediency, on the principle that any means can be justified by the end alone. It is vital to an understanding of the distinction between authentic and inauthentic Marxisms, that the principle of 'the inclusion of counter-instances under a rule' should be sharply distinguished from this expediency and I cannot end this essay without some explanation of this distinction.

III

The principle of expediency, far from being identical with my principle, is exactly what my principle is designed to exclude. On a purely causal conception of the means/end relationship it will not, of course, matter at all whether it is by tolerating or by refusing to tolerate that the required result is achieved, so long as it is achieved. Scientistic Marxism, however, represents itself as nothing but a highly elaborated causal theory of the social mechanisms, and the theory of ideology is a sub-theory about the causal conditions in terms of which the social effects of bourgeois morality are explained. Consequently, the concern of the theory with morality itself is self-limitingly confined to those aspects of its symbol-conveying capacity which are related to its social results. This Marxism is just a special case of the fetishism of 'what works', plus an unusually elaborate theory of social agency. Perhaps it can tell us what will be the result, whether progressive or reactionary, of torturing or not torturing class enemies in particular circumstances, and it may even be capable of generalising from particular cases to strategies permissive or intolerant of torture in general terms. But scientistic Marxism refuses to acknowledge that in addition to the strategy of using means which are effective of the required ends (and supposedly justified by those ends alone), essential to morality is the strategy of using means which are related to the end not just causally, but also as part of a pattern of behaviour which is related symbolically to the result which it causes.

There is all the difference in the world between these. Indeed the difference is that between there being and there not being a moral world at all. We enter the world of morality only when we acknowledge that action has to obey the laws not only of causal adquacy but of symbolic adequacy as well. There is all the difference, therefore, between an outlook which justifies violence because of its predicted social outcome and an outlook which justifies violence only when without violent action the attempt to love will necessarily fail, where the refusal of violence will destroy the capacity of the behaviour to exhibit the meaning of love. It is the difference between saying: 'This act of violence is justified against *N* because he is the class enemy' and saying 'This act of violence against the class enemy is justified because there is no other way in which I can show what it means to love.' The first is a pre-moral response: the second may be the *sine qua non* of the survival of moral talk itself.

And so we have come to the central point of distinction between that Marxism which can and that Marxism which cannot claim to be what morality is. Authentic Marxism refuses to accept, as having the capacity to make moral demands on it, that bourgeois morality which it criticises. But the form of that criticism is neither that of a moralism which claims knowledge of an alternative moral order, nor is it that of an amoralistic positivism which denies that there are any moral claims laid upon its conduct of the class struggle. For neither take real history seriously; the first, by supposing that what can only be won in and through the historical struggle is already given to it a priori, the second, by supposing that no previous history has won anything at all by way of moral advances.

Authentic Marxism is related to the moral order of capitalism as its 'rescued truth'. It must, therefore, presuppose that there is a truth to be rescued within bourgeois morality. If not, then there is no morality to be known. For if Marxism knows anything of morality at all, it knows only that which it can wrest from the contradictions and anomalies of ideological morality. What it can wrest from ideology, it may claim to 'know'. But what it knows from the moral point of view, it lies under the authority of.

But if this is how the distinction between authentic and inauthentic Marxism is to be made out, then a question is raised as to what is left to differentiate authentic Marxism from authentic Christianity, and, connected with this, there is the question as to how morality, whose shape is identified in the authentic Marxist tradition, is to be justified. And here I can only gesture towards the possibilities of an argument which there is no place here to conduct. If genuine Marxism is to be able to distinguish itself from its amoralistic deformations, if it is to be distinguished from moral expediency and is to make moral sense of the strategy of non-tolerating as toleration, or of justified violence in order not to betray love, it will be only in so far as it allows for the possibility of something which it cannot itself justify, that there are some actions which we can perform now, in *pre*-communist conditions, which make real in the present — make 'really present' — those values, those conditions of life which our actions of love, of sacrifice, of toleration at the same time 'heuristically' anticipate in their absence. For if we cannot say this, then we cannot say that that future is *present* in the form of its absence, but only that it is absent. We could not then make that future the present basis of our actions in history, for it would have the character merely of an abstract, not yet realised 'norm' of action, at best, if any theory could show this, causally dependent on our present action.

For even within authentic Marxism those positive symbols which heuristically point towards what we might mean by 'love' or by 'toleration' or by the 'pacification' of a contradictory social reality, those symbols whose *materiality* demands the abolition of capitalism as a condition, are all wrested from those very capitalist conditions which Marxism seeks to abolish. Within capitalism those symbols are to be found only in a disordered relationship with the social world which has generated them and they cannot do the work which, as symbols, they signify. Marxism, however, must presuppose that to create the material conditions in which those symbols are retrieved from ideology is to create conditions in which people can more really engage with the world than they can in ideology. As it stands Marxism cannot justify this, it can but hope that it is right. For even when Marxism is happy to wrest from ideological sources the moral symbols which it criticises, it can justify what it borrows only by way of negation: it can justify its criticism of bourgeois morality only in terms of that morality's incapacity to realise its own truth. In this sense all Marxism is morally negative — the necessary negativity of morality — in that it is one fascinatingly elaborate *ad hominem* argument against capitalism. It is the irony of morality pitted against bourgeois moral cynicism. It is nothing more.

But if morality is of itself nothing more than this, it surely needs something else as its basis. Irony, like Marxism is essentially parasitic upon what it ironises, even if it also transforms what it feeds on. For irony is the disclosure of an innocence in the subversion of the cynicism which suppresses it. But to justify that irony, and so to justify the moral form of it, we need to know more than that it strips away the reifications of cynicism. We need to know that the innocence disclosed will set us in a more secure relationship with reality, that it is not just another form of illusory relationship with it. At best Marxism does not justify that proposition which it must presuppose, that love is not an illusion. For it does not possess the terms in which to show this. At worst, in the crudity of its scientism, Marxism does not even know that there is any question of it.

It may be that nothing can justify this proposition, with whatever necessities Marxism must presuppose it. It may be that at best we must act not knowing whether our actions can be justified. It may be, however, that the Christian can establish the right to say more than this, and if so, not merely because he is not made of such stern existentialist stuff as the Marxist. Perhaps the Christian can give grounds for his belief in the future reality of that which is glimpsed in the critical struggle with capitalism. Perhaps, moreover, the Christian can accept that the partial and fragmentary disclosure of the demands which that future makes upon our present actions of achieving it is the disclosure of a revolutionary socialist morality. If the Christian can accept this implication of solidarity with Marxism, then perhaps he will be able to convince us that the goal of that solidarity — communist society — points to a reality which has another name, the name of the creator God, whose 'presence in the form of his absence' is the mode of his creative activity. If the Christian can show this it will be only because he has abandoned all the theological, ritual, ecclesial and moral apparatus which inhibits his engagement in the Marxist struggle with history. But if he can show this, then he will be saying to the Marxist that because the Marxist's response to the demands of history is to acknowledge the demands of the creator, that response is shown to be our access to reality. In any case, it is only if he can show this that the Christian can justify that most

Christian and non-Marxist belief, that a death met in the course of that struggle is the ultimate form of that access.

IV

All this, however, is another story, to be told on another occasion. In the meantime enough has been said about what needs to be done. For we live in a world which generates more fundamental moral problems than we have the discourse or the praxes with which to cope. The urgency with which the task must be faced of generating the required discourse and practice lies in the fact that undoubtedly some lives and everyone's happiness depends upon our being able to do so. For we live in a world dominated by two facts mainly, a fact of 'Marxist' moral expediency and a fact of bourgeois moral cynicism, neither of which we can allow to make those claims upon us which we could unambiguously call 'moral'. In that world there is a third force, Christianity, which in much of the West is of diminishing significance — and it deserves no better fate, if only for the reason that its endless incantations of 'love' as the solution have to be treated, as Marxists rightly do, with contempt.

Marxists might just be able to make Christians see, if they are willing to look, that love is no solution, for it is the problem, one which can be solved *only by revolutionary means*. When they come to see this, then perhaps Christians will talk less glibly about love than they do when, unaware of the price of such talk, they express their cheap preferences for love over the class struggle. For love, transcendent, spiritual, ultimately transforming as it is, in the meantime bears the weight of its historical materiality and so is fraught with all the ambiguities and uncertainties out of which our present conditions are made. The problem is as simple as this question: how are we to love within the struggle to win the class war? It is also as complex as that question.

But Marxism is not the ultimate answer either, although it is the present form of that answer. What Marxism 'knows' it cannot know the true name of, that is God, and so it cannot know the name of that which, if anything does, would justify

the reality of its own praxes. Marxism knows but the absence
of God. It does not know how that absence is the characteristic
form of the divine presence.

If Christians have not been spectacularly successful in
convincing Marxists of this, it is simply because they have not
had any right to carry conviction. Their 'god' has been a
mockery equally of God and of history. What is everyone's
ideology is in addition their idolatry. And it matters that
they acquire that right, not from some narrow 'Christian'
point of view, nor from the point of view of a sectarian
Marxism, but because, as I have said, the state of the one world
we all share demands a moral response for which we do not
have the discourse. That discourse awaits creation. My proposition is that it is within the dialectics of the praxis of 'strong
compatibility' that the materials of that discourse will be
forged, or not at all. And there is nothing to guarantee that
we will forge them.

NOTES

1   K. Marx, *The Eighteenth Brumaire of Louis Bonaparte*, in K. Marx
    and F. Engels, *Selected Works* (one volume), London, 1968, p. 97.
2   See chapter 10, pp. 181–3.
3   I have now made this point twice. It should be noted that this is
    not meant as a historical remark, as if Soviet Russia were the
    product of some theory, or even of the deviation of some theory.
    I mean only that, for whatever reasons, Soviet praxis could be
    justified only on a perversion of Marxism, one of whose character-
    istics would be a scientistic positivism.
4   See chapter 8, pp. 122–4.
5   Cf., for example, the chapter on 'The Working Day' in Karl Marx,
    Capital, I, translated by S. Moore and E. Aveling, London, 1970.

Index